WITHDRAWN

THE TORRANCE KIDS AT MID-LIFE

THE TORRANCE KIDS AT MID-LIFE

SELECTED CASE STUDIES OF CREATIVE BEHAVIOR

Garnet W. Millar

FOREWORD by E. Paul Torrance

PUBLICATIONS IN CREATIVITY RESEARCH

Joan Franklin Smutny, Series Editor

Ablex Publishing

Westport, Connecticut
London

Library of Congress Cataloging-in-Publication Data

Millar, Garnet W.
    The Torrance kids at mid-life : selected case studies of creative behavior / Garnet W.
    Millar ; foreword by E. Paul Torrance.
        p. cm. — (Publications in creativity research)
    Includes bibliographical references and index.
    ISBN 1–56750–606–2 (alk. paper)
    1. Creative ability—Longitudinal studies. 2. Creative thinking—Longitudinal
    studies. I. Title. II. Series.
BF408.M52   2002
153.3'5—dc21   2001022178

British Library Cataloguing in Publication Data is available.

Library of Congress Catalog Card Number: 2001022178
ISBN: 1–56750–606–2

First published in 2002

Ablex Publishing, 88 Post Road West, Westport, CT 06881
An imprint of Greenwood Publishing Group, Inc.
www.ablexbooks.com

Printed in the United States of America

∞™ The paper used in this book complies with the
Permanent Paper Standard issued by the National
Information Standards Organization (Z39.48–1984).

10 9 8 7 6 5 4 3 2 1

Copyright Acknowledgments

The author and publisher gratefully acknowledge permission to use the following material:

Figure 3.1 on page 17 is reprinted from *E. Paul Torrance: "The Creativity Man"* by Garnet W.
Millar, published in 1995 by Ablex Publishing. This figure is reprinted by permission of Ablex Publishing.

The photograph of Dr. E. Paul Torrance on page 32 is reprinted courtesy of the Hargrett
Rare Book and Manuscript Library/University of Georgia Libraries.

The obituary on page 83 of Dr. C. W. Lillehei is reprinted by permission of *The New York
Times*. Copyright © 1999 by *The New York Times*.

The Friendship Garden newspaper article on page 217 is reprinted by permission of the
Minneapolis *Star Tribune*.

contents

figures and tables

In *The Torrance Kids at Mid-Life: Selected Case Studies of Creative Behavior*, Garnet Millar has written a book that is at the same time insightful, interesting, and useful. It is of interest to parents, teachers, counselors—especially vocational counselors—elementary and high school administrators, and college and university teachers. The participants tell their stories of their struggles and lessons learned by experience. Throughout, discussion of the "Manifesto for Children" is dominant.

Let us take a look at what I call the "Seven Commandments of the Gospel According to Paul" for creative development. This Manifesto was formulated on the basis of the struggles of the participants, shown in the 1980 follow-up. From the responses of the participants I tried to grasp the essence of their struggles. In the 40-year study, we have tried to validate the Manifesto. This book tells most of the story.

The Seven Commandments are as follows:

1. Don't be afraid to fall in love with something and pursue it with intensity.
2. Know, understand, take pride in, practice, develop, exploit, and enjoy your greatest strengths.
3. Learn to free yourself from the expectations of others and the games they impose on you. Free yourself to play your own game.
4. Do what you love and can do well.

5. Find a great teacher or mentor who will help you.
6. Don't waste your energy trying to be well rounded.
7. Learn the skills of interdependence and gladly share your infinite creativity.

The Manifesto has served many functions since its creation in 1983. With parents, there has been relief, especially with the commandment, "Don' t waste energy trying to be well rounded." Many of the participants tell of the pressures they experienced in trying to be well rounded. A multitalented young man complained that he was *too* well rounded. Even he displayed some one-sidedness. He was highly talented in creativity, intelligence, music, art, and writing. He received his doctorate in the philosophy of education, but he had enough credits in history and physics to earn undergraduate degrees in those fields. He earned his college expenses through his music—his rock and roll band—his writing and editing, and his art—as a medical illustrator. However, he was not gifted athletically. In the foreign service of the State Department he has achieved high rank and has made excellent use of many of his talents. However, he has not had time to pursue his science-fiction writing, music, acting, and art. He will soon retire from the State Department. Then he plans to go to Hollywood and Los Angeles in order to find outlets for his music, writing, art, and drama.

Garnet Millar also describes the participants' struggles to find work that they loved and could do well, and their struggles to deal with the expectations of their parents and teachers and "to play their own games."

Most of the males experienced high expectations, and most of the females suffered from low expectations. One young man, the son of a world-famous heart surgeon, could never fulfill the expectations of his father. He had a highly gifted and competitive older brother. However, he has been listed in the last two editions of *The Best Doctors in America* and has made his own innovations. The low expectations of some of the females were even more serious. One girl's parents told her, "You will never be able to complete elementary school." Yet, she graduated from college and attained her master's degree. Her parents would not waste one penny on her college expenses. Fortunately, her grandparents recognized her ability and financed her post–high school education. Another girl was told by her parents, "You will never be able to hold down a job as a clerk at Woolworth's." She, too, completed college and has gone on to a successful business career.

Garnet Millar's interviewing style comes through clearly. There is even the laughter of the interviewer and the interviewees. His interviewing style makes the readers feel as though they were there. The photographs and other illustrations contribute much.

This book validates the value of the Manifesto as a good guide for developing creative and satisfying careers.

E. Paul Torrance
Athens, Georgia
November 21, 2000

acknowledgments

Many individuals gave of their time to talk with me or assist in some manner:

- The Torrance Center for Creative Studies, University of Georgia, provided a research fellowship to the author so that the research could be conducted. In particular, Dr. Juanita Morgan-Matthews, Director, was helpful. Also, Drs. Bonnie Cramond and Tom Hebert provided assistance with statistical analyses.

- Dr. E. Paul Torrance, for providing complete access to his files on the longitudinal study and the case studies. His vision 40 long years ago has made this study a reality. He was always available to provide answers to my endless questions and was prompt in responding to e-mails or mail.

- Joan Franklin Smutny, Director of the Center for Gifted at National-Louis University at Evanston, Illinois, for her encouragement and support to complete this study.

- The 18 individuals who were selected for case study were extremely cooperative in giving freely of their time and in reading the transcripts of the interviews. Ten individuals were selected for in-depth case study. The cooperation demonstrated by these individuals is deeply appreciated. Permission was granted by all to use their actual names to tell their stories.

- Dr. Berenice Bleedorn of Minneapolis, who helped "find" the individuals that were selected for case study. She continues to be my Minnesota link to the case studies.

- Former teachers at University Elementary School in Minneapolis, Dr. Roger Zimmerman, Dr. Rod Myers, and Dr. Wayne Kirk provided insight into the philosophy and curriculum of the school in the late 1950s and early 1960s.
- Dr. Grace Schlosser, University of Alberta, for her assistance in analyzing the interview data and her dissertation on "Eminent Women in Canada and Finland."
- Sandra Mukai, for the arduous task of transcribing approximately 27 hours of tapes of the interviews.
- Word processors Sandra Mukai, Susan Wilson, Ann Bradley, and my spouse, Shirley Millar, who remained patient through several revisions.
- My spouse, Shirley Millar, for her support while I was either in Athens, Georgia, or Minneapolis conducting the research, or was "holed-up" writing in my office at home.

part one

INTRODUCTION AND BACKGROUND

At age 20 in 1964, I faced my first class of students—it was a split class of 18 students placed in grades 5 and 6 in Westwood School, Kenora, Ontario. To complicate my teaching assignment, I was "given" a grade 4 student early in the year who had been giving "trouble" to the equally "green" teacher in the grades 3–4 class. I wondered how I would teach all the programs of study to all three grades. I soon realized that they were all such different personalities, some wanting to be in school while others did not.

I still remember the names of them all—Susan, Greg, Roger, Sandra, Pam, Ron, Mike, and so on. As I reflect on my success with them, it was due to the fact that I treated them as individuals and soon learned and grew to value their different thinking and learning styles.

I wondered at the time what would become of these students who had such varied strengths. By now, most would be approaching 50 years of age. How have Sandra and Ron fared over the course of their careers and lives? I remember that Sandra called me "tenrag" (which is my first name spelled backwards), while Ron called me other unmentionable names. Could I have predicted from their school behavior what they were to become? What contributions would they make to their family, career, community, and so on? What influences or factors have determined their work, hobbies, marriage partner, and other life decisions?

Teachers have no easy way to know what will become of their students. A study of the same individuals over a long period of time allows one to understand the factors or influences that shape and affect what they will become. This type of study is called a "longitudinal study."

This book describes such a study that was initiated by Dr. E. Paul Torrance in Minneapolis some 40 years ago. As a professor of educational psychology and director of the Bureau of Educational Research at the University of Minnesota, he undertook the study of creativity in students and how it would influence the type of person they were to become and the career they would choose. Dr. Torrance wondered, "Could a test to measure creative potential predict creative achievement later as an adult?" and "What other factors influence, predict, encourage, or sustain their creativity over time?"

one

CREATIVITY

AN ESSENTIAL SKILL FOR ALL

"Creativity! Me creative? No way!" is a common response from many people. "I've not produced a great piece of art, composed music or writing, or fashioned a violin of the quality of Antonio Stradivari." That creativity is only for the gifted few is a myth that needs to be dispelled. The truth is that creativity is not just for geniuses. Creativity is for each of us individually. Harvard psychologist Howard Gardner talks about "small c" creativity and "Big C" creativity. There are those who make creative contributions ("Big C") that are world influencing, and those who are creative ("small c") in their daily activities at home, work, and personal interactions. Kirton (1987) calls this difference—adapters and innovators—a continuum from "small c" to "Big C" creativity.

What is *creativity*? I like to think of creativity as a form of energy seeking to express itself in all people. Others have called it an innate capacity for growth and empowerment. It is the energy that allows us to think a different thought and to express ourselves in a novel way. Torrance (1971) has said: "It takes courage to think differently—for as soon as we do, we're in a minority of one." Creativity enables us to view life as an opportunity for exploration, discovery, and a new sense of who we are. We must embrace creativity for its power and not be intimidated by it. Creativity enables individuals to release their potential. A good deal of our potential is buried, hidden, imprisoned by fear and the hold of convention.

Creativity involves displaying a certain disposition/attitude; awareness and understanding of the process; and learning and applying specific essential skills.

THE PROCESS OF CREATIVITY

Creativity is relatively independent of the concept of intelligence. Intelligence deals with a constellation of specific abilities; for example, arithmetic, vocabulary, block design, and picture arrangement in verbal and performance areas. All these component abilities deal with convergent thinking and *do* predict success, especially in a school environment. Creativity, however, is the production of something new or unusual via the process of sensing gaps, forming ideas or hypotheses, testing the hypotheses, and communicating the results. These abilities deal with divergent thinking and relate to success in careers and life.

ATTITUDE TOWARD CREATIVITY

Research shows that a person must believe that creativity is important and be committed to it in order to embrace it as a "behavioral style." Creative motivation, both externally by asking people to be creative—to think of lots of ideas and the like—and internally—that is, wanting to be creative—all contribute to the actual creative behavior. Paul Torrance has designed a *Creative Motivation Scale* (1995) that predicts creative behavior. For example, teachers cannot be creative with children if they only provide creative activities; rather they must be motivated or committed to teaching creatively.

BENEFITS OF CREATIVITY

What are the benefits of working and living creatively? Isn't it enough to be intelligent and hardworking? Creativity equips people to *deal* more effectively *with the future.* Hoffer (1973, p. 22) wrote: "In a time of drastic change, it is the learners who inherit the future. The learned find themselves equipped to live only in a world that no longer exists." The skills used in creative problem solving (identifying challenges, selecting an underlying problem, producing solution ideas, selecting criteria, applying criteria, and developing an action plan) equip individuals to better deal with the future as it presents itself. The Future Problem Solving Program was designed by Paul Torrance in 1974 and helps students to creatively identify and solve world and community problems. World situations, such as the geopolitical restructuring of former countries such as the Soviet Union and Czechoslovakia, and depletion of natural resources such as oil, gas, and forests will require novel and elegant solutions. Creativity will be required to deal with these kinds of world problems.

IMPORTANCE OF CREATIVITY FOR YOUNG PEOPLE

Mental Health

If creativity is stifled in the home or school, a great deal of tension and stress is caused. Creativity is one's most valuable resource in coping with daily stresses. Mental health is most relevant today, considering the harassment and violence witnessed in many schools. It may be that divergent behavior as exhibited by some students is ridiculed by students and unwittingly neglected by staff.

Fully Functioning Students

Schools mainly teach to the intellectual domain, to the detriment of students' creative abilities. Students are marginalized if they cannot apply their creative abilities and will not be prepared to deal with the challenges that life-after-school will inevitably present. Students need to practice the creative abilities involved in awareness of problems, thinking up solutions and testing them.

Creativity enables people to accept divergency in others and perceive their differences in constructive ways. People have four primary thinking styles (Black, 1985): directive, intuitive, negotiative, and meditative. The *directive thinker* is high-task focused, consistent, accurate and right, and systematic; the *intuitive thinker* is imaginative, fun, challenging, multitargeted, and exploratory; the *negotiative thinker* is team-focused, caring, sensitive, and easy to be with; and, finally, the *meditative thinker* is very precise, thorough, analytical, and very focused. We need to be aware of these thinking styles and understand our students or the people we work with in order to make things happen in a creative way. Recognizing and using divergence are fundamental to helping people understand their value and contribution.

Another benefit of our knowledge about creativity is in the identification of special children who, if identified early as having creative promise or potential, will likely make creative achievements in later life. The case studies presented in this book illustrate that identified creative potential early in life and other supportive factors such as having a mentor make all the difference later on.

At school, teachers, counselors, and administrators can provide a "safe" environment for creativity to flourish; be a mentor; recognize creative talent; help students understand divergence; recognize creative talent and help parents understand creativity in their children. Easy to express, certainly, but not always easy to implement and follow through!

CREATIVITY EXPRESSED IN LATER LIFE

Creativity can contribute to physical well-being as we age. Cohen (2000) has said that "creative expression fosters positive feelings that prompt a positive outlook and sense of well-being." Creative expression in many forms of art will serve to reduce stress. As the world becomes more of a global village through technological advances, we will become more aware of myriad problems and will need to use creativity to deal with them.

For personkind to successfully adapt to world change and advancement will depend in large measure on the creative endeavors of world citizens.

CREATIVITY IS LIFE LONG

Research that says "you can't teach an old dog new tricks" is not so. Old dogs—people—can learn a tremendous amount in the second half of life. Research shows that if the brain is challenged it will respond biologically in positive ways, regardless of age. Science has shown that new growth can occur in individual brain cells if the individual is in a stimulating environment. Production of a chemical called acetylcholine occurs in the brain, which helps to improve memory and thinking functions. This brain growth can occur in individuals from their early 50s to late 70s. Some famous people who have been very productive in their later years are as follows:

- Pablo Picasso, at age 86, produced a remarkable series of 347 etchings (*Suite 347*)
- Alfred Hitchcock, at age 73, directed *Frenzy*
- Dr. Suess, at age 82, wrote *You're Only Old Once*
- Mahatma Ghandi, at age 77, successfully completed negotiations with Britain to grant independence to India
- Sigmund Freud, at age 67, published *The Ego and Id*
- Daniel Defoe, at age 59, wrote *Robinson Crusoe*
- Antonio Stradivari, in his early 90s, fashioned two of his most famous violins.

Cohen (2000) has identified four phases of creativity. He speaks of wisdom as a possible developmental mix of age, knowledge, and practical experience that become integrated to achieve insight, which can be applied to a variety of life circumstances. Cohen speaks of four developmental phases—reevaluation, liberation, summing up, and encore—that shape the way our creative energy grows and the way we express it in our later years:

1. *Reevaluation phase* (age 50+): Our creative expression is intensified by a sense of crisis or quest. Most adults at this age are engaged in a quest for ways to make their lives and work gratifying.
2. *Liberation phase* (age 60–70): Creative endeavors are charged with the added energy of a new degree of personal freedom that comes psychologically from within us and situationally from retirement (or refirement!).
3. *Summing-up phase* (age 70+): Feel a need to find a larger meaning for our lives through a process of looking back, summing up, and giving back.
4. *Encore phase* (age 80+): Reflects the energy of advancing age: to affirm life, to take care of unfinished business, and to celebrate one's place in the family, community, and spiritual realm.

The "Torrance Kids" represented in the case studies are just about to enter the first phase of creativity—the reevaluation phase—at approximately age 50. It is our intention to continue to follow them during other phases of their careers and lives.

PRINCIPLES OF CREATIVITY

1. Creativity is ageless.
2. Everyone *can* be creative (you don't have to be Einstein!).
3. Creativity is a continual process, 24 hours a day.
4. Failure is the mother of all creativity.
5. To be creative, you have to be incredibly positive.

SKILLS OF CREATIVITY

Torrance's pioneering work on measuring the skills of creativity have enabled behavioral scientists to identify the skills that make up creative behavior. These skills can be learned and practiced by everyone, regardless of age. Developmentally, we know that children are naturally creative in their play, and afterwards become less creative as they progress through the school system. However, creativity can be nurtured by teachers who are committed to teaching creatively and who value creative thinking in children. These skills deal with certain factors (fluency, flexibility, originality, elaboration, openmindedness) and several strengths. These are explained in more detail in appendix A.

Paul Torrance, as a young psychologist in the late 1940s and early 1950s, learned a great deal about creative behavior from his work with the U.S. Air Force Advanced Survival School after World War II and with fighter pilots during the Korean War. In both cases men were confronted daily with survival and extreme stress, and in aircraft combat with situations for which they had no practiced or learned solution. They had to resort to their own resources or creative ability to deal with the emergent situation—in order to survive. There are certain skills that one can use (ideational fluency and creative problem-solving) to extricate oneself from these life-threatening situations. It was not enough for fighter pilots in the U.S. Air Force to rely on luck, eyesight, good equipment, and a fine aircraft. They needed to be resourceful and creative to survive. Torrance (1954a) found that pilots who were considered to be "aces" were more creative than those who were not. The jet aces displayed a strong drive (achievement, motivation, and striving for success) to be the best they could be and were men "who met life head on." Their imagination and creativity scores were higher than those of the nonaces as measured on biographical (Life Experience Inventory) information and a projective test (Rorshach Test). Torrance's (1954b; 1954c) description of the personality and physical makeup of the ace is interesting: "Somewhat smaller than the average American male, unusually articulate, friendly, soft spoken, enthusiastic, intensely alive, and a cigar smoker." Torrance goes on to say that, in comparison to pilots with no kills, the ace seems much more colorful and emotionally alive.

A colleague of mine was faced with the task of identifying the skills considered to be essential for students in the public/separate schools of a large province in Canada. These skills were considered to be important to students in preparation for careers. A host of skills was quickly identified for working, learning, and living in four major categories; namely, building personal capacity; interacting and communicating; planning and managing; and using data and computer technology. I proposed that creativity be put forth as an essential skill. It was accepted and went forward for the approval of education officials. Schools need to be committed to teaching creatively and valuing student expressions of creativity. More will be said about the importance of creativity in the school environment.

SOME EXERCISES TO "WAKE UP A LAZY BRAIN"

There are many exercises to help you think creatively. A few samples are given below. In an information age, individuals will need to become more technologically capable and find ways to use the Internet and World Wide Web as possible sources of information.

Ideational Fluency—"Exercise Your Brain"

- see how many yellow (or green) vegetables that you can name in 30 seconds
- count backward from 100 by 6s without making a mistake
- visualize a golf (or tennis or _____) game you've just played. Can you remember each shot and the course hazards you needed to consider?

Keep an Open Mind

Listen to different kinds of music, even those you don't like. Creative people like diversity, and different kinds of music stimulate different parts of the brain. I may even appreciate the musical groups that my sons enjoy (Gorilla Biscuits and Fuzzy Sprouts).

Take a Nap

Some of the most creative insights occur in your dreams. I often "leap out of bed" with a new thought or insight. Write them down immediately.

Keep a Record of Questions

As you incubate on ideas and problems, questions arise that need to be examined. These questions will come to you at different times and situations—while taking a walk, driving in the car, having coffee with friends, and so on. Record them or "trap" them in a notebook.

two

E. PAUL TORRANCE

A TOAST TO "THE CREATIVITY MAN"

E. Paul Torrance (c.1995), "The Gentle Genius of Georgia"

On the occasion of his 80th birthday and the book launching of his biography on October 5, 1995, I gave the following toast to E. Paul Torrance at the Hargrett Library, University of Georgia (Millar, 1995b):

> It is my honor and privilege to propose a toast to E. Paul Torrance. Many have known you, Paul, in various roles over the years: teacher; counselor; principal; psychologist; researcher; professor; sociodramatist; administrator; and writer.
>
> During the writing of the biography, I've known you as a mentor and friend. In fact, you've been my alter ego!
>
> I would like to say a few words about 4 or 5 of your personal attributes that have impressed me most as your biographer. I have had the privilege of knowing you personally as a result of staying at your home during brief study periods over the past 5 or 6 years.

Firstly, you helped me understand the importance of having a mentor and a network of supporters. Because of your extensive network of friends, colleagues, and students, I was able to contact them to obtain information about you and your work. In fact, two of your colleagues led me to Ablex Publishing Corporation—the company that published your biography. Those helpful colleagues are Joan Franklin Smutny (Evanston, Illinois) and Mark Runco (of California).

Another attribute that impressed me is your punctuality. I know of no person who is more punctual than you. I would often ask you about a certain article or book (perhaps written years ago) when I was at your home and within hours, it would be on my desk. And, as many people here would attest, your response to letters of inquiry is uncommonly swift. I know, also, that the volume of your mail is staggering.

Your consideration and emotional support is greatly appreciated. Whenever I stayed with you, you would happily make meals for me and even wash my socks! I remember clearly three years ago when my sister passed away while I was staying with you, you called me at the Torrance Center to inform me of the situation and when I arrived at your home an hour later, a sympathy card was on my desk in the Pansy room with a comforting message.

Joe Renzulli once said that your H.Q. (Humility Quotient) was as large as your intelligence and creativity quotients. Your humility is uncommon and admirable. Despite your international status as a renowned researcher and writer, you have remained accessible to those of us who ask for assistance. This is a rare quality today.

Finally, your productivity in your special field of study is remarkable and incomparable. Anyone who has written nearly 2,000 articles, tests, and books is worthy of the description—exemplary Beyonder—a term coined by you. Another way to think of your productivity is the statistic that you have written, on average, an article or book every week for the last 30 years. As Pearline Yeatts-Thomas said to me, "The Paul Torrances are the candle in the dark of the night."

Ladies and gentlemen, please join me in celebrating *"the Creativity Man, the Gentle Genius of Georgia,"* E. Paul Torrance.

Paul Torrance is respected, valued, and loved by countless students, colleagues, and others throughout the world. He has "touched the creativity" of individuals, through his writing and mentoring, in countries such as South Africa, Japan, Korea, Spain, Malaysia, Canada, and Mexico, and this human network influences countless people.

At age 85 he continues as advisor to the Georgia Studies of Creativity in Athens. Currently, he is engaged in completing a book on his 40-year longitudinal study. The study involves a sample of 391 individuals who were administered a variety of creativity tests while in elementary school from 1958 to 1965. He has been a prolific writer and has approximately 2,000 publications (books, chapters in books, and articles) to his credit. His primary achievements, documented in Sheehy, Chapman, and Conroy (1997), include:

1. Development and refinement of a battery of tests of creative thinking that have been translated into 35 languages.

2. Discovered that the developmental characteristics of most creative-thinking abilities are different from those involved in intelligence tests and logical-reasoning tests.

3. Showed that the common "fourth-grade slump" in creativity could be offset through clever use of instructional materials.

4. Showed that the use of intelligence tests *only* to identify gifted students misses about 70 percent of those who are equally creatively gifted.

5. Found that children identified as creatively gifted, but who fall short of the I.Q. cutoff for gifted classification (e.g., I.Q. of 130+), tend to out-achieve as adults those who met the I.Q. criterion of giftedness and failed to meet the creativity criterion of giftedness.

6. Having a mentor is significantly related to adult creative achievement.

7. Having a childhood future-career image—"being in love with something"—and persisting with it is related significantly to adult creative achievement.

8. Having certain teachers in elementary school increases one's chances of adult creative achievement.

9. Creative-thinking ability tests appear to have little racial or socioeconomic status bias.

10. Founded the Future Problem Solving Program, which is used by an estimated 250,000 students throughout the United States and several other countries.

His daily schedule of commitment to his work would be grueling for a man even half his age. He gets up at 4:30 A.M., reads the newspaper and does personal chores, works on writing projects and answers correspondence, including e-mails, and finishes his day at 11:00 P.M.

three

THE "CREATIVITY SCENE"

UNIVERSITY OF MINNESOTA (1958–1965)

On the occasion of his election as president of the American Psychological Association in 1950, Dr. J. P. Guilford suggested that creativity be considered for serious study. According to Guilford, at that time only a fraction of 1 percent of the literature in psychology was devoted to the study of creativity.

Paul Torrance was aware of the importance of creativity as a result of his wide reading on the subject and his experience as a psychologist with the U.S. Air Force (USAF) Advanced Survival School. During the USAF survival-research program, Torrance learned that an underlying element of survival is creativity, and that risk taking and other creative skills are essential for producing constructive behavior and unusual achievements. In a personal letter, Torrance reflects:

> Many of my ideas emerged from my survival research with the USAF. It was not until my retirement that I realized how much I have been influenced by this. . . . In the survival schools, the goal was to train men to behave effectively in emergencies and extreme conditions. *I have held that whenever one is faced with a problem for which he has no practiced or learned solution, some degree of creativity is required.* [This came to be known as Paul's simple survival definition of creativity; emphasis

added.] Of course, they were taught many solutions that others had used—from the American Indians to polar expeditions to survivors of World Wars I and II. I became a firm believer in experiential learning, cooperative learning in small groups, learning in all modalities, tolerance of disagreement in groups, the extreme importance of motivation and creative thinking.[1]

When Paul Torrance was hired as director of the Bureau of Educational Research at the University of Minnesota, Dean Walter Cook gave him a challenge: "Whatever research and teaching that you engage yourself in, it must be made famous!" Paul took him literally and did just that, over a distinguished career at Minneapolis that was carried on later at the University of Georgia in Athens. His research on creativity is extensive and provides the foundation for creativity study today.

Dean Cook wanted to develop a research climate at the College of Education at the University of Minnesota and would always challenge the professors at his faculty meetings by saying, "At least 50 percent of what you are teaching your classes is untrue, and it is time you found out which half that is!" Paul's initial mandate was to initiate a 25-year pioneering research program on giftedness in children. To do this, he needed to know what was happening in the United States and Canada for gifted children. He was instrumental in organizing three Minnesota conferences on the gifted and invited the leading scholars of the day to present papers. These are well documented (Torrance, 1960, 1961; Torrance, Wilk, & Harmon, 1960). He had wanted to study various kinds of giftedness, much like the work on multiple intelligences by Howard Gardner of Harvard University today. However, he started with creativity and never left it! Torrance and his graduate students began to review the literature on creativity and studied the biographies of famous people to determine fruitful areas to explore and research.

DEFINITIONS OF CREATIVITY

Three definitions of creativity have been developed by Torrance that have guided his research studies and form the conceptual basis for the development of his tests. Each is briefly discussed here. For more elaborate discussion, see chapters 3 and 4 of my book, E. Paul Torrance: "The Creativity Man" (Millar, 1995a).

"Survival" Definition

Whenever one is faced with a problem for which he has no practiced or learned solution, some degree of creativity is required.

"Research" Definition

Creativity (Torrance, 1962, p. 16) is the production of something new or unusual as a result of the processes of:

- Sensing difficulties, problems, gaps in knowledge, missing elements, something askew
- Making guesses and formulating hypotheses about these deficiencies
- Evaluating and testing these guesses and hypotheses
- Possibly revising and retesting them
- Finally, communicating the results.

Embedded in this research definition are the major features of other definitions that have been previously proposed. Specifically, other definitions of creativity include such notions as "the production of

Rendering of the "research" definition of creativity hanging in Paul Torrance's office

something new" and "adventurous thinking"—permitting one thing to lead to another—and "truth"—shedding bias and being willing to discover the world as it actually is.

"Artistic" Definition

Karl Anderson, a student in Torrance's class while he was teaching at the University of California at Berkeley during the summer of 1964, created an "artistic" definition or description of creativity. Paul liked it immediately because, consisting of simple line drawings, it meaningfully communicated the essence of creativity. Paul has lost the original Anderson drawings but Nancy Martin redrew the visuals in 1985, and they closely approximate the originals. To make the drawings meaningful, one has to look upon them as analogies. Figure 3.1 displays the drawings in an analogy that has inspired an infinity of meanings and ideas about creativity.

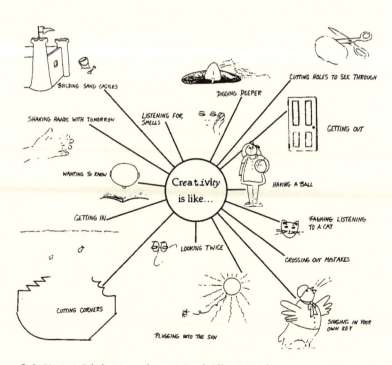

FIGURE 3.1 "Artistic" definition of creativity (Millar, 1995a).

A large number of exploratory studies on creative behavior, creative skills, instructional materials, and a cross-cultural study on creativity was conducted between 1958 and 1966. There is not space to discuss them all here. The interested reader may wish to refer to chapter 4 of E. *Paul Torrance: "The Creativity Man"* (Millar, 1995a). A climate for the fostering of creativity was established and Torrance and his graduate students began the task of measuring "creativity" in children. A description of the development of the Minnesota Tests of Creative Thinking follows.

Underlying the creative tests are skills that have been identified by Torrance through review of the literature and by exploratory studies in schools. Four main factors of creativity emerged—fluency, flexibility, originality, and elaboration—and some 13 creative strengths such as humor, unusual visual perspective, and so on. These are described in detail in appendix A.

NOTE

1. Personal communication from Dr. Torrance to Garnet Millar, December 25, 1991, in possession of the author.

four

BOOKS ON THE TORRANCE LONGITUDINAL STUDY AND REVIEW OF THE LITERATURE

This volume on selected case studies, *The Torrance Kids at Mid-life*, is the second book written about the 40-year follow-up of the Torrance Longitudinal Study of Creativity. The purpose of this book is to illustrate how specific test scores and other life factors affect creative achievements and individual careers. It affords us the opportunity to integrate all of one's experiences and how they impact the shape of a person's life. The ten case studies represent both those with high creative potential and those with average potential. It enables a researcher to discuss factors that influence a person's life other than simply test performance at specific times in that individual's life. Factors unexplained by childhood test performances, such as early experiences, being in love with something, having teachers who value creativity, and having mentors, are discussed.

The first book, *The Manifesto: A Guide to Developing a Creative Career* by Torrance (2001), describes the 40-year follow-up of elementary school students who were originally tested with a research version of the *Torrance Tests of Creative Thinking* (Torrance, 1974) in the 1958–1965 period. In addition to a thorough analysis of the predictive validity of such predictors as measures of intelligence, the effects of such variables as having a mentor, the changing attitudes about gender differences, cultural changes, the passage of time, and occupational changes, are analyzed.

The book also describes the responses of 211 young adults who had attended two elementary schools in Minnesota from 1958 to 1964. They had been administered some creativity tests each year, and they were followed-up in 1980. On the basis of their questionnaire responses, the Manifesto was developed to describe their ongoing struggle to maintain their creativity and use their strengths to create their careers and to provide guidance to children. In 1998, they were followed-up again in order to understand their creative achievements and to validate the Manifesto. A total of 101 questionnaires was obtained. Some of the 101 participants had attained eminence, while others had attained only mediocre careers. The struggle had continued.

The ten chapters of the book by Torrance are:

1. Origins of the Manifesto
2. Background and Overview
3. Procedures and Subjects
4. Major Statistical Results
5. Falling in Love with Your Work
6. Learning to Know Greatest Strengths
7. Expectations and Playing Your Own Game
8. Being Well Rounded
9. Loving the Work You Do
10. Learning Skills of Interdependence and Sharing Your Infinite Creativity.

The *The Manifesto: A Guide to Developing a Creative Career* describes the struggles, successes, and failures of the subjects following the guidance of the Manifesto. Most of them have had some career they loved, although some of them had not done so until recently. A larger percentage of them had found a mentor since the 1980 survey. The data also revealed that having a mentor is an aid to achievement.

These two books on the longitudinal study of creativity will be useful to, and have implications for, several global audiences: universities, colleges, public/private education, and the general public.

A REVIEW OF THE LITERATURE

The review of the literature in this area is easy. There is no longitudinal study of comparable length. The Terman (1925–1959) longitudinal study is concerned with the persistence of intelligence over time and other factors that influence the career and life of individuals. Terman and Oden (1959) studied 1,528 individuals at various intervals in their lives. They found that both heredity and environment had effects on achievement. Cox (1926), in volume II of the *Genetic Studies of Genius Series*, cites the frequency of eminent parents among her subjects. She notes also that the influence of environment revealed itself in an especially positive family attitude toward education. The study is still being conducted on individuals from the original sample.

Terman and Oden (1947) in *The Gifted Child Grows Up* (volume IV in the series) make an interesting reference in their conclusion to the creative achievement of their gifted case studies. They stated: "The task ahead is not simply that of finding how gifted children turn out; it is the problem rather of utilizing the rare opportunities afforded by this group to increase our knowledge of the dynamics of human behavior, with special reference to the factors that determine degree and direction of creative achievement" (p. 381).

five

UNIVERSITY AND SIDNEY PRATT ELEMENTARY SCHOOLS

"CREATIVE PLACES" FOR CHILDREN

The two schools involved in the longitudinal studies with Paul Torrance and his associates during the 1958 to 1964 period were "creative places" for children to grow, and were considered very progressive at the time. Neither functions today as a school but both are used by the university and community for other purposes.

Both University Elementary School (UES) and Sidney Pratt Elementary School were extraordinary in terms of teachers and students. The teachers were mainly doctoral students at the time and the students were quite normal but not quite average. Many of them came from professional families. Both schools adhered to progressive methods of elementary teaching. As a young man and teacher-in-training at Lakehead Teachers' College in Port Arthur, Ontario, I can vividly recall the words of Norman Kleven, a master of child psychology. The year was 1963; he said: "Dr. Paul Torrance and his associates at the University of Minnesota are engaged in important work in the area of identifying and unleashing the creative potential in students." I had no way of knowing then that I would be assisting Dr. Torrance with his work and engaged in his longitudinal study nearly 40 years later.

The University Elementary School was planned as a service agency of the College of Education at the University of Minnesota. Accord-

University Elementary School—Pattee Hall, July 1998

ing to the *Alumni News* (1961), it was envisioned by the late dean of education, Wesley E. Peik, to be "an experimental setting for both old and new methods" of teaching. The article states that "mistakes might even be dared in the pursuit of ultimate improvement in education." The first kindergarten class began in 1946, and in each successive year a new grade was added until grade 6 was established in 1952. The school was located in Pattee Hall on a corner of the University of Minnesota campus. Recent personal correspondence with three of the teachers involved with Torrance and his associates gives us a good glimpse of the philosophy and operation of the school at the time.

Dr. Rod Myers, a grade 4 teacher and doctoral student at the time, recalls the progressive nature of the school with these observations:[1]

1. "Students (pupils) were enrolled usually before they entered kindergarten. They came largely from professional families. (Many were the children of professors.) I can only recall two in my class who weren't from a professional family—but one was Jim Young."

2. "We had a marvelous principal [Dr. James Curtin] and one teacher for each grade. Most of our teachers were doctoral students. I replaced a man who went on to become a member of the education faculty at San Diego State."

3. "The main purpose of the school was as a demonstration ("lab") school. Classes from the university visited or watched behind one-way mirrors. (In my case, it was a screen that served the same purpose.) Occasionally, we gave a demonstration lesson. Parents could also come whenever they wanted to watch their offspring and not be seen by them. Experiments

Sidney Pratt Elementary School, now a community center, July 1998

were conducted, and students were sometimes asked to leave class in order to participate in the experiments."

4. "Class size was usually optimal—I had 25 pupils in my fourth grade. The average I.Q. for my classes was over 130. So the classes were not the average or typical groups found in the public schools."

5. "The members of the school staff were all members of the university faculty, and the university administered the program."

6. "Usually only one student would be missing from one year to the next, as when a parent went on a sabbatical."

7. "P.E. classes were conducted in a gymnasium very close by. A Spanish teacher came in once a week, as well as a music teacher."

Myers was an excellent teacher and made a tremendous impact on the students in his classes. In fact, he is described in an article (Torrance, 1981) as a "teacher who made a difference." Interestingly, he still corresponds with three of his former students and is considered their mentor—nearly 40 years after teaching them!

According to Wayne Kirk, there was really no stated philosophy of University Elementary School. The principal, Dr. James Curtin, selected the teachers and then they functioned according to their beliefs. Kirk stated:

> I had just completed three years in a very organized large public school system in Racine, Wisconsin. It was noted for curriculum development. Suddenly I was teaching in a school with few rules or suggestions. Each teacher really did his or her thing. Except for a math series and a few language-arts books, I really developed the curriculum along with student interests.[2]

He apparently realized that he was teaching an exceptional group of students who had such expansive backgrounds. Therefore the philosophy of education, as the teachers came to know, was really one of a very liberal view.

As each teacher developed his or her curriculum, there was overlap and some voids. Teachers taught to their strengths. Perhaps one teacher was strong in creative thinking but did not stress some basic skills. What seemed to "save" the staff was that they worked well together and were really quite outstanding. Although the administration had a hands-off policy, it was supportive and always gave encouragement. In a sense, according to Kirk, the secretary "managed" the school.

One of the overall goals of University Elementary School was to support the College of Education at the University of Minnesota and provide a setting for exceptional students. It was a great place to teach for young people with "no one to look over your shoulder."

Roger Zimmerman (now Dr. Zimmerman), a grade 5 teacher at the time, presents in a letter to the author an interesting view of the curriculum, the attempts to teach for creativity, and the uniqueness of University Elementary School. Regarding the curriculum, the only subject common across the grades was mathematics. The teachers all used the same textbook series. Beyond mathematics, the teachers had a great deal of freedom. Dr. Curtin, the principal, was the quintessential model of a teacher and learner. When the teachers approached him for curricular advice regarding language arts, he would direct them to some resources and trust them to come up with something. Zimmerman says that "at the time I wanted more specific help, but the end result was positive for the students in grade 5 and me."

Charlotte Miller was a primary school teacher at the school who was particularly interested in creative writing and drawing. She encouraged the students to display their productions such as the dinosaurs created by Jim Young and the inventions of William Reed.

Content acceleration was common throughout the school and was used extensively in grades 5 and 6. In mathematics and some foreign languages, the University High School followed-up and allowed accelerated students to begin at their level of competence rather than at the grade 7 level. As a result, some students were taking classes at the University of Minnesota while being a junior or senior in high school. This happens frequently now, but was progressive in the early 1960s.

Roger Zimmerman used flexible ability grouping for reading, math, and spelling as a result of content acceleration. Social studies and science were taught with the whole group. He used small groups as learning experiences for the students before the Johnson brothers introduced cooperative learning. Resources were used according to student ability; some used, for example, high school biology text-books, while others used a grade 5 science textbook. Now this is called "compacting" the content of the curriculum and is advocated by Renzulli (1977) and others as a means to accommodate the ability of bright students at school.

Zimmerman did make deliberate attempts to teach for creativity, saying,

> sometimes opportunities to do that were thrust upon me. Dr. Torrance and/or his graduate student(s) would come to UES classrooms to do a lesson or try out a new idea. Often the teacher became involved in the lesson or in the follow-up lessons. For one year the fourth grade teacher, located next door to my classroom, was R. E. Myers. I was not into "creativity" to the same degree as Rod, but just being exposed to his ideas caused me to try some of them with the fifth graders. On my own, I did quite a bit with creative writing. The impetus for that came when Dr. Curtin pointed me to some resources. My own interest and a small measure of talent in visual arts prompted me to encourage student creativity in that area.[3]

University Elementary School was most likely ahead of its time. An example of the uniqueness of the school is demonstrated by the class that finished grade 6 in 1963. They held a class reunion only a few years ago—dinner was arranged on a Saturday evening and the students had an all-day picnic on Sunday. That reunion may high-light what made University Elementary School so unique. Perhaps it was not the principals, the teachers, the curriculum, or the methods of instruction. Perhaps it was the blend of children. How many sixth graders will organize a 25th-year reunion on their own? During con-versations at that reunion, Roger Zimmerman heard the students speak about why University Elementary School was special: teachers who allowed them to explore and teachers who both encouraged and challenged them, and the special talents of the students.

Sidney Pratt Elementary School also served children from mainly professional families that lived in Prospect Park, a neighborhood of

Minneapolis. It was also staffed by teachers working on advanced degrees and wanting to try out progressive teaching methods.

NOTES

1. Personal communication from Rod Myers to Garnet Millar, September 20, 1999, in possession of the author.

2. Personal communication from Wayne Kirk to Garnet Millar, December 2, 1999, in possession of the author.

3. Personal communication from Roger Zimmerman to Garnet Millar, December 4, 1999, in possession of the author.

six

LONGITUDINAL STUDIES

Longitudinal studies are rare. Several reasons can be advanced for this statement: lack of financial support; difficulty in maintaining contact with and interest of subjects; requires a good deal of work; and changing interests of investigators.

What is a *longitudinal study*? According to Stratton and Hayes (1993), a longitudinal study "is a study that takes place over a period of time and is concerned with studying some form of development or change which occurs over time." Longitudinal studies have been valuable in challenging many erroneous or commonly held beliefs. For example, longitudinal studies of the relationship between aging and intelligence suggest that intelligence, if used, continues to develop and increase throughout life rather than decline with age, as was once thought.

The Torrance longitudinal study of creativity deals with the predictive quality of the *Torrance Tests of Creative Thinking* (TTCT) and other factors or influences that may account for or promote and sustain adult creative achievements.

In fact, there are several uses of longitudinal studies advanced by Torrance and his associates. Prediction is the one regarded by most scholars as the only or major use of longitudinal studies. Test developers always want to report on the predictive validity of a test instrument; that is, does a test predict at a young age that same ability at a later age? In the case of the *Torrance Tests of Creative Thinking*, does high creative potential as measured by the *TTCT* as a child play out or foreshadow high creative achievement of that same individual as an adult? Although this is important to behavioral scientists, there are many other important uses of longitudinal studies.

Other influences in a person's career and life can be studied longitudinally. How children see themselves and their environment is the stuff of longitudinal study. Part of the environment involves the perceptions held by others—parents, teachers, siblings, and peers. For example, what influences do mentors have on creative achievement? Social change and historical events may influence creativity. How will the effect of time relate to the prediction of creative achievement? Will changes in attitudes concerning gender differences affect creativity? What struggles will the children experience to maintain their creativity? Do elementary teachers influence the creative achievement of their students? What is the influence of early life experiences on creative achievement? Some answers to these many questions will emerge from the 40-year study and from analysis of case studies. How will creativity be developed, measured, sustained, promoted, "squashed" over a 40-year period? This is "the stuff" of the Torrance longitudinal study of creativity.

seven

GENESIS OF THE "TORRANCE TESTS OF CREATIVE THINKING"

The instrument used to collect information during the initial stage (1958–1964) of the longitudinal study, from which the case studies reported here were selected, was the Minnesota Tests of Creative Thinking. This battery of tests later became the *Torrance Tests of Creative Thinking* (1966; 1974; 1993). It has been translated into approximately 35 languages.

Creativity, like intelligence, is very complex and difficult to quantify on some discreet measure. Torrance chose a battery of tests that represented the most important aspects of creative thinking. After considerable review of the literature on the topic of creativity, he and his associates designed a battery of tests that purportedly measured the essence of creativity. It is important to remember that these are only "best guesses" or approximations of what creativity may actually be.

In table 7.1, the verbal and figural tests designed by Torrance some 40 years ago and refined since then are presented. These tests are described below. The table delineates the name of the subtest or activity, describes it, states its rationale, and finally, the factors that it measures. This summary is derived from a *Research Review of the Torrance Tests of Creative Thinking* by Torrance (2000).

The *verbal test* is composed of six word-based-designed exercises that measure three mental characteristics (creative factors: fluency,

TABLE 7.1a

Description of the *Torrance Tests of Creative Thinking* (TTCT): Verbal

Name of Test and Subtests	Description	Rationale	Creative Factors
Activity 1— *Ask and Guess*	This activity requires the person to ask questions from drawings on the page	The *Asking* activity reveals the person's ability to sense what a person is unable to find out by looking at the picture and to ask questions that will enable a person to fill in the gaps in one's knowledge. Curiosity is the indispensable element of inquiry and scientific creativity	• Fluency—relevant responses • Flexibility—different categories/shifts in thinking • Originality—uncommon, original responses
Activities 2/3— *Guessing Causes* and *Guessing Consequences*	These activities require the person to make guesses and consequences of happenings related to a drawing on the page	The *Guessing Causes* and *Guessing Consequences* activites are designed to reveal the person's ability to formulate cause and effect	
Activity 4— *Product Improvement Activity*	The person thinks of as many possible ways to change a toy animal to make it more fun to play with	This activity taps the person's ability to develop and play with ideas	• Fluency • Flexibility • Originality
Activity 5— *Unusual Uses Activities*	The person devises as many uses as possible for objects, such as tin cans or cardboard	This activity is a test of the ability to free a person's mind of a well-established set	• Fluency • Flexibility • Originality
Activity 6— *Just Suppose Activity*	The person predicts possible outcomes and consequences of an improbable situation	This activity is a test for the ability to "play with" ideas and consequences, and often is an indication of degree of fantasy	• Fluency • Flexibility • Originality

flexibility, and originality). Currently, it has parallel forms, A and B, and measures the following essential components of creativity: curiosity; cause-and-effect relationships; the ability to "play with" ideas and consequences; "freeing" of the mind from rigid, "set" thinking; and the ability to fantasize.

The *figural test* is composed of three activities designed to measure seventeen mental characteristics (creative factors: fluency, originality, abstractness of titles, resistance to premature closure and elaboration, plus thirteen creative strengths). (For a description of the factors and creative strengths, see Millar [1995a, appendix C, pp. 353–57].) The figural test also has two parallel forms, A and B. It measures the following essential components of creativity: the ability to impose meaning on a situation or stimulus where none exists; to structure, integrate, and present an object, scene, or situation; and the ability to perceive similar stimuli in different ways.

During the six-year period (1958–1964) covered by the initial testing, a variety of alternate forms, known as the Minnesota Tests of Creative Thinking, were used. They do not vary significantly from the current activities contained in the *Torrance Tests of Creative Thinking*.

TABLE 7.1b

Description of the *Torrance Tests of Creative Thinking* (TTCT): Figural

Name of Test and Subtests	Description	Rationale	Creative Factors
Activity 1— *Picture Construction*	The person constructs a picture using a pear shape or jelly bean shape as a stimulus on the page. The shape must be an integral part of the composition	This activity gets at the tendency toward finding a purpose for something that has no definite purpose and to elaborate it so that a clear purpose emerges	• Originality • Abstractness of titles • Elaboration • Checklist of creative strengths
Activity 2— *Picture Completion*	This activity requires that a person use ten incomplete figures to make, and to name (label), an object or picture	This activity calls into play the need to structure, integrate, and present an object, scene, or situation	• Fluency • Originality • Abstractness of titles • Elaboration • Resistance to premature closure • Checklist of creative strengths
Activity 3— *Lines and Circles* (repeated figures)	This activity consists of three pages of lines or circles and the person is to make objects or pictures using the lines or circles as a part of their picture. They are to add titles/names at the bottom of each picture	This activity requires an ability to return to the same stimulus again and again, perceiving it differently each time, disrupting structure to create something new	• Fluency • Originality • Elaboration • Checklist of creative strengths

Dr. Torrance conducting a test with a child

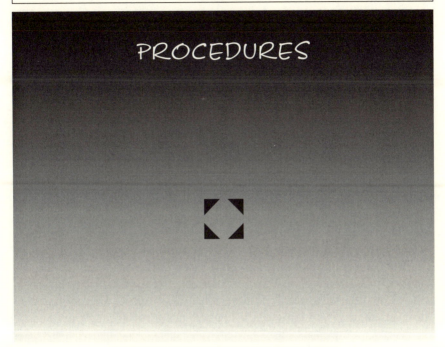

eight

PROCEDURES

SELECTION OF INDIVIDUALS FOR FIELD STUDY

Individuals selected for in-depth case study were chosen by Dr. Torrance and the author from the original sample and from those who responded to the first follow-up questionnaire in 1980. Efforts were made to randomly select individuals who lived in the same geographical region and those who "had a spark of something interesting" and were distinguished in some way. An equal number of females and males was chosen, for a total of 18 persons.

Original Sample of Elementary Students

The longitudinal study was initiated in 1958 by Torrance while he was director of the Bureau of Educational Research at the University of Minnesota. During the period from 1958 to 1964, all the children enrolled in grades 1 through 6 at the University Elementary School (*N*=170) and Sidney Pratt Elementary School (*N*=221) were tested with the Minnesota Tests of Creative Thinking. These tests were in the process of development by Torrance and his associates. They are described in table 7.1 in chapter 7.

The sample of 391 students from the two schools represented 204 girls and 187 boys. In the 1980 follow-up, 211 students (116 females, 95 males) responded to a questionnaire, while in 1998, 101 students (56 females, 45 males) from the original sample responded to a questionnaire. Problems inherent in a longitudinal study of 40 years made location of the subjects difficult. The most promising way to find the subjects was by using a former address and then using electronic (computer) means to reach them. Directories on the Internet were used and many were located by telephone.

Interviews were arranged with 18 of the individuals who responded to the 1998 follow-up questionnaire. Fifteen interviews were conducted by the author in the Minneapolis-St. Paul area during the first two weeks of July 1998. The interviews were held in a mutually convenient location: the home of the individual, office location, or in a hotel meeting room. Three telephone interviews were also conducted. Usually, the interview lasted from one to one-and-a-half hours.

The interview questions covered five main areas: early influences on creativity, career paths and transitions, creative accomplishments, questions related to the "Manifesto for Children," and general questions on creativity. A copy of the specific questions ("Interview Form") is located in appendix E.

TREATMENT OF THE INTERVIEW DATA

The interviews were all recorded on a Sony Microcassette-corder and transcribed from a Sony Microcassette Dictator/Transcriber. Each individual in the case study had an opportunity to read the transcript of the interview and make revisions.

Each transcription of the interviews was analyzed by a qualitative data procedure known as "meaning units." This method is described by Strauss and Corbin (1990). Another useful resource was *Qualitative Interviewing: The Art of Hearing Data* by Rubin and Rubin (1995).

The protocols of the interviews were listened to and read through simultaneously to get a feel for the perspective of the individual selected for case study. A chance to "relive" the interviews was helpful in the development of themes and in becoming aware of details that may not have been noticed in the actual interview process. Each verbatim transcript was analyzed according to meaning units. Meaning units consisting of unities of data—phrases, sentences, or paragraphs—were identified as the basis of analysis. The meaning units were paraphrased and codes or tags were used for labeling them. The process of thematic analysis was a long procedure involving several in-depth readings of the transcriptions and clusters in each of the five categories of questions (as shown in appendix E). The last step of the analysis involved searching for commonalities in the five categories across all case studies.

The meaning-units analyses were conducted separately by a University of Alberta doctoral student and experienced teacher, who was expert in using the method, and by the author. The two separate analyses were then combined as one and represented the conceptual essence of each interview. Additional analysis was conducted by the author to determine the themes and trends in the 18 interviews. It represents the patterns of responses by all case studies. That analysis forms the essence of part three of this volume: "Themes from the Case Studies."

DATA FOR CASE STUDIES

The data for each case study were derived from the files of Dr. Torrance. He has maintained careful files and records of all the test protocols, scoring results, and correspondence over the years for all the individuals in the longitudinal study. I had free access to those materials and to Dr. Torrance himself while writing each of the case studies. The Torrance Center for Creative Studies at the University of Georgia provided a research fellowship for me to study, organize, and write this book of case studies. Dr. Torrance was always accessible to me via e-mail and letters while I wrote at home (in Edmonton, Alberta) or in person while I was working in Athens at the university.

THE FOLLOW-UP QUESTIONNAIRES

1980

Two questionnaires were used in 1980. Copies of these are located in appendix C. The first questionnaire dealt with questions divided into three areas: general information, educational information, and career development:

1. *General information:* age, marital status, number of children, and political preferences.
2. *Educational information:* educational attainment and achievements, future educational plans, academic honors attained.

3. *Career development:* employment history, career-related honors, present position, career ambitions, projected career changes, time-out experiences, high school creative achievements, post–high school creative achievements, self-assessed most-creative achievements, spurs and obstacles to continued achievements, experience with a mentor, satisfaction with various areas of life, current frustrations, and dreams for the future.

Those who completed the first questionnaire were sent a second one titled "Supplementary Information" designed to capture information on personal or "creative style of life" areas. The purpose of this questionnaire was to gather information on creative achievements that were more personal in nature. The following types of information were collected: recollections of "teachers who made a difference" in their careers, a recent example of everyday creative behavior, information on support systems, sharing household tasks, creativity and ingenuity in dealing with household tasks, and so on. Women were asked to report on special problems in realizing their creative potentialities.

1998

The 1998 40-year questionnaire was designed cooperatively by Dr. Torrance and the author. A copy of it is found in appendix D. Its purpose was to update information from the 1980 questionnaire. The following information was obtained:

1. *Personal information:* address, telephone number, marital status, number of children, and occupation.
2. *Educational information:* educational attainment and awards and/or scholarships.
3. *Career information:* jobs since 1980.
4. *Creative achievements:* public achievements and personal creative achievements.
5. *Questions related to the "Manifesto for Children"* (love of work, mentors, "well roundedness," greatest strengths, playing your own game, doing what you love and can do well, interdependence) and availability for a personal interview.

MEASURING ADULT CREATIVE ACHIEVEMENTS

In both the 1980 and 1998 follow-up questionnaires, the individuals in the sample were asked to indicate their achievements, both public and personal. These were then rated to determine an index of creative achievement.

Throughout the longitudinal studies of creative achievement, the qualitative rating has seemed to be necessary. Surely an important invention, an excellent book, a hit song, or an important medical discovery is worth more than conducting in-service training or making suggestions regarding the workplace. Although a quality rating is subjective, an effort was made to make the quality rating more meaningful by considering the following aspects of creative achievement:

- importance
- originality
- creative "leap"
- amount of creativity involved.

It was recognized that raters vary in their values of what is important. To correct for this, at least three raters have been involved, using raters from different backgrounds. For example, in the 1980 follow-up, a nurse-educator, a graduate student outstanding as an actress, and an educational psychologist and author were raters. All three had extensive backgrounds in creativity. In the 40-year study this variety was not available. However, all of them had considerable training and study in creative research and theory.

Five indices of adult creative achievement were derived from the 1980 questionnaire responses:

1. number of high school creative achievements
2. number of publicly recognized and acknowledged post–high school creative achievements; for example, an invention, an award for creative art production, scientific or medical breakthrough, and so on
3. number of post–high school "creative style of life" achievements (not publicly recognized)
4. ratings of the quality of highest achievements described
5. ratings of the creative quality of the aspirations and future career images described.

In 1998, one index of adult creative achievement was derived from the questionnaire responses, which was the number of publicly acknowledged creative achievements.

nine

DESCRIPTION OF SAMPLE—
PERSONAL PROFILES

The 18 case studies selected for in-depth field study and interviews were chosen by Dr. Torrance and the author. Selection was based upon availability and willingness of the individuals to cooperate. They all live in the same geographic location—Minneapolis-St. Paul and surrounding areas—with the exception of three who were interviewed by telephone and mail. All were identified as "having a spark of something interesting" and were distinguished in some way.

AGE

It turned out that there was an equal number of females and males. The average age of the case studies at the time of the interviews was 48, ranging from 45–50 as shown in table 9.1.

MARITAL STATUS AND NUMBER OF CHILDREN

Sixty-seven percent (N=12) of the individuals in the case studies are married; 28 percent (N=5) are single; and 5 percent (N=1) are divorced. The average number of children produced by individuals in the case studies is 1.4, ranging from 0 to 4.

TABLE 9.1

Average Age* and Range of the Case Studies

	Females (N=9)	Males (N=9)	Total (N=18)
Average Age	47.6 years	48.1 years	47.9 years
Ranging from	45–50 years	46–50 years	45–50 years

*At the time of the interviews (July 1998).

POSITION IN THE FAMILY AND SIZE OF FAMILY

The vast majority of the individuals in the case studies were either first- or second-born children. Table 9.2 illustrates the specific family positions. The average family size for this sample in the early 1950s was 4.3, ranging from 1 to 10.

TABLE 9.2

Position in the Family

	First-born	Second-born	Third-born	Fourth-born
Females	3	3	2	1
Males	3	6	0	0
Total	**6**	**9**	**2**	**1**

SCHOOLS ATTENDED

The majority of individuals in the case studies attended the University Elementary School (UES); specifically, 13 (72%) attended UES, while 4 (22%) attended Sidney Pratt Elementary School. One individual attended both schools—at different times.

POST-SECONDARY EDUCATION STATUS

All case studies hold a post-secondary credential or degree, ranging from a certificate to a doctoral degree. Specific credentials are shown, for females and males, in table 9.3.

TABLE 9.3
Post-Secondary Accreditation of the Case Studies by Gender (N=18)

	Cert.	B.A.	B.F.A.	B.Ed.	B.Sc.	M.S.	M.F.A.	J.D.	M.D.	Ph.D.	Total
					Credentials						
Females (N=9)	1 (CPA)	3	1	1			1	1		1	9
Males (N=9)		1			2	1	1	2	1	1	9
Total (N=18)	1	4	1	1	2	1	2	3	1	2	18

CURRENT OCCUPATION OF CASE STUDIES

The majority of individuals are involved in professional careers. One is currently unemployed, while two have taken early retirement. The most common occupations are: lawyer (3), librarian (2), and actor or actress (2). Table 9.4 lists the occupations by gender.

TABLE 9.4
General Occupations of the Case Studies

Females	Males
Librarian (f=2)	Lawyer (f=2)
Actress/Writer/Singer	Medical Researcher
Lawyer	Professional Actor/Teacher
Cable-splicer/Telecommunications	Neurologist/Professor
Purchaser–Printing	Architect/Builder
Psychologist	Neuropsychologist (unemployed)
Family Manager	C.E.O./Medical Equipment
Certified Public Accountant	Foreign Service Officer

f = frequency

PARENTAL OCCUPATIONAL BACKGROUNDS

The overwhelming majority of individuals in the case studies came from professional families. The mothers also had been trained to work in a professional field, although many of them had chosen to stay at home as homemakers. It must be remembered that these "mothers" were raising their children after the Second World War. Table 9.5 lists the various occupations, by gender, of the parents of the case studies.

TABLE 9.5

Schooling and Occupations of the Parents of the Case Studies

	Parental Schooling, Parental Work/Occupation (Father)	Parental Schooling, Parental Work/Occupation (Mother)
Females (Case Studies, N=9)	High school, two years of college	Homemaker and community volunteer upper management
	Masters degree (civil engineering), CEO—Fisher Nut Company	Masters degree, foster-care worker
	D.D.S., M.S., professor/head, dental school	B.A., administrator—University of Minnesota
	Management, farm machinery (industry)	B.A., elementary teacher
	Professor—medicine	B.A., homemaker
	B.Sc., owns chemical supply company	High school and some college, homemaker
	Ph.D., professor, bio-physical chemistry	Ph.D., clinical psychologist, homemaker
	Masters degree (architecture)	B.A., homemaker
	M.Ed., civil-rights worker	Ph.D., school psychologist, homemaker
Males (Case Studies, N=9)	Professor—geography	Two masters degrees, librarian
	Physicist–mathematician	Homemaker
	Professor, American studies	Four years of college
	Heart surgeon	Nurse
	M.B.A. (Harvard), real estate salesman	Homemaker
	University professor	Homemaker
	German teacher in high school	Homemaker
	Medical doctor	Ph.D., speech pathologist
	Restaurateur	Homemaker

INTELLIGENCE

The average intelligence quotient (I.Q.) of the individuals in the case studies is 127, ranging from 108 to 147. The scores are based on one of the following tests: Stanford Binet Intelligence Test, Wechsler Intelligence Scales for Children, or the California Test of Mental Maturity. Specific average scores for females and males are reported in table 9.6.

TABLE 9.6
Average I.Q. Scores of the Case Studies

	Females (N=9)	Males (N=9)	Total (N=18)
Average I.Q. score	127	126	126.5
Ranging from	121–130	108–147	108–147

CREATIVITY

The estimated creativity quotient (C.Q.) or score of the individuals in the case studies is 104, ranging from 84 to 125. The scores are based on the Minnesota Tests of Creative Thinking, designed by Torrance during the 1958 to 1965 time period. These scores are based on students who were tested in Minnesota schools at that time. Dr. Torrance[1] has indicated to me that these scores cannot be interpreted in the same way that the *Torrance Tests of Creative Thinking* are today. He states that approximately 10 points would have to be added to the Minnesota scores to make them comparable to national norms of today. Specific average scores for females and males are reported in table 9.7.

TABLE 9.7
Average Estimated C.Q. Scores of the Case Studies

	Females (N=9)	Males (N=9)	Total (N=18)
Average C.Q. score	108	99	103.5
Ranging from	93–125	84–117	84–125

QUALITY OF CREATIVE ACHIEVEMENTS

As rated by experts in the field of creativity, the average score for quality of public creative achievements in 1998 for the individuals in the case studies is 5.5 out of a possible 10, ranging from 1.0 to 9.5. Specific averages for females and males are shown in table 9.8. In 1980, the average score for the case studies was 6.5 out of 10, ranging from 2 to 9. Averages for this time period for the genders are also shown in the table.

TABLE 9.8

Comparison of Average Scores of the Quality of Public Creative
Achievements for Genders over the Follow-up Periods
(1980 and 1998) (f value=16.03*)

	1980 Follow-up	1998 Follow-up
Females (*N*=9) average score	7	4
Males (*N*=9) average score	6	7

*$p<0.01$

A repeated measures analysis of variance indicated a significant ($p<0.01$) interaction between the quality of public creative achievements between males and females. The females have dropped and the males have increased significantly over the two time periods.

The ten selected case studies that follow serve to illustrate the predictive validity of the *Torrance Tests of Creative Thinking* and, perhaps equally or more important, the intervening variables or factors that support and sustain creativity as individuals live out their lives.

NOTE

1. In discussion with the author, April 2000.

part two

CASE STUDIES

Of the 18 individuals identified for in-depth follow-up, ten were selected to illustrate the predictive validity of the *Torrance Tests of Creative Thinking* and to validate the "Manifesto for Children." Although
the case studies follow a similar format, the individual lives present
very different careers that have been shaped by a variety of influences. The themes that emerged from these lives are discussed in part
three of this volume.

ten

WENDY HENRY

"CREATIVE PERSON-AT-LARGE"— RENAISSANCE WOMAN

"My most creative achievement . . . is myself!"—Wendy (1998)

Wendy Feder, circa 1958

Wendy Charlene Henry is clearly one of the most creative students in the longitudinal study. She states that creativity is "part of my life all the time." She does not compartmentalize her life—her career and work are not separate from her hobbies. Wendy's career at the present time could be described as building and creating a healthy, joy-filled self through nourishing relationships and creative works, and sharing what she has learned with others so that they too can live deeper and happier lives. She truly has learned the skills of interdependence and is gladly sharing her infinite creativity.

Wendy is a professional actress with multiple talents in several areas: writing (stories, poetry, monologues), singing, song writing, making music (cello, piano, guitar), painting, skiing, drawing, photography, dancing, and ceaseless home-improvement projects. She is obviously doing what she loves and can do well. She doesn't worry about being well rounded, but rather knows, understands, takes pride in, practices, develops, exploits, and enjoys her greatest strengths.

Currently, she and her husband, Stuart Henry, have just had their first child—or, rather, children: twin boys, Jake and David! They are excited about bringing children into the world and helping them to grow creatively and to realize their potential. As a mother, Wendy will undoubtedly "fall in love" with her new role as parent and will "pursue it with intensity," as she has in so many other areas of her career.

Wendy's creativity potential as measured in elementary school predicted high creative achievements as an adult, but there were also several other important factors that sustained her creativity as she developed, such as learning to free herself from the expectations of others and to walk away from the games they imposed on her.

SCHOOL YEARS

Wendy Feder (now Henry) was raised as a middle child in a family of three children in St. Paul. Her father was vice-president and then president of the Fisher Nut Company and her mother worked in social services. As a student at the University Elementary School she was assessed by a variety of creativity and intelligence tests over the period 1958 to 1962 while attending grades 1 through 4.

Her creativity tests while in elementary school show that she was in the superior range, with high scores in the factors of fluency, origi-

Grade 4, May 14, 1962

Grade 2 doodle

nality, and elaboration. Other creative strengths over that period of time included unusual visual perspective and extending/breaking boundaries. She did not experience the fourth-grade slump in creative production, as did most of her peers. Her intelligence score placed her in the bright range (120+). Her drawing of herself in grade 4 illustrates not only her articulateness in drawing, but also a joyful Wendy with a peaceful cat at her side. In grade 3, with Mrs. Taplin as a teacher, Wendy indicated that she wanted to be an artist when she grew up. She was always drawing and doodling. Her future career image was emerging.

FIRST FOLLOW-UP

At the time of the 22-year follow-up, Wendy was 27 years of age, married, and was working as a journalist-reporter-photographer with the *Navajo Times* in Window Rock, Arizona. She had completed a Bachelor of Arts degree, cum laude, from Stanford University (1974), majoring in psychology with a minor in art. Wendy had done some graduate work "at large" at Arizona State University (1975–1976) in acting musical theatre, painting, and ceramics for her own growth and stimulation. She was not enrolled in a degree program at that time.

Wendy was involved at this time in a number of training programs. She had worked as a picture framer after college in 1975 and had enjoyed the simple, manual work. She remembers most loving the creative part of selecting mats and frames that would enhance the beauty of the art. She spent the summer of 1971 in Israel, taking a drama workshop, and performed lead roles in many shows—university theatre and community theatre. She had nine years of musical training in the cello and four years on the piano.

Since graduating from high school, Wendy had worked as a factory worker in the Fisher Nut Company in Minneapolis during the summer of 1970. After graduating from college, she worked as a saleswoman in the fall of 1975. During the late 1970s Wendy was a reporter/editor for the *Navajo Times* on the Navajo Indian Reservation in Arizona. She received "special recognition" many times for her writing from the Navajo community. Wendy's career ambitions at this time were to apply to theatre schools for graduate study, and she longed to return to writing songs and doing artwork again.

Wendy had achieved a number of accomplishments in high school. She participated in two summer programs for high school students sponsored by the National Federation of Temple Youth (NFTY), traveling to Israel in 1968 and to Europe in 1969. She shared the lead and had other minor roles in school plays; she played cello in several performances of the school orchestra; and organized and sang in a girl's barbershop septet. In high school, Wendy was elected vice-president of her junior class and graduated with honors. While there, Wendy and her two brothers collected donations from students, raising $1,400 to help people in Israel after the Six-Day War in 1967. While in college, Wendy and three other students put together and taped a series of songs about the Holocaust that was presented to Elie Wiesel, the writer and survivor of a concentration camp. This project was not related to a school requirement.

Wendy's creative achievement score was 8.0 out of 10.0—much above average for the case studies as a group. Since graduating from high school, she indicated a number of noteworthy achievements:

- published several feature stories
- performed several lead roles in plays
- composed several pieces of music
- published artwork in a newspaper
- created several advertising ideas
- volunteered in various political campaigns
- organized her own business—designing brochures for local artists
- conducted several in-service training sessions for co-workers.

Wendy indicated the following three creative achievements since high school:

- wrote and presented a series of songs about the Holocaust
- reaching a level of excellence in journalism while working on the *Navajo Times* newspaper
- her performance as "Beatrice" in a community-theatre production titled *The Effects of Gamma Rays on Man-in-the-Moon Marigolds.*

In the 1980 questionnaire, Wendy stated that her greatest spur for continued achievement was herself—her need to fulfill her own potential and use her talents. Her greatest obstacle to continued achievement was, again—herself! Wendy expressed a fear of failure and inability to put her needs above those of friends and family. She had no mentor at this time and expressed her current lifestyle as somewhat-to-very-satisfying (4 out of 5).

Wendy, circa 1998

Wendy does bring ingenuity to household tasks. Her best cooking comes from "made-up recipes." She invents "gourmet" dishes such as soups, vegetarian lasagnas (filled with everything from broccoli and olives to sherry wine) and her stir-fries and brown-rice casseroles are most famous. Because she basically hates housecleaning, she often makes up little games with rewards for herself to get it done. For example, she will watch a particular television show if, during the commercials, she can "run" into the kitchen and get at least ten tasks done. Wendy and a friend used to do their housework together. They would work together on one house first, and then do the other one. It made a social event. They also would switch leftovers—that way, each family had some meal variety.

Finally, Wendy expressed the primary frustration in her life. She felt that women, generally, are dealt a "bad deal" in society—not so much in lack of opportunity or societal discrimination, but more in conditioning. Women, she stated, are encouraged to be more warm and nurturing to others than to fulfilling their own potential.

For the next ten years after college graduation, Wendy wished to become a competent actress, singer, and musician and to earn a comfortable living doing what she loved best. She ended this period in 1980 by reporting that she had been accepted into a Master of Fine Arts (MFA) theater program at Brandeis University, to begin in the fall of 1980. She moved to Waltham, Massachusetts during the summer.

MIDDLE AND LATE CAREER

In the 1998 questionnaire, Wendy indicated that she had remarried since the last follow-up and was working as a freelance actress and artist. She had completed the MFA degree in from Brandeis in 1984. Wendy was awarded an artist-in-residence position at Brandeis University during the 1983–1984 academic year.

Then she moved to New York City, where she studied with the noted acting teacher Uta Hagen. For a while she worked as a sort of music therapist/activity person at a nursing home in a very rough part of Brooklyn, singing old songs along with her guitar in an attempt to engage elders suffering from organic brain syndrome and other severe age-related conditions.

She moved back to Minnesota in May of 1988. She performed in a number of shows in Minneapolis theaters, and had a working relationship with Illusion Theater doing educational theater, dealing with issues such as diversity, primarily for corporate groups. She performed "The Shame of It All" during 1992–1994, a two-person touring show for which she co-wrote the music and collaborated on the script. She had a small role in the ABC television miniseries *Son of the Morning Star* and was a "day player" in a feature film. Sample poems and songs written by Wendy have been included at the end of this interview.

Wendy's score of 9.0 out of 10 for creative achievements was the second highest of the group selected for the case study in the longitudinal study. Her public creative achievements in acting, composing music, and delivering keynote speeches are too numerous to list, and her personal creative achievements involve her artistic pursuits, some of which are designing greeting cards and unusual gift wrapping, which Wendy refers to as "making silk purses out of sow's ears," and writing poems, monologues, and stories. Her latest creative foray is consulting with the corporate world as a communications coach and creativity consultant-mentor. She recently "coached" her husband for a presentation he delivered at an international quality-assurance conference in Orlando, Florida. She helped him with his presentation and wrote some of the lyrics for a blues song, which he sang with a blues harmonica that he plays. Many rated Stuart Henry's presentation to be the best in the conference.

Wendy indicated that she is "in love with her work," but what she loves most is reaching and moving people through her creative expression. Other people depend on Wendy for support, "mothering," insight, advice, creative ideas, encouragement, figuring out solutions, and cheerleading them out of seemingly impossible situations. Her creative goal and aspiration for the future are "to have my own children as they are the future and our treasure chest."

INTERVIEW, JULY 11, 1998

The interview with Wendy Henry was conducted in Minneapolis. She reflected on the early influences on her creativity, her career path and transitions, her creative accomplishments, and, finally, some general comments on creativity. Her own words tell her experiences best. (*Note:* The bracketed or footnoted information was added by Wendy after she read the transcript for verification of information, December 18, 1998.)

EARLY INFLUENCES ON CREATIVITY

At what age were you first aware of your creativity, of your resourcefulness, if you like?

I guess I'd have to say that one goes back as far as my memory would go. What I know now is that I was sexually abused as a child, which I didn't remember at that time, but I know I always drew; I always loved to. There was a game I would play. My favorite thing was to have somebody draw a doodle. I'd say, "Mommy, draw me a doodle." Drawing a little, any kind of a squiggle, and I would make pictures out of it, I would make something out of it. I remember making very creative cards, even early, early on, I remember, probably somewhere in the basement. They've probably been saved [GWM laughing], ones that I took eggshells or whatever I had and created cards. When I was living in New York I designed a series of cards for a card business, which I never did publish. I make my own cards and I send them to people now. Some people say it was a safe place for me [referring to a safe place to retreat with myself—from my abusive reality, which as a child I couldn't consciously face] but I can't remember not being like that.

What influence do you feel your schooling had on your creative ability?

I don't think that schooling was the greatest influence. As I mentioned before, I started at the University Elementary School, I believe when I was two. They had a nursery school that was in Pattee Hall that is no longer there. I remember that there was one room where there were one-way mirror windows and I knew that we were being watched. I remember being taken over next door— there was a psychology department that was next door. Grad students would do a series of tests on us. I don't know if they were Rorshach or not, but I remember being taken over to the University of Minnesota and I remember feeling observed.

There was a professor who was a piano teacher and I think that it was through the university because he took some apparently creative kids which I was one of those, and we were put on television, where we'd come and clap our hands and do rhythmic things. But he was a very cruel piano teacher. I think I started piano in first grade. I just remember playing and he'd have a ruler and when I'd do something wrong he'd slap it on the piano right next to my fingers so that there was this very loud sound. It really scared me.

I'm very, very musical. Oh, I remember that I really wanted to play the flute and somebody at the university told me, "Oh, you don't have the lip for it." It was very strange, because now I know that these lips are fine. [GWM laughing.] It was not true. But I stopped playing piano. Beginning in fifth grade I played the cello for about nine years. I'd volunteer for anything creative at all and pull it off because I'm creative and smart. That's how I started playing the cello. It was actually when I changed schools. In fifth grade, somebody came to the class and said, "The orchestra needs cellos. We're looking for somebody to play." I was a new student, and wanted friends, so I put up my hand not even knowing what a cello was and ended up playing for nine years. [GWM laughing]. I went to college on my essays about playing the cello. I had a dream in college that I was climbing in Yosemite with the cello on my back and it was a big burden. I set it down and I basically stopped playing.

My father played piano and he had this idea that there was a right way to do things and a wrong way to do things. I don't think that helped, but I found my way through it and beginning in college, I taught myself guitar. I have played close to 30 years without ever learning the names of the strings [laughing]. I played the music and now actually in the last couple of months, I'm taking some lessons to learn some of those things, so I can get some structure that I need to be able to do the job. I would like to accompany my husband because he plays harmonica. I started writing music and I'd play the chords on my own; started singing what I felt and lyrics came out. I reacted against or responded to a kind of rigid training.

What specific incidents can you remember in your childhood which enabled your creativity to develop?

Well, I have to say that at home my artistic abilities were recognized early on and that I got a lot of support there. I think in later life I resisted that,* because I have an extremely competitive mother who sang on the radio once when she was a kid and said, "You don't know what I could've been" and a family that liked to box you into your own little territory.† I think I resisted that. I'm professionally trained as an actress. I'm finding my way back to art,

---

*This refers to the fact that my family, particularly my mother, *specifically* supported/encouraged me in my *visual* artistic abilities (painting, drawing, etc.) even though I was talented in the others as well (music, acting, etc.) because, in a way, that was a "slot" that wasn't taken—or wanted by others. My mother sang a song on the radio as a kid and I believed harbored some secret fantasy of the great actress and performer she could have been. My father played piano and much was made of the hours he practiced as a kid and the fact that he taught some piano to help support his college education. He was THE musician. I remember a few years ago, I was over at my parents' house and I sat down at the piano and played "Somewhere over the Rainbow." My mother walked by and instead of remarking on how well I played, said "What a wonderful tribute to your father." (My father is alive.) So I believe that because both my parents are so extremely competitive—and competitive with their children, they chose to encourage and "box me in" to an area of my talent that didn't compete with their territories. That is what I resisted. I became an actress, singer, songwriter, performer. . . .

†I believe nothing seeks more to destroy creativity than sexual abuse. But I wanted to amend that to say this—at least in my experience, my creativity was never destroyed. As a matter of fact, I believe it saved my (inner) life. It gave me a means to express and to heal—as evidenced by some of the songs and poems I've written about my pain and/or my healing process.

What sexual abuse destroys—at least 'til healing occurs—is the *joy* in the ability to create, not the need to do it. But an abused or neglected child will forget, essentially, who she really is—and forget, in her hopelessness, that she can still be found—and comfort can be found through her creativity.

For me, I feel one of the ways I carried on my own abuse and neglect was by depriving myself of art.

"Harvey"

as it happens, in the same darn way I started to play the cello. The director of a play needed somebody to do a painting, a portrait. He was playing the lead character and "Harvey", which is a giant, invisible rabbit. Of course I said, "Well, I'll do it." [GWM laughing.] I've never painted a portrait in my life. I ended up doing a 30 inch by 40 inch painting which amazingly enough really looks like him.

Was there any influence at elementary age that you now recognize as having had an impact on your subsequent career or your chosen field of work?

A number of years ago I was doing some painting. I was experiencing the joy of art in being able to do that. So I'd have to say that being a very lonely . . . I was very lonely at University Elementary School, and this had an effect. I lived in Highland Park. We were in St. Paul, so we had to carpool and we were taken to the university everyday so I didn't have any friends in the neighborhood. The only time that I could ever see kids was when there was a sleepover. And so I remember being extremely lonely and I have a memory from fourth grade. I felt it was really significant to me. I remember walking around Pattee Hall and I just felt completely alone. I remember feeling very old and just this sort of profound aloneness. I felt very much older than a kid.

I had one particular best friend who I played with every day. That friendship probably saved my life from fifth grade to tenth grade. She came into my life actually when I was in fifth grade. I remember she came over to my house. Her name was Kathy Bass. She lived a block over. She'd just moved from Winnipeg, Canada, and I had this toy that was called a Vacu-Form. It created heat to melt a bit of plastic over a form and so you could make these plastic things. We were in my basement and Kathy didn't know how to use this and I said to her, "You don't even know how to use the Vacu-Form?" She said, "I'm from Canada. We don't have those." [GWM laughing.] That was her excuse and she was my Canadian friend. She was my first real best friend . . . from the fifth to tenth grade. And then I changed schools because I wasn't learning enough.

The new school was called Summit School. It had small classes and I went to visit with this girl that I had grown up with, Mimi Ravits. I went to these classes with ten or twelve girls. It was so exciting. We had to do entrance exams and all that stuff and I changed schools again in the eleventh grade. I never studied harder than I did in that eleventh grade in high school. It was the most exciting year of learning for me. I was sure I was gonna flunk out and I was actually first in my class. I thought I was flunking out.

[I have no idea what this was about but I just remember how significant it was to be in a girls' school where appearances didn't matter—there were no boys to impress and we all dressed alike in uniforms so it didn't matter, you couldn't tell who had money and who didn't—and the classes were small so I felt much more visible and important. Also, I noticed that all of the girls and I were much more verbal and engaged in our education—I believe I was far less self-conscious and more willing to be bolder and "out there" without boys around.

I went to Summit School for eleventh grade. It merged with St. Paul Academy for my senior year and I was in the first graduating class of "Saint Paul Academy and Summit School" (S.P.A.S.S.).

When I started at Summit School, I had just returned from spending seven or eight weeks in Israel. I was so thrilled with it; I almost Israeli-danced my way into the school! So I never noticed, nor knew, until many years later that there was quite a bit of anti-Semitism in the school. I guess because of my innocence (or ignorance!), lack of defensiveness, I ignored and thus overcame what could have been obstacles, and succeeded both scholastically and in friendships. As I mentioned before, the discrepancy between my intelligence, talents and competence, and my sense of esteem was immense. I studied hard, fearing I would flunk out of the school and not only did I not flunk, I was first in my class my first semester there. I was also elected vice-president of my class at the end of that first semester. I feel very proud about this particular success as I look back. Or perhaps touched. I mean I got to be both smart and successful *and* well liked and respected. How wonderful is that? And it all was quite unexpected by me. Years later, when a classmate told me that, not only was there anti-Semitism, but the Jewish kids were particularly resented for being at the top of the class, that experience became even more striking and meaningful to me.]

I remember a specific event in high school that affected my future career. Probably very much [laughing]. I mentioned that the interest in theater was there earlier. There was a play called "A Company of Wayward Saints." My brother was cast in it, my boyfriend was cast in it and all of my best friends were in the cast. I remember just feeling so, so, you know, so left out, so . . . something. So, I was so left out, it's still painful for me when I hear the music for some reason. I was on the outside of it. There is a specific memory of my boyfriend and a woman who later on became a professional actress. They had been practicing an audition for another play and were going to do a scene from "A Company of Wayward Saints." I remember coming in and seeing them acting on stage as I sat in the dark at the back of the auditorium. There they were in the light and on the stage and thinking, that's where I want to be. I think that being left out and having that experience had a huge effect on my ultimately choosing theater for my career.

The next thing that happened was when I was 28 years old. I'm gonna go back four years from then. I was living on the Navajo Indian reservation working as a reporter. I was married, my first marriage, and I was watching a soap opera called "Ryan's Hope" and there was that same woman from high school on this soap opera. She was now a professional actress. I found myself thinking, If I were 95 and looking back on my life, would I regret it if I didn't try acting? So that's when I decided to audition for theater school. But anyway, I know that I'm jumping farther ahead. I'd not done any kind of "just go for it things." I mean, I was living on an Indian reservation and decided okay, I'm wanting to go back to school, go back to theater, so I went back down to Phoenix where I'd been a graduate student-at-large after college to talk to an acting teacher about theatre schools. I said, "What are the best schools in the country? He laughed and I said, "I might as well start at the top." I ended up flying out to San Francisco to audition for the "League" schools, the best schools in the country. I had memorized two monologues and had my editor at the *Navajo Times* take a photo of me at my home. We developed it at the newspaper office for my headshot. I was accepted to two schools and was wait-listed at a third, Brandeis, where I ultimately went.

What would you say, Wendy, was the most important lesson that you learned with regard to your creativity?

[Pause.] All that keeps coming up is that creativity is the greatest strength I've ever had. It is something that can become blocked but can't be killed (laughing). There's a freedom of your spirit in creativity that I feel is very closely connected to the spiritual part of us. I really think that as you get older, people become stuck and get more and more blocks, and wear more and more masks.

I don't know if that is a lesson but I think it's what has saved me in my life. You know, that (creativity) and love are the things that sustain me.

How would your peers in the elementary grades have described you?

Well, my impression of how others kids spoke about me, was they liked me but I was really smart so I think I was therefore on top of the class. I wanted everybody to like me, to be friends with me. I was a major approval seeker.

[I think other kids would have said I was very smart, very talented, sweet and warm, but quite insecure. They might have noticed that I longed to be liked and to be included.]

CAREER PATHS AND TRANSITIONS

What is your present job?

Well, right now, I'm not exactly, officially, gainfully employed. Which is sort of fine with me. This is sort of private so I don't know if you want me to say it or not. For the last few years, my husband and I have been trying to get pregnant, using every means known to man and every procedure. That has taken all our time. I mean every form and amount of creativity that we have.

I'm still called occasionally by Illusion Theater to do outreach kind of stuff. But at the moment, I'm just kind of not doing that. I've done keynote speaking. I coached my husband in a presentation that took place at a national computer conference [laughing] last fall. And I am beginning to mentor people. [Coach corporate people on communications and giving presentations.] Actually we presented a proposal together on giving presentations and the importance of how you prepare and face the audience in this case.* I'm in the process of starting to coach people on presentations, communications, how to present yourself [laughing] and be personal with a group of people. It's the same thing whether you need to reach across this divide and connect with another person in order to communicate something and how you bring that into a larger kind of setting. So I think that I will probably call myself a communications coach and start more officially working with corporate people. I mean, on keynote speeches, presentations or with actors on monologues.

It almost seems trite for me to ask you: How do you apply creativity to your work?

I'm a creative person-at-large. That's what I am, that's just what I do. I realize I do it all the time.

I taught undergraduate acting after I got my degree. I was an artist in residence at Brandeis University and then I moved to New York City. I worked there as an art therapist in a nursing home, where I really did more music therapy. I would sing old songs, like "Let Me Call You Sweetheart." I worked with people that had a lot of organic brain syndrome and like, there was a woman who hadn't spoken in years and all of a sudden, she sang, sang the lyrics of this old song. So music had a way of getting the job done. I've done that.

I lived on a Navajo Indian reservation for six years and I got a job as a reporter for the Navajo newspaper. I'd never taken a class in journalism, and on the first week (which was my first issue,

---

*Since this interview, my husband and I have presented together at two computer conferences—one national and one international. The first was here in Minneapolis in October, the second in Orlando, Florida in November. We have been hugely successful. We were rated "Best in Conference" at the first, and were so popular in Orlando that they asked us to do it a second time two days later! They are talking about bringing us back next year in a keynote position, we have submitted to two more conferences (Orlando and San Antonio), and we just sent out a proposal to a Phillip Morris in Virginia, who approached us at the Orlando Conference asking us if we might consider doing a communications workshop with their Quality people. I'm enclosing a sheet describing the basics of what we're beginning to do. . . . It's great fun! We both speak and utilize music, theater and all but the kitchen sink! Obviously the corporate world is craving creativity and warmth!

I'm at the helm when it comes to the coaching and seminars.

since it was a weekly paper), I had the front page story which was about a train hitting a flock of sheep. [GWM laughing.] I learned; I just started doing it. The same way I did many things, volunteer—I volunteer and then I do it. That's why I can talk to you about a million things but I couldn't do the questionnaire.

The same thing happened in college. I took two quarters of Italian, didn't interest me. Then I went for six months to Italy and I had to talk to people about all kinds of things.

Somehow I do whatever it takes and my resolve creates.

[In other words, it is so important to me to connect with people; the language came easily because I *needed* it. I wanted it. I *had* to reach those people.]

So I was also a photographer, when I was a reporter for the *Navajo Times*. That's where I got very interested in Navajo rugs and Navajo weaving. I started spending all my money, in collecting all these rugs. I just sort of didn't know what to do.* Here in Minnesota, I invited a bunch of people to my parents' house and brought these rugs and started teaching them about how the craft happens and how the wool begins with the sheep, how it's cleaned, spun, dyed, woven and becomes a rug because I was so interested. It is such an incredible art form, how these rugs come out of the minds of the Navajo people.

There was a community theater of which I eventually became president. One of my favorite things that I've ever done was to direct a production of *A Streetcar Named Desire*. It was multicultural. And then I got this woman who I just thought, "This woman has talent," a black woman to play Blanche. And I remember the production was wonderful.

I conducted an acting workshop with seventh and sixth graders at a Bureau of Indian Affairs boarding school, I don't know how I . . .

---

*I guess this would be a good example of how I've often watched other people, asked them questions about how *they* do things and in that way, I suppose, let lots of people in the world be my mentors. There was a woman on the reservation who had started a Navajo rug business. She wasn't much like me and her motivations were different from mine—she was a businesswoman interested in making money and I was more interested in getting closer to more and more of these beautiful things and the craft and to support and meet those wonderful weavers (there were only so many rugs I could collect! It seemed to me, that if I could sell them to others, I could keep buying them!). Anyway, I watched how she did it—she set up Navajo rug shows in people's homes, taught about how they were made and then sold them. I asked her lots and lots of questions and then I tried it myself.

[I believe I was handing you a resume from around 15 years ago that I had put together to apply for jobs teaching acting in colleges. Jobs were scarce; I sent out a number of resumes with no luck and never pursued it further.

I think that was for the best. I think, now, that an academic structure may have been too confining for me . . . who knows?

It feels today like I like to pull things out of a big, open space and put something together. Possibilities that begin without limit . . . does this make any sense? In a context of rules and with my ever-lessening, but still present need for approval, belonging and connection, it may have not been the best place for me.]

I wrote speeches for a man who was elected tribal chairman. I met a woman living on the reservation, Maely Trimiar, who told me she actually wrote, "Lady Sings the Blues." She said, "Darling, you have so many talents, you can really write," so she wanted me to write her book. I said okay. [I taped some conversations with her talking about her life, which I probably still have somewhere, but we never completed it and she died.]

I was a journalist. I did an interview on this girl who was a barrel-racing champion and it was published in the *World of Rodeo Magazine.* [GWM laughing.] I was a good writer, so I just learned to do it. But I think that's the way they would teach in journalism school.* I've learned how to do stuff creatively.

I directed shows when I was an actor and an artist-in-residence. I team taught with the head acting coach.† Let's see . . . composer, guitarist, cellist, composed a song that is performed and composed some ballads. Same thing as this portrait, something comes up, something needs to be done. "It's a doodle." That's appropriate [laughing].

---

*I know in journalism school there's a particular writing formula that has a shape like an upside down triangle ∇ to describe starting with what's most important and tapering down to what's least important. My common sense (or creativity) told me that if I just pretended I was writing a letter to someone I cared about, I would *naturally* communicate this way—so that's what I'd do! At the typewriter, I would literally type, Dear So-and-so, and tell them about what had happened. I would then erase the "Dear So-and-so," do some editing, and there would be my story!

†This is what happened: I offered to help teach. Ted Kazanoff (the head acting coach) suggested splitting his class into two sections. Now, I was afraid that those who spent time in my section would be angry or disappointed, because Ted Kazanoff was quite well known and highly respected and many acting students came to the school in order to study with him. When the class *voted* to have me continue teaching them, I was extraordinarily touched and gratified.

Just tell me what you need and I'll do any work necessary. Performing, performances, I did a show, a clown show when I was in grad school, where I brought out the cello that I played. I was the cellist in the marching band. I would then sit and play the cello with a live cockatiel on my bow. [GWM laughing.]

When I was in college, there were four of us performing together. One was a fellow who wrote music about the Holocaust. He later became a rabbi. There was a fellow who played piano and another fellow who played the guitar and I sang. Two of us were Jewish, two of us weren't. We put together this original music, called "Night." [Based on the book *Night* by Elie Wiesel, a Holocaust survivor who has written many books about his experiences and has spoken all over the world for over 40 years. We presented the finished tape to him when he came to Stanford.] The same group came back and got together after I graduated and put together another series of songs called "Warsaw."

I was in a miniseries on TV. I went to Montana to go to the wedding of a boyfriend's brother. I found that there were these auditions and took my resume. I auditioned and got called back. I ended up being cast in the mini-series.

Let me ask this question here then, about changes that you've made. You've talked a lot about the number of things you've done in your life up to now. When you made changes in your working life, was there anyone whom you relied on for support and advice?

I think I've always relied a lot on other people for the changes. I've always probably been seeking mothers [both laughing]. So I've always talked to a few friends a lot or therapists, or teachers, or people that I thought were the experts and knew more. Or later in life, a close friend of mine who is a psychic. I've looked to the outside for guidance in my life a lot.

[I think what I was saying here was—perhaps because of the profound level of abuse and emotional neglect in my background, I've always craved connection and have looked to other people for lots of things—for guidance, for warmth, for reassurance, for safety, for *connection*.

This quality in my personality, a sort of dependency, perhaps, which grew out of trauma, has also been a great gift to me in my life. I have many friends and my greatest joy comes through my connections with people.]

CREATIVE ACCOMPLISHMENTS

What would you consider to be your most creative achievement to this point?

My most creative achievement? Myself.

Yourself?

My most creative achievement is that—myself [both laughing]. Who I am, the fact that I'm creative and funny and smart and liked. A person that loves other people despite what I've gone through and the fact that I have depth. I have a marriage, I love somebody and I work on it. So I'd have to say that is the greatest one. I'm proud of my portrait and I'm proud of the shows that I have directed. I'm proud of the movies and of painting, the things that come out of me. I'm proud of a couple of my poems.

In what area now of your life do you feel you are most able to be creative?

Well, I guess it ends up being in relationships again. My husband and I want to have children. Kids love me [laughing] because I'm good at going into the imagination realm in life. My creative strengths come into play. I hear what seems to be going on with other people's lives and I think that I'm able to look at things differently.

I have done things that are creative and that make money. I have made money as a journalist and as an actress. I'm lucky that I'm not poor, so I don't necessarily have to work. The things that are the most creative I think are the way I am all the time. I would think it was creative coming in here and meeting you and deciding I want to know more about Dr. Torrance's study. I needed to do it for me. I brought my guitar in case you wanted to hear me sing.

Let me ask you this, Wendy, about your close associates and you have quite a few friends, by the sounds of it. How do they describe your creative attributes?

My friends think I'm unbelievably talented and that I should be winning Tony Awards. I have this one friend who has two daughters that I'm very close to, she told me she'd love it if her daughters grew up like me and she admires my intelligence and wit and creativity. So my friends think I'm extraordinarily talented and funny. They think I'm extraordinarily wonderful and smart. [GWM laughing.] They wish that I could see myself as they see me. My friends really, really see it. I've been supported by people like Uta Hagen, the famous acting teacher. When I left New York and moved back to Minnesota, she said, "I'm sure you know how talented you are. I was afraid your intelligence would get in the way but it didn't. I knew that I was watching a flower bloom, I'm sure you know how talented you are." Somebody overheard it and said, "God, I could go for ten years if she ever said that to me." My greatest weakness, I think, is my own lack of trust in people, in myself and in my art.

What influences guide or constrain your creativity?

I guess what guided it could be a little kid saying, "Wendy, you know, I need some help, what do you think of this? Or how do you do this?" It's questions from people like, "How would I get a portrait for this show?" It's questions because that creates the doodle. The doodle is presented and I have to make something out of it. I find that springs me forth into creative activity. It's a question of the personal aspect. If there's a personal element then it's not a vague, square, impersonal thing. It's not institutional questions. It's like a person; here you are, here's this human being who I can see wants to hear, believes in something. You believe in something that you're doing, and I'm moved. I could be here all day. That's what inspires me the most is the personal contact.

What constrains my creativity? What stops me and gets me to feel hopeless is not having an outlet for it. I don't know where it's supposed to go. I mean if somebody said to me, "I want to see your pictures, could you do a show of your artwork?" I'd say, "YES." So when nobody asks for it, it doesn't have importance, sitting there it doesn't matter. So I say the inspiration *is* the *question*, asking for it. Then I know how to give it. The constraints are the rules—maybe that's how I experience the questionnaire that you and Dr. Torrance sent me. Other constraints are judgment and criticism and singular ideas of right and wrong. Where it's you feeling a need to fit me into what you want me to be, as opposed to what I want you to see.

GENERAL QUESTIONS ON CREATIVITY

If you could provide educators advice for nurturing creativity in children, what would you share with them?

I would share what I shared with you. Respect kids. Motivate them to be creative. What is it you would teach? Well, I would never talk to my child in a way I wouldn't to my best friend. Children are people. They may be in little bodies but they're huge people. Approach them with interest as you would a treasure chest filled with stuff that you want to discover and ask, "Who are you?" Don't assume anything. I don't believe you should assume much about anyone. Assume that there are jewels to be found in a child and that you have the privilege to approach them with a key. Find the place in yourself where you can do this in a genuine way. Because it's wonderful what comes out.

What advice would you give to parents to nurture the creativity in children?

I would say that it's your task and job to give the child a safe place. As a parent, it's your job to give your children a safe place, which means that you need to set limits for the purpose of that child feeling safe. You need to treat the child with at least the respect that you would a friend and you can come to your child's level and play or help draw things out in play. A child needs to know that you have things under control. You need to do the grown-up stuff. You need to allow space for a child's creativity. You also need to set limits. The child needs to know that there are consequences for things and choices for things and that structure is really important. I would say that there's a structure that's important in a classroom, too, but it's something that's not a rigid thing. There needs to be a structure that allows respect. Children should be allowed to be different and wonderful and from that they will learn to respect one another.

What advice would you give mentors who may work with highly creative children?

[This is what I believe is important for mentors: Share your own experiences, your struggles, how you overcame them . . . this will connect you and allow someone else, in a way, to see a light on a path ahead. As mentors, we are no better; we've merely walked a little farther along a certain path. I never got much help from people who told me what to do. It was, and is, those who were willing to share themselves that have helped me the most. I am empowered when I can see myself in someone else's sharing.]

If you could design a time capsule that represented you as a creative person, Wendy, what would you include in that time capsule? Say 5, 6, 7 items?

This is what it would be. My capsule would be like on *Star Wars* where Princess Leia was a hologram. I would have to be doing it all with the hologram. The hologram would be me [laughing] talking about how I feel about creativity. I would probably put a child [laughing] in with my hologram. I'd be talking. I would be showing my artwork. I would be playing a song, but I would be explaining it myself because I think that's me, and the way I communicate things and express who I am creatively.

Thank you, Wendy.

This was written during a therapy group of mine. I was describing how I was feeling at that time, which was February 1995.

POEM

To be direct it is clear to me
As Einstein's relativity
There's nothing more complex, you see
Than an act of pure simplicity.

There's so very much I'd like to say
I wish it didn't take all day
If only you could give a push
That would stop my beating 'round the bush.

If I sound dramatic, well, hell it's true
Oh God, here comes the other shoe
My problem is, well here's the deal
I'm not so clear on what I feel.

When I get scared, my eyes get glazed
I can't respond, I'm in a daze
I want so badly for you to know
If only I could make it show.

It's as if I am behind a screen
That translates words from what I mean
To look like someone my parents see
Who has very little to do with me.

But what makes even lesser sense
Is that I am in the same audience
Watching and judging that phony girl
Is it any wonder I don't feel real?

—Wendy Henry © 1995

This is pretty dramatic and harsh but this has to do with obvious stuff, okay?

Okay.

And it has a rhythm and I don't know if I'll do it. It's called "Pissed at God" or "Fuck You, I'm Entitled" or "Don't Blame Me for Acting like a Victim But You Made Me That Way." That's my sense of humor, okay [laughing]?

POEM

If I count up all the hours
Of the time I spent in showers
It's a wonder I have any skin at all.

I keep scrubbing where the dirt is
Trying to get at where the hurt is
But the real shit just keeps sticking to my craw.

Will it leave me if I name it
doesn't help me if I shame it
And the blame I send just will not stick at all.

I just can't win for losing
Grandpa wasn't of my choosing
And my memories are cloudy even now.

God, I need your best support here
Or isn't my report clear
Can't you see that I am up against the wall?

Have I really been so selfish
To deserve a life so hellish
Or is your scoring really kind of shot?

You served me quite a menu
Home for me, your favorite venue
Among your guests were Mr. Nut and Scott.

Mom and Dad were really losers
Better dressed than common boozers
But the parents (let's just say it) straight from hell.

Then along came Bill who proved it
If it moved he'd go and screw it
Really God, with me you're doin' pretty swell.

That's why I feel entitled
My rage is still unbridled
A miracle's the least I would demand.

A full range of emotions
Check your list of magic potions
Something simple that will even grief with joy.

Then pull me from my fear spot
Will you stay within my earshot
Oh, come on, don't be such a big killjoy.

Just restore my heart to normal
A sweet life nothing formal
A love who'll share a life with me that's real.

I know you're pretty busy
But I tell you, God, I'm dizzy
And Goddamnit, I deserve a better deal.

—Wendy Henry © 1995

And this has been my philosophy which is similar to Dr. Torrance's "Manifesto."

SONG

Can it really be so simple as standing in your shoes?
I'll try it, there is nothing I can lose . . .
Just a simple little lesson, but one to set us free
When I'm loving you, I'll be loving me.

SUMMARY

Wendy Henry is clearly one of the most creative persons in the Torrance longitudinal study. Her greatest strengths are kindness, warmth, depth, sensitivity, an ability to communicate and make friends, a sense of humor, intelligence, talent, courage, commitment, and creativity. Her creativity permeates her career, life, and family. It is not measured in numbers of books and paintings, but rather through the lives that she has touched and will touch in the future. Wendy uses her creativity to respond to the needs of people. In response to expressed needs, she has written poems, composed songs, created paintings, and made music, and has been a mentor to many people. Schools and society can learn from Wendy's approach to solving problems—seek out the needs of children and adults and attack these needs creatively.

In a recent letter[1] to Dr. Torrance, Wendy wrote, "I realize that what you have been doing has been for the purpose of protecting, preserving, and nurturing creativity and children, so that they will grow up to live free, rich, and fuller lives."

What Wendy has to say about children is instructive: "Children are people, they may be in little bodies, but they're huge people. Approach them with interest as you would a treasure chest filled with stuff that you want to discover and ask, 'Who are you?'" At middle age now, Wendy and her husband Stuart have just had their first children, twin boys. She now can apply her creative skills to raising her own children and being a supportive mother.

When asked about what would be included in a time capsule to represent her as a person, Wendy responded that she would be a hologram, like Princess Leia in the movie *Star Wars*, and talk about her feelings about creativity—her artwork, singing a song, swing dancing—all in the company of a child(ren). Wendy Henry had an opportunity to express herself creatively in person on behalf of the "Torrance Kids" when she presented the annual Torrance Lecture in October 2000, in Athens, Georgia. The text of that lecture is reprinted in appendix B.

NOTE

1. Letter to Dr. E. Paul Torrance from Wendy Henry, personal communication, July 15, 1998.

eleven

KEVIN O. LILLEHEI

A "BEST DOCTOR IN AMERICA"— EXPLORING "INNER" SPACE

"I had conflict within myself because I was not able to meet the high expectations of my father"—Kevin (1998)

Kevin Lillehei, circa 1958

One of the most successful students in terms of career achievements is Kevin O. Lillehei. In spite of Kevin's average creativity score and high intelligence as an elementary student, his career choice was influenced greatly by the positive role model and support of his parents and family—especially his father, who was a world-renown heart surgeon, and his brother, Clark, who died of a brain tumor.

SCHOOL YEARS

Kevin Lillehei was the second youngest of four children raised in St. Paul. As a young student at University Elementary School, he was assessed by a variety of creativity and intelligence tests over the period 1960 to 1964 while attending grades 2 to 6. His creativity tests showed that he was average, with a relative strength in the area of flexibility. Other creative strengths over that period of time included: resistance to premature closure, expression of feelings and emotion, putting things in context, movement and action, expressiveness of titles, unusual visualization, breaking boundaries, humor, richness, and colorfulness of imagery, and fantasy. He experienced no fourth-grade slump in creativity production, as did most of his peers. His intelligence score placed him in the high average range (120+).

In grade 5 Kevin indicated in written form that he wanted to be a doctor or an astronomer when he grew up. His future career image, prophetically, was that of a medical person (like his father) or a "star gazer." Admiration for his famous father was recorded in grade 3 when he responded to the question "Of all the people in the world, name the ones you would most like to be?" in this way: "1. Kevin, 2. Kim, 3. Dad." He also indicated at that time (November 8, 1961) that the people he would imitate the most would be his brother, Craig, and his father.

Kevin's father was Dr. Clarence Walton Lillehei, known in the medical world as the "Father of Open-Heart Surgery." He was the first to develop a technique to keep the patient's blood circulating and oxygenated in the body, enabling a surgeon to work on the interior of the heart. Dr. Lillehei performed the first successful open-heart surgery, on a five-year-old girl in 1952. In addition, he developed a wearable pacemaker that sends electrical impulses to the living heart in order to maintain a steady beat. He also invented four different artificial valves that were used in vessels entering the heart. As a professor of medicine at the University of Minnesota, he trained a thousand doctors in heart surgery, including Dr. Christian N. Barnard, the South African surgeon who in 1967 performed the first heart transplant in history. Kevin's father was clearly a strong, positive role model for his son, who became a neurosurgeon, and for his brother, Craig, who became a pediatric surgeon. See the obituary reprinted at the end of this case study for further information about Kevin's renowned father.

FIRST FOLLOW-UP

At the time of the 22-year follow-up in 1980, Kevin was 26 years of age, single, and doing an internship in general surgery at the University of Michigan. He had obtained a Bachelor of Science degree (cum laude, Dean's Honor List) in physics and chemistry from Cornell University (1975) and received his medical degree (MD) from the University of Minnesota (1979). He had worked as a research assistant at Cornell University in New York during the summers of 1973 and 1974 after graduating with honors from Marshall-University High School in Minneapolis in 1971. Kevin spent short periods of study in cardiology at Harvard Medical School and undertook a medical elective at the Royal Free Hospital in London before assuming neurosurgery residency training at the University of Michigan Medical Centre in Ann Arbor in 1980. While immersed in medical studies and practice during this period, Kevin found time to be captain of the wrestling team at Cornell University and also listed backpacking, electronics, and auto mechanics as hobbies. Kevin's older brother Craig also attended Cornell University and took his medical training at Harvard University. He is now a pediatric surgeon in Boston.

Kevin indicated the following two creative achievements since high school:

- Designed a high-speed, high-voltage switch to use in a research experiment while in the Department of Physics at Cornell University
- Designed a commercial switch for lights activated by sound.

Kevin's score on the quality of creative achievement in 1980 was 6.0, which was within the average range for the case-study group.

In the 1980 questionnaire, he stated that his greatest motivation for continued achievement was his desire to never get bored, and that his greatest obstacle to continued achievement was his inability to speed read. He also stated that he did not have a mentor in his occupational field who "took him under his or her wing." The primary frustration in his life in 1980 was not having enough time to do all the things he'd like to do. His future career image was clearly stated as being neurosurgery, in clinical medicine as well as research.

His final statement in the 1980 questionnaire revealed his intense focus: "During high school and college, most of my energies were directed toward athletics, allowing little if any time for outside achievements."

Kevin, circa 1998

MIDDLE AND LATE CAREER

According to the 1998 follow-up questionnaire, Kevin was working as a neurosurgeon at the Denver General Hospital in Colorado and as an associate professor in the training program for neurosurgeons at the University of Colorado Health Sciences Center. He had achieved his future career image since the 1980 follow-up and had completed his residency at the University of Michigan in 1985. Kevin Lillehei was now 46 years of age, married, and a father of a 14-year-old girl.

His score for creative public achievements was 9.5—the highest score as compared to others in the study group. His *curriculum vitae* reveals his prolific research and writing interests in his special field of brain-tumor study as well as involvement in the organizational aspects of medicine. His younger brother, Clark, to whom he felt very close, had died of a brain tumor. It may well be that Clark provided the motivation for Kevin to choose and pursue with passion his field of medical specialization: brain-tumor research.

Kevin was cited in *The Best Doctors in America* (1996–1997)[1] and (1997–1998)[2] for neurological surgery. This referral guide lists approximately 7,300 doctors nominated by their peers as outstanding within their medical specialty. The question asked of doctors is: "If you had a close friend or loved one who needed a neurological surgeon [for example], and you couldn't perform the operation yourself, for whatever reasons, to whom would you refer them?" The referral guide is a "picture" of the medical profession at a given moment—not a monument to reputations. Kevin was also listed in the "Top Doctors in Denver Region—Neurosurgery" in *5280 Magazine* for 1998. Both of these referral guides attest to his competence as a surgeon and respect from colleagues in his field.

His research activities involve harnessing the immune system to fight brain tumors. He is or has been involved in 18 research grants, contracts, and agreements either as the principal investigator or as co-investigator. He has two chemical/drug patents that are pending that would help eradicate or treat "solid tumors." His publications include 48 professional journal articles, six book chapters, two book reviews, and 43 abstracts. All these concern innovative research in brain-tumor immunotherapy. Kevin conducts in-service education and training for co-workers on a regular basis. He also has received four awards for leadership since 1980. In addition, he finds time to give invited lectures at the local, national, and international levels. He has been invited to deliver lectures on his research in Norway, Canada, and Switzerland in recent years. Dr. Lillehei established the neuro-oncology program at the University of Colorado and is its current director.

In addition to the numerous public creative achievements cited above, Kevin indicated the following personal achievements of his since 1980:

- designed and taught a course
- designed a garden
- completed a poem-story-monograph that has not been published
- became seriously involved in a new sport and hobbies (guitar playing and stained glass).

Kevin indicated that he is "in love with his work," and his greatest strengths are his abilities to work hard and to relate to other people. He stated that his parents and teachers had very high expectations for him to perform well during his medical training and early education. He reported that he was not completely free to "play his own game" and has encountered some conflicts by not meeting the expectations of his father. He still did not have a professional mentor, and regretted not having one. He felt that a mentor would have been of great help. When asked to report on his skills upon which other people depend, Kevin stated: "Specialized surgical procedures and organizing and coordinating a multidisciplinary research group."

INTERVIEW ON AUGUST 24, 1998

This interview with Kevin Lillehei was conducted over the telephone and added to later via mail. Kevin was reached at his office in Denver. He reflected on the early influences on his creativity; his career path and transitions; creative accomplishments; and finally, general comments on creativity. His own words tell his experiences best.

EARLY INFLUENCES ON CREATIVITY

At what age were you first aware of your creativity? How did this show itself?

I am not entirely sure at what age I first felt that I was creative. However, at a very young age, I recall putting on plays, building forts, and building un-motorized go-carts with my brothers and neighbors. This would have started at age 5 or 6.

At elementary age, what influence did your schooling have on your creative ability?

I attended University Elementary School in Minneapolis. It was a unique school in that it was a laboratory school and the teachers were certainly enthusiastic about their work.

What specific incidents can you remember in your childhood, which enabled your creativity to develop?

I vividly recall being given an assignment, in the third grade, to write a fiction story. I had never really before that time undertaken a big project where I actually put words on paper and did so using only my imagination. I got quite taken away with the assignment and remember writing a very long story that I was quite proud of. I don't really remember how well received it was by the teacher.

Was there any influence at elementary age that you now recognize as having had an impact on your subsequent career or chosen field of work?

I feel my parents were very influential on my career. Although both my mother and father were in the medical field, they never really encouraged me to go into medicine. I feel I ultimately chose this field because I had been very exposed to it and enjoyed what I saw.

What were the qualities/skills/behaviors of your parents?

My mother was very creative, energetic, and self-reliant. My father was very hardworking and dedicated to his profession.

What would you say was the most important lesson you learned with regard to your creativity at this age?

I'm not sure I can recall any specific lesson I learned at that age with regard to creativity. In retrospect I feel I was fairly creative at that time in my life, but at the time, I had no clue of this.

How would your peers have described you at that time?

At that age, my peers would have described me as follows: I was of average intelligence, did average in my schoolwork but was a good athlete. I tended to be a leader on the playing field and quiet in the classroom.

CAREER PATHS AND TRANSITIONS

What is your present job?

I am a practicing neurosurgeon and a professor in the training program for neurosurgeons at the University of Colorado.

How do you apply creativity to this work?

I think that creativity is very applicable to the work I do. I initially chose the field of neurosurgery because it in many ways is the most primitive of the medical fields. Although many of our procedures are quite sophisticated, our actual knowledge of the workings of the brain is still very rudimentary. This allows for a great deal of creative thinking in areas where you are really on the frontier of knowledge. The old dogma on how to treat the various diseases of the brain continually needs to be re-examined based on the new facts available. In the treatment of brain tumors, my particular area of interest, we are continually looking for new approaches, both from a surgical standpoint as well as in the use of our adjuvant therapies. My interest has been in harnessing the immune system to help in eradicating these malignant tumors.

Have you had other jobs? If so, were you able to work creatively while in these jobs?

I have had odd jobs as a teenager. I worked at the Red Barn Restaurant; in constructing parade floats, and in a research lab. I was able to apply my creativity especially to the construction job. Decorating the parade floats enabled me to be creative.

What major changes/transitions have you experienced in your working life? What caused these transitions?

In the last four to five years, I realized I was a workaholic and that I needed to spend more time at home with my daughter. My daughter, who is fourteen years old, needs my attention. The years from zero to ten went very quickly.

To achieve this goal, I have had to learn to still remain very active and productive at work, yet allow time for my family. To do this requires a great deal of discipline and a good deal of organization. It is a very difficult task to put your family first and work second, but as I have grown older, I feel I am getting my priorities better in tune with their importance in my life. Surprising that it should be any different, but in our society, we tend to define our self-worth by who we are in the workplace and not who we are at home.

When you made changes in your working life, was there anyone whom you relied on for support and advice? If so, what did they do which was most helpful for you at these times?

Good question. I have never really had a mentor. Although a doctor at the University of Colorado was interested in my career, he was in a different field/specialty.

Why is it that you've not had a mentor?

I'm not sure . . . however it may be due to my personality. I'm more introverted and do not, or have not, sought out a mentor. I don't go out of my way to talk to colleagues or seek out potential mentors. Unfortunately, I have had a very difficult time developing close relationships with my professors. Although I can think of a number of individuals I have admired over the years, I have rarely sought out their opinions or help concerning my own direction in life. There is really no particular individual I feel has served as a mentor to me. This probably stems from my being relatively introverted. At this stage of my career, I regret not having developed a close working relationship with at least one individual I could call a *mentor*.

How are you able to integrate relationships, as a parent, a partner, and as someone's child, into your working life?

I think it's tough. You've got to be aware of it all the time. We're so caught up in the immediate that it always takes over. Balance in your personal life is difficult to maintain. It's more important to think of your various roles. I'm starting to work on it.

CREATIVE ACCOMPLISHMENTS

What do you consider to be your most creative achievement?

At this time, I feel my most creative achievement has been publishing numerous peer-reviewed journal articles. However, I take the greatest pride in my research on the use of the immune system for the treatment of brain tumors. If this research ultimately turns out to be a useful clinical therapy, it will clearly be my most creative achievement.

In what area of your life are you most able to be creative?

In my work, I can apply creativity to my research (immune therapy) and in surgery—to minimize visible injury to the brain. In my private life, I can apply my creativity to playing the guitar, stained-glass projects—things I don't get to do very much.

What do you consider to be your creative attributes?

Willingness to question what is accepted (challenge existing dogma) and little fear to try a new medical technique.

How would your close associates describe your creative attributes?

Pretty much the same.

What influences guide or constrain your creativity in, for example, overall life purpose, career goal, and financial burdens?

Clearly the obligations of everyday administrative work and the time commitments required for patient care significantly limit the time available to pursue creative work. If you think too much about this, you become very frustrated. However, in an academic setting, there is ample opportunity to conceive of questions and go about finding some answers—creative problem-solving can be applied in my teaching and work with medical students.

GENERAL QUESTIONS ON CREATIVITY

If you could provide educators advice for nurturing creativity in children, what would you share with them?

To really challenge students in specific areas. In my work, medical students find it boring to just do rounds with doctors—they needed to be challenged—pushed to work hard in certain areas. Give them specific topics and time periods to complete/present them. Students at school need to be pushed or challenged in specific areas.

If you could provide parents advice for nurturing creativity in children, what would you share with them?

Maximize areas of interest and open opportunities for them in areas of expressed interest. My daughter is more artistic, not science-oriented like me.

If you could provide guidance to mentors working with highly creativity youngsters, what would you share with them?

I would want them to seek out relationships with the withdrawn student who has real potential.

If you could design a time capsule that represented you as a creative person, what would you include in this capsule? Five to ten items?

Copies of significant research in brain-tumor study; samples of contributions in the clinical aspect of brain research and new treatment strategies; proof that I was a good role model for students as a physician; proof that I was a good inspirational father; proof that I was a good husband.

What are your creative goals and aspirations for the future? Please describe.

To be a better parent—that is very important to me—try to maintain a positive relationship with my daughter—it will take a lot of careful planning; to do basic research with brain tumors; to continue my clinical activities.

SUMMARY

Kevin Lillehei is clearly one of the most successful and accomplished students in the sample. Although he had a good deal of creative and intellectual potential as a student in elementary school, the positive and supportive role model of his parents has had an enduring effect on his chosen career and success within it. Even though Kevin states that he had difficulty with the high expectations of his father, he took on those same characteristics in his career. Kevin has indicated that his medical students need to be pushed to work hard and be challenged in certain areas—just as his father did with him. Kevin is a pioneer in medicine and is embracing the challenge to explore the "inner space" of the immune system to fight brain tumors—he is on the frontier of knowledge. His recognition by colleagues as a "best doctor in America" attests to his eminence in his field of neurological surgery. It is likely that the death of his brother, Clark, due to a brain tumor, motivated him to tackle the field of brain tumors and chemotherapy.

Kevin's career has been characterized by dedication, hard work, willingness to question or challenge existing dogma, and he exhibits little fear in trying new techniques. At this time of his life, he is pretty much "free to play in his own game" and "sing in his own key" within the limits of his responsibilities as a full professor at a medical school. Certainly, no one directs his research or influences the cases he takes on within the practice of neurosurgery. Coming from a strong medical family, he was always interested in medicine but didn't really consider it a career choice until his senior year in college. He was always looking for something that might be more interesting. After entering medical school, while taking his first-year neuroanatomy course, he realized that whatever he did he wanted to work with the nervous system. This was when he fell in love with neurology, and eventually neurosurgery.

In his personal life he has struggled with the concept of mentoring and never felt he was able to develop a relationship with one of his teachers in order to truly benefit from having a mentor. He wonders, "how do you develop such a relationship if by nature you tend to be more introverted?" He clearly feels that a student–mentor relationship can be very powerful in an individual's career.

Kevin is free to concentrate on his work because of the strong support provided by his wife. He says: "My wife has been very supportive of my efforts in neurosurgery since I started my internship in 1979.

She has always been a very good listener and has the uncanny ability to break down what initially appears to me to be a complicated situation into its basic tenets. She keeps my feet on the ground and my expectations in touch with reality." Kevin's wife provides the stability in his life so that he can unleash his creative strengths in his work.

It is likely that Dr. Lillehei will continue in the years ahead to make important contributions in his medical specialty of eradicating brain tumors by way of chemotherapy. Like his father, Kevin is on the frontier of medical research. An added challenge for him, as for so many other creative individuals, will be to balance his personal life as a father and spouse. He does have a career image of the "Big Picture"!

NOTES

1. Naifeh, S., and G. W. Smith (1996–97). *The best doctors in America*. Aiken, SC: Woodward/White, Inc.

2. Naifeh, S., and G. W. Smith (1997–98). *The best doctors in America*. Aiken, SC: Woodward/White, Inc.

DR. CLARENCE WALTON LILLEHEI

'Father of open-heart surgery' behind ingenious inventions

Devised pacemaker and helped design artificial valves

Dr. Clarence Walton Lillehei, who has died aged 80, was a surgeon whose pioneering techniques made open-heart surgery possible; he also was an inventor of considerable ingenuity, devising the first wearable electronic pacemaker and contributing to the design of four artificial heart valves.

On Sept. 2, 1952, Dr. Lillehei and a five-year-old heart patient named Jackie Johnson made medical history when the little girl became the first person to undergo successful open-heart surgery. Dr. Lillehei and his team of surgeons took 19 hours to lower her body temperature, wrapping her in rubber blankets that conducted a cold alcohol solution and cutting off all blood flow in her body for 5½ minutes while they worked inside the heart.

Until then, it had been considered impossible to perform critical operations within the human heart. There was no viable substitute for the natural process that places oxygen into the bloodstream and circulates blood throughout the body. Heart surgery was thus limited to disorders that could be remedied without entering the heart itself.

Dr. Lillehei set out to overcome that obstacle, initially using a technique called "cross circulation," in which the bloodstream of the patient undergoing surgery was linked by tubes to the bloodstream of a healthy donor. The process worked, but was risky for the donor, so later abandoned.

The turning point came in 1955 when Dr. Lillehei and a colleague, Dr. Richard A. Wall, performed successful surgery using a heart-lung machine, called a helix reservoir bubble oxygenator, which bubbled oxygen through the blood during the operation.

The machine ultimately made heart-transplant surgery possible. For his efforts Dr. Lillehei was dubbed the "father of open-heart surgery."

Clarence Walton Lillehei was born in Minneapolis and graduated from the University of Minnesota in 1939. He received his medical degree there in 1942 as well as a master's in physiology and a doctorate in surgery in 1951.

He went into private practice as a general, thoracic and cardiovascular surgeon in 1945 after wartime service in the Army Medical Corps in Europe, where he rose to the rank of lieutenant-colonel and won a Bronze Star. He joined the department of surgery at the University of Minnesota Medical School as a full-time instructor in 1949 and trained some 1,000 doctors in heart surgery, including Dr. Christiaan N. Barnard, the South African surgeon who in 1967 performed the first heart transplant in history, and Dr. Norman E. Shumway, who devised the technique for such transplants.

Dr. Lillehei played a prominent role in other breakthroughs that made treatment of once-fatal heart conditions possible. One of these, known as heart block, occurs when the body fails to produce the small electrical signals that regulate the heartbeat.

By 1957, Dr. Lillehei and his colleagues in Minnesota had worked out a method of hooking wires directly into the living heart, supplying the electrical signals from a battery-powered electronic device, a pacemaker, small enough to be worn under the clothing and providing pulses for a firm, steady heartbeat. The device proved effective for long-term maintenance of non-surgical heart patients.

Dr. Lillehei and his associates also contributed to the design of four prosthetic heart valves, including the widely used St. Jude Medical Mechanical Heart Valve.

Dr. Lillehei is survived by his wife of 52 years, Kay Lindberg Lillehei, and three children.

Wolfgang Saxon, The New York Times, with files from The Associated Press

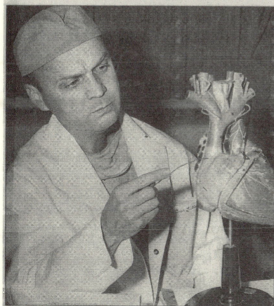

THE ASSOCIATED PRESS

Dr. Clarence Walton Lillehei in 1957

twelve

CATHY GORLIN

FROM GRADE 6 CLASS PRESIDENT TO "SUPER LAWYER"

"The most important relationship in my life has been all the support from my parents, who cared so much about me and wanted only the best for me"—Cathy (1998)

Cathy Gorlin, circa 1965

Cathy Ellen Gorlin is a good example of a case-study individual who has succeeded in her career, including home life, due to the tremendous support of her parents—especially her mother and also a few minor mentors.

Cathy is able to maintain a healthy balance between work and personal/home responsibilities. She is presently a partner in a successful law practice. She is able to apply her skills of communication and listening and problem finding and solving to her work and also to her husband and children. To maintain this balance, she has learned the art of saying *"no"* to many requests where one has an option.

SCHOOL YEARS

Cathy is the elder of two children raised in a suburb of Minneapolis. As a young student at University Elementary School, she was assessed by a variety of creativity and intelligence tests during the period 1959 to 1964, while attending grades 1 through 6. Her creativity tests showed that she was above average, with a relative strength in the area of originality. Other creative strengths over that period of time included: abstractness of titles, resistance to closure, expression of feelings, putting things in context, movement and action, unusual visual perception, extending/breaking the boundaries, humor, and richness and colorfulness of imagery. She experienced the fourth-grade slump in creativity, along with most of her peers. Her intelligence score of 130+ at that time placed her in the superior range.

In grade 5 Cathy expressed a career interest in helping mentally ill, crippled, or blind children. This interest persisted in grade 6 as well. However, in grade 9 she investigated a career in law for a school project. This foreshadowed her eventual career as an attorney.

FIRST FOLLOW-UP

At the time of the 22-year follow-up, Cathy was 25 years of age, single, and was practicing law with a mid-sized firm in Bloomington, Minnesota. She had graduated from law school with her J.D. (Doctor of Laws) degree from the University of Minnesota in June 1978. Cathy was granted a Bachelor of Arts degree (magna cum laude) from Wesleyan University in Middletown, Connecticut in June 1975. While attending Wesleyan University, Cathy was awarded a number of honors:

- chosen teaching assistant for constitutional law class
- grant awarded for honor's thesis
- chosen Wesleyan representative to U.S. Conference on International Affairs at West Point
- nominated for Root Tilden Scholarship Application (New York University Law School).

While attending law school at the University of Minnesota Cathy was chosen as a member of the Law School Grievance Committee, and an honorary member of the American Judicature Society.

During her formal education Cathy served as an intern in various political offices, including Congressman Donald Fraser and Senator Hubert Humphrey in Washington during 1974, and later as a law clerk in the offices of the Minneapolis and Bloomington city attorney. In her position as a judicial clerk, she was involved in memo writing and research for a family judge. Her career ambition was to become a partner in a small- to medium-sized firm and be active in many legal and community organizations. In 1980, she even aspired to be a judge someday.

Cathy had not taken any time off from full-time study since high school. She indicated that her current interests and hobbies were: photography, a reading club, and racquetball. She had a real interest in photography and took every photography class offered at the university and in her community. Photography enabled her to "see" things differently.

Cathy's creative accomplishments in high school are summarized as follows:

- poems and articles published in high-school newspaper
- editor of literary magazine
- placed third in state speech contest
- elected to student-council office
- awards for leadership.

After high school, Cathy was elected chairperson of the third-district Young Democrats and chosen as American Field Service Student to France. She also received an award for high-school journalism. Since high school, Cathy has achieved the following:

- edited a literary magazine
- held, along with other participants, an exhibit of photographs
- created educational materials with others
- received recognition for leadership
- wrote a brief for the Minnesota attorney general to the U.S. Supreme Court.

She stated that her greatest spur for continual achievement was to be productive and to be a contributing member of society.

Cathy indicated that she had a mentor who was an attorney-at-law, who set an example for her as an honest, forthright, intelligent lawyer. She adopted from her mentor certain verbal expressions, methods of negotiating, and methods of presenting a viewpoint. She also emulates his even-tempered and optimistic outlook. Cathy stated that she would turn to her parents for assistance and encouragement on a difficult project or in a time of crisis, or for "morale building." Her father was a regents professor in the medical and dental school at the University of Minnesota, while her mother was an administrator at the same university, as well as being a mother and homemaker.

Cathy stated in 1980 that, although she hoped to get married and have children, she was content with her current situation and lifestyle. She indicated that she planned to get back to her creative outlets by writing poetry and taking photographs. Her career image for the next ten years was to become a partner in a public-interest law firm.

Cathy, circa 1998

MIDDLE TO LATE CAREER

In the 1998 follow-up questionnaire, Cathy was working as an attorney (partner) in a medium-sized law firm. Eighteen years ago, she had planned to have this particular position in law. Cathy had achieved her future career image since the 1980 follow-up. She was now 45 years of age, married, and the mother of two children, ages 10 and 13.

Her score for creative public achievements was 6.0—higher than average for the case-study group. Cathy's *curriculum vitae* reveals a modest number of publications (15) since 1979, but 23 speeches delivered over the same time period through Continuing Legal Education Programs. Her written publications deal with communicating existing and new legislation that affects family-law practice. Her speeches deal with similar content, but use a different medium to reach more people. She has conducted several in-service/training sessions for co-workers. Cathy acts as a resource person to the Twin Cities Step-families Association. She also has been very involved with professional organizations in her special field of family and divorce law. She is listed in the *Who's Who of American Women*, *Who's Who in American Law*, and *Who's Who in the World*. Her continuing leadership is exemplified in the following positions and achievements:

- editor of *Minnesota Law Practice Manual*
- chosen as chair of the State Bar Family Law Section
- chosen as chair of Hennepin County Family Law Section for two separate terms
- chosen as leading Minnesota Attorney in Family Law
- named "super lawyer" by *Law and Politics Newspaper* and articles were written about her work in the business section of a Minneapolis newspaper.

Besides the above creative accomplishments, Cathy considers raising two children as perhaps the most creative of her personal activities. They present a constant challenge to her creativity. Cathy describes her career as a love-hate relationship. It affords her much freedom to attend to her children, who require a good deal of her time now. She states that her greatest strengths are her listening ability, strategizing, loving her kids and family, and helping people in a one-on-one setting. She has always felt the weight of the expectations of others to be the best that she could be and to work hard and produce. Her mentor is probably her mother, a very strong woman who was an active volunteer although she was not employed until Cathy was practically in college. She also mentioned other more minor mentors such as her husband and other lawyers and judges.

When asked to report on her skills upon which others depend, she says, "conceptualizing the tasks that need to be done."

INTERVIEW ON JULY 15, 1998

This interview with Cathy Gorlin was conducted at the Minnesota Athletic Club. She reflected on the early influences on her creativity, her career path and transitions; creative accomplishments; and, finally, general comments on creativity. Her own words tell her experiences best.

EARLY INFLUENCES ON CREATIVITY

At what age were you first aware of your creativity?

I don't think I was aware of my creativity at all. I think I was aware that I was a good listener, that I cared about people, and that people would listen to me. I would say, maybe, even as early as first grade. But in terms of, in thinking of myself as creative, I don't think that I ever, in elementary school, thought of myself as creative. I have this recollection in sixth grade of being told to be creative when writing a story. And [GWM laughing] you know, just feeling absolutely at a loss that I could not be creative [both laughing] in writing a story. But then another thing that happened in the sixth grade was that I was elected the president of the class.

And that came after, there was a history of all boys being president. And all the boys would only nominate boys to be president and so there would only be boys as president of our class.

So this was really a breakthrough.

So it was a breakthrough because we were creative. The girls were creative in terms of how we got a girl to be president of the class. We decided that we were going to bullet ballot for the president, which means that we would all agree that we would all vote for one girl. The problem was that no boy would nominate a girl, and the existing president, a boy, would call only on boys to nominate. The trick was how do we get a girl nominated to be president. And so we figured out we'd bribe a boy a nickel [both laughing] to nominate me. Somehow they came up with me; I don't remember how I was the one chosen. I don't think I was totally the leader in creating this system, but obviously there was some problem solving and I was the one who ended up being president of the class after that.

At an elementary-school age, what influence did your schooling have on your creative ability, as you think back now?

In second grade, my father went on a sabbatical to Denmark. And it was my first situation where I had to go into a completely new situation with all new kids for a short period of time. It was an international school and I spent two weeks away from home when my class went on a trip to this little island north of Poland. It was a whole new experience. In terms of teachers, I always liked and got along well with teachers. Each year at U.E.S., my class had the same kids. There were 25 kids at the most. The teachers could really spend time with and know the students in the school. I always was a kid who felt close to teachers. I don't remember any teacher doing anything in particular to take me under his or her wing. I always felt pretty much a closeness to teachers as opposed to thinking teachers were something that you run away from [laughing].

What specific incidents can you remember in your childhood which enabled your creativity to develop? Either at school or in the home environment.

Well, I always had very supportive parents. And their number-one focus was my education and my development in all areas and I knew that they cared about that and I knew that they were very supportive in what I wanted to do. So I was not singing my own tune, really, but I felt very supported by them. Maybe throughout my career I was trying to please them, to a certain extent. And yet learning a lot from both of my parents and . . .

Tell me a little bit about your parents.

My father was a regents professor at the University of Minnesota. He retired a few years back, but he really has never stopped working, so the same sort of thing as maybe Paul Torrance. His field was medical. I didn't follow in those footsteps, in terms of wanting to go into medicine.

Yes.

My mother, although she wasn't working *per se*, was always a very active volunteer and was very involved in politics. It was like full time; it was like a job, although she definitely was there for us, and my brother and I were her number-one priority.

Right.

She made it clear—both parents made it clear, that our education and our careers and our development were first and foremost.

Was there an influence at an elementary-school age which you now recognize as having had an impact on your subsequent career and chosen field of work?

Well, I always knew that I wanted to strive for the best. I sort of knew [laughing] that I was going to be a lawyer or doctor, probably from an early age. I remember doing something in high school, maybe ninth grade. There was a career project and lawyer was definitely among my choices of future careers. I'm not sure that I really know at what age I was influenced by my mother's interest in politics although I know it was in elementary school. I was also turned away from ever going into politics [laughing] or being a politician because I saw too much of it [both laughing].

I knew that my mother had had an interest in going into law school. Maybe I was fulfilling a dream that she had, too, for herself, and yet I realized that it was a career that would be good for me, too.

What were the qualities or behaviors of your mother in particular, who had a strong influence on you at this time?

First of all, my mother exhibited toward me, clear, unconditional love. She was very supportive, both in her listening to me and her availability for me. I saw that, even though she was not working, that she was a very strong woman. She was very strong, self-assured.

Sort of independent in herself.

Independent, right. She was a good role model.

I remember having, at one point in college, a letter she wrote to me where she was worried about the women's movement. She had a lot of feminist friends that she felt were going too far; that there was still a need for mothers raising kids. I remember saying, "Mom, I can do it all. I'm going to college for a reason, and I don't want to waste that education." I remember having these discussions with her about what was right. I think that even though she may have said at times that I could be just a mom raising kids and that that was okay, that I always knew that she wanted for me to be an independent, career woman.

You work at balancing your family with your workload?

I do, I do, but still, it's a full-time job that I have and I'm a partner in a medium-sized law firm and so by anyone's standards, it's not like working part-time and balancing. It's working full time and [both laughing] balancing, too. I've got terrific kids and there are lots of times when I go off to work and I really want to spend the time with my kids. I've always made time, and to a certain extent, the practice of law has a lot of flexibility. That's why I have liked it, too. I can just mark my calendar to go on a field trip this Friday with my kids in school just like I can mark it to go to a court appearance.

Right! Or being interviewed.

Or being interviewed, exactly. So, I do have that flexibility. Obviously my law firm wants me to produce a certain number of dollars per year [laughing] and my clients want me to accomplish certain things for them, but within the day, it all can be juggled. Unless I have to be in court.

What would you say was the most important lesson that you learned with regard to your creativity at this age?

Just that both teachers and parents told me all the good things that I was doing. All the kudos that I got throughout those years. Those were the important feelings, you know, the pushing . . .

They all kept you moving forward.

That's right. The praise kept me moving forward. I didn't feel that I couldn't do things eventually. I'm sure that I had some doubts at times [laughing]. I remember taking all these tests and [laughing] at times not feeling comfortable or feeling that I was inadequate. But it was generally the encouraging comments that people made to me, that either teachers made to me or that parents made to me that were an influence on my success. The extended family sort of thing.

How would your peers have described you at that time?

As a good kid. I wasn't a troublemaker at all. I remember in seventh grade (this is getting a little bit older), I wanted to be like my peers. The other kids were trying cigarettes and I tried one. They would laugh at me. [GWM laughing.] "Oh, you're too much of a goody-goody to even take a puff." I was in tears that I couldn't be included in the cool group. Yet, I felt free to tell my mother that I had smoked a cigarette and it was . . .

It's an adult thing.

Right. I mean, telling her in tears that they wouldn't accept me, even when I smoked to be like them [both laughing]. My own daughter would just keep quiet, she wouldn't tell me [both laughing]. But in terms of how I'd be described by peers, maybe a little shy. But yet I did things like become the president of the class.

CAREER PATHS AND TRANSITIONS

Can you first of all tell me a little about what you're presently doing?

I'm a lawyer with Best and Flanagan. We have about 50 lawyers, so it's considered a medium-sized law firm. Here in Minneapolis. I'm a partner. I head up my department, which is family law. It's a field that a lot of lawyers would hate to be in because it's basically "divorce" law. Clients are at their worst emotionally. Even the best people can be crazy when going through a divorce. [GWM laughing.] So it's a field that there's no pat way to do it. Absolutely every case is different. There are no two cases alike. Even two clients that both have a pension plan, a house, and earn $50,000/year. No two cases are alike. So the cases definitely demand a different approach for each client that is involved.

Are you able to apply creativity to your work?

I think that I am. After I listened to your definition of creativity, I think that, that there probably are many creative approaches that I take on a daily basis. It's not something I think about. It's just something that is intuitive. There are problems that have to be resolved, continually, all day long. When I was younger, I did a lot more producing articles and giving speeches, but those were not something that I felt were creative even though I created many articles and speeches. They were not a passion. It was almost as if I needed to produce because it's required, you know, because other people are putting pressures on me to do written things and then I was a good kid and did them [laughing].

So it really wasn't a spontaneous sort of thing, I guess you're saying.

Not really, I had to push myself to do all of the writing that I did. But I found ways in which I could do that writing. I did a lot of articles for magazines, professional magazines, but they were things that didn't take. . . . They took a lot of work, yet not, overly. I did a lot of writing about the judges and the new people coming into family court. It was fun for me. But my creative work is in how I deal with every case that I have. And how I manage my department, and all of those things, but primarily in the daily work that I do.

Have you had other jobs in law other than the one that you're presently in?

I had two other main jobs after law school. I worked for a judge, two different judges, in family court. That was my first main job that lasted any significant time. I was a law clerk in family court and that taught me about my field. When I graduated from law school, I wasn't at all sure that I wanted to do family law. And in some sense it was a fluke that I ended up in family law. I knew that I wanted to do some sort of law, probably involving litigation, which includes family law. That's what I do, I litigate, I'm a trial lawyer. A lot of my cases will settle before we actually ever go to trial, but I am still considered a litigator, in terms of law. So I started off not knowing I wanted family law. Even in law school, I thought that I didn't want family law. And I stayed away. I avoided taking any family-law classes. I stayed away from family law, thinking that this is a field that was too emotional [laughing] and not seriously respected. All the family problems. I probably didn't give it too much thought in law school, but then I got a job as a law clerk. I was with a terrific judge and that judge was a kind of a mentor to me. And I just took it upon myself at that point to really learn everything I possibly could about family law and then I watched him, I watched other family-law attorneys in the courtroom. I decided that there was room and need for a female family-law attorney who was a high-class family-law attorney. There were a lot of family-law attorneys that I thought were not very good. But there were not enough attorneys who were really going to do a great job and be known. And be part of a big firm. So I decided there was room in the field and that I was going to join the field. I applied for work to these attorneys who I watched and admired. I was in a position where I lucked out because I got a job directly with a law firm, which maybe I wouldn't have ended up in, had I not worked as a law clerk first. It helped me end up doing what I'm doing and feeling so competent at what I do. I saw and learned from all the other lawyers that would come and practice in family court. This is the time that they were at their best. So I saw how they litigated and how they negotiated. There was a couple of years of working as a law clerk, and then, at that point, I was really wooed by law firms. And was hired by a large law firm named Larkin, Hoffman, Daly and Lindgren. I worked there for four years and was wooed away by Best and Flanagan, which is where I am now. After law school, I must've sent a million resumes, not a million, I'm exaggerating, a lot [laughing]. A lot of resumes, all rejected. Getting hired out of law school by a good law firm was a very discouraging process, but then I lucked into getting a job with a terrific judge from whom I learned a lot and was able to watch other lawyers, from whom I learned a lot.

Let me just put the question like this. When you made those changes in your career in law, was there anyone whom you really relied on for support and advice?

My husband is a significant person in my life. He was very supportive when I made the transition from Larkin, Hoffman to Best and Flanagan. When I was being wooed away from Larkin, Hoffman, I had to make a decision to leave. That decision to leave was very hard because it wasn't like I was really thinking about leaving before. I was being asked to come to a new law firm and then all of a sudden, I had to make a decision. There were things that happened at Larkin right about that time that helped me make that decision. My husband gave me all the support that I needed in terms of actually making that move. I think I'm somebody who, once I find something that kind of works for me, I'm not somebody who is looking to change. For instance, a friend of mine suggested some makeup in college and I've used that same makeup ever since. I'm not somebody who's searching for the new thing out there always. Another thought: When I went to my first college (I went for one year at Hampshire College in Amherst, Massachusetts), it was a new college that was really on the leading edge of education. I don't know if you've heard about it, but it was too much on the edge for me. It was trying to be the most creative in education; it was too much innovation for me. I needed a more traditional education. So then I transferred to Wesleyan University in Middletown, Connecticut, which was an established, old-time university and probably I needed more of that classic base; I needed that base.

How are you able to integrate relationships into your working life?

Even though I'm a full-time, dedicated family-law attorney, I probably have to say that my family comes first, even in the end of all that. And so although I've had nannies in my children's early years, I've worked very hard to try to be there for my kids and be very involved in their lives. My husband is a very busy lawyer in his own right, probably more busy in his work than I am. To balance my busy life, I needed to learn to say *"no."* It was

---

a peer who actually taught me to say *"no."* Which is, *no* to some demands of others.

How did she teach you that, to say "no"? Just by talking?

Yeah, just by telling me. She is somebody who probably has her career first and foremost in her life and she's going constantly and doing all kinds of things. And the other thing that I learned from her is goal-setting. She was one year ahead of me, so a peer, but with a little bit more experience, not lots of years ahead, but really just right there where you are. She taught me the benefits of goal-setting, which I find hard to do [laughing]. I've always been taken with how well she did that and so was inspired by that. Although it always takes work for me to do and doesn't come naturally, I really do goal-set. Most of my goal-setting takes place in the back of my mind.

CREATIVE ACCOMPLISHMENTS

What would you consider to be your most creative achievement to this point?

I know that when I wrote the answer to the questionnaire, I probably said my kids, and I still believe, that they are my most creative achievement. They might be just the same [laughing] . . . regardless of what I have done. I'd like to think that, just like I deal with my clients and their daily problems in a creative way in whatever problem solving, needs to be done at home, too. Even though my family life takes priority, it's been a creative achievement to become a partner in my law firm, where I'm also the head of the department in my law firm. I'm also on the distribution committee, which basically shows that I have a lot of respect from my peers, to be able to decide how much money they all receive. So it's a group of five of us out of fifty. The distribution committee is a committee of five lawyers who decide what everybody gets paid.

I don't know how creative I am [laughing], I'm trying to figure that out. I try to be creative in that problem solving, too.

In what area of your life are you most able to be creative?

I think it's dual, it's my career and it's my kids.

What do you consider to be your creative attributes?

[Laughing.] Problem solving at a very personal level. [Pause.] Listening, you know, I think that a good part of it is really listening and hearing and then communicating to people and giving advice, making others feel like they're part of the decision-making process.

How would your close associates that you work with describe your creative attributes?

I think it's pretty much the same.

What influences guide or constrain your creativity?

Time [laughing]. [Pause.] And in terms of career . . . it's the other pulls, I guess. It's the other areas of creativity that are pulling me away from career. I mean, my husband seems like he could spend all day and all night doing it. For me, there's a limit on how much enjoyment [laughing] I can get from working in my occupational career. I need the enjoyments in my other areas of creativity.

There are times when maybe you spend more energy on one area or the other?

I need time away from career to do my best and to be my most creative in my career. I also need the time away from it because it's so emotionally demanding. People are going through so much that . . .

You kind of need to recharge.

Right, I do. And spending time with family and doing those other things really help me then to be able to be creative and help the people that I need to help.

QUESTIONS RELATED TO THE "MANIFESTO FOR CHILDREN"

Would you say that you'd be in love with your work or do you have a passion for it?

Well, to a certain extent, but I'm not sure that I have it in the same sense that I've seen other people have it. So I do my job well, I enjoy it. I wonder every once in a while, is there another field that would have been better for me if I hadn't gone to law school? I might have felt a pressure to go to grad school, and probably felt the direction from my parents which steered me to law school. I perceived it myself, too, that law was a good area for me to go into. And I've thought as a lawyer, would there have been a better career for me? Would I have enjoyed advertising [laughing] or creative writing or something, better? When I think about my daughter and the kinds of things that are available to her. Is there something other than law? But I haven't concluded that there is anything different that I'd rather be in. There are probably days when I'm pulling my hair out and saying, why am I doing this [laughing]. I definitely get a lot of good feelings from what I do. But it's not something I feel like I need to do all the time.

What are your greatest strengths?

I'm a good listener, I'm a good sympathizer. I know quickly what the problem is, and can cut to the chase. Sometimes I want to cut to the chase too soon. I think I can put together what needs to be put together to solve the problem and/or to present the case to the decision-maker. I think that those are my strengths.

In what ways is your creativity affected by the expectations of other people? Or do you feel able to "play your own game," "sing in your own tune," like you said before.

Yeah, yeah. Maybe it's my interpretation that's . . . "singing your own tune." If anything, I guess I was pushed along and supported and maybe did things that were not "singing my own tune"; I wasn't rebellious.

I think it's just being fairly independent.

Yeah, fairly independent and, I'm trying to think of the times that I was independent. [Pause.] Like telling my mother that I could do it all, that kind of thing. But on the other hand, I think that she really was always pushing me to have a successful career of my own. I guess I feel more that I was singing other people's tunes and just finally, that I succeeded and I feel . . .

That you were able to make some variations, maybe, now.

Right, that I got very flexible and I'm able to feel successful and confident in the area and so [laughing] maybe that's why I'm not absolutely passionate [laughing] about having to be a workaholic in the area. But in a sense my creativity has allowed me to be able to enjoy a field that maybe I wasn't meant to be in [laughing].

Right. Been flexible and you can move within it.

Right. Right. And perhaps "sing my own tune" because I can mostly call my own shots and really be my own boss.

What relationship has been most instrumental in helping you to achieve your potential?

I would think all parental support that I've had, I think is so important. And there were people along the way who encouraged me—support from my husband and all that. But most important was all the history and all the support all along from my parents who just cared so much about me and wanted only the best for me.

What do you feel for mentors?

Well, I feel love, I mean I feel very close to my parents. My mother says that we argued about issues and politics during my adolescence. I don't think I had as strong an adolescent rebellion as other kids. And I don't know if any of that figures in or not. I feel hurt when my daughter, she's thirteen, is going through this adolescent rejection of mom and, it's tough on me. But I try to think back. Was I like that and I might be just totally suppressing it all? I even asked my mom. She suppresses some of it, too, but I think I listened more to my parents. I think I may not have had a strong adolescent rebellion as a young kid.

In what ways do you interact with others to enhance their career or personal lives?

In work, I work with associates and I try to guide them, both in giving suggestions of groups that I think that they should join to help boost their careers, as well as talking to them on all kinds of things. So I make a commitment to help young lawyers in my office. I made a commitment to interview kids applying to college for Wesleyan University, so that's been my connection at this point and throughout the past ten years to students in high school. I like to be a role model, even if it's just for the half-an-hour interview that I'm doing with them. Wesleyan University sends me five names during the application period, and I may go meet them somewhere for the interview. Mostly they do come to the law office, so I think that that's good for them to see the law office at work.

With regard to my own kids, I definitely want to supply the best support for them. Then the question is, can I give the kids, my kids, what my parents gave me in terms of all the love and support. I definitely try to do that. There've probably been times when I felt the pull; I think it's harder when kids are younger. My kids are now thirteen and eleven, so they are just beginning to be independent now. I think no matter how old they are, I want to try to be there for their needs. I think of myself as a very available mom, even though I work. Then, also, my mother is still there for my kids. My kids go to her house after school. She lives a block away from the school, so after school, they're with the extended family.

Would you describe yourself more as well rounded, or more able at some things than others?

Oh, that's hard [both laughing]. I think of myself as well rounded, I guess. I know that one of Paul Torrance's rules for creativity is that you don't have to feel like you have to be well rounded. However, the well rounding may be important for creative parenting. Although it's good if kids see a parent with a passion, I think that's good, too. But it all depends on what well rounded is. Clearly my efforts went into law and a law career and there were lots of areas that I have not spent any time on. A lot of things, just because the time demands are so much, that I was starting to do, like photography, went by the wayside. I mean, I hardly take a picture of my kids now [laughing]. And who knows if I'll ever go back to them. I still want to. It has to do with this balancing of passions. I don't know if I really have one passion. I don't feel like I put all my energies into the law. I don't know if that's me really.

GENERAL QUESTIONS ON CREATIVITY

What are your goals and aspirations for the future?

To continue to be as best as I can in doing what I'm doing now. I guess I still see myself as being in the present law firm until my kids really need me to be available to be a grandparent for them. [GWM laughing.] That's definitely going to be an important part of my life, when they have kids. Being available to be part of that whole part of their lives. I do get enjoyment out of what I do for the law firm. I don't have any aspirations to run for office. Maybe I have goals of producing more in terms of making more money and being able to pick and choose more of the cases that I take on. Basically that's just a small thing—in terms of making the practice a nicer practice for me. Even the big cases involving a lot of money don't necessarily not have crummy people involved [laughing]. Many times, you cannot know that clients are really jerks until you're in the middle of the case, so [both laughing]. So I think I have a pretty good intuition for a lot of that.

If you could provide advice to educators for nurturing creativity in kids, what would you share with them?

In a creative way? I'm a big supporter of praising kids, and lots of pats on backs, too. A lot of individual pats on backs is important, for every kid as much as they possibly can provide. Obviously it's getting harder and harder, with bigger classrooms, for teachers to be able to spend the time, but teachers should, as much as they can, give individual attention to kids and let them know that they're there for them and listen.

What advice would you give to parents for nurturing creativity in their kids?

[Pause.] Well, just being there, unconditional love, being supportive, all real general [laughing], real general things. For me, it was just sort of feeling all that support to try different things. Also, open up as many opportunities for your kids as you possibly can. So they know that there's just a lot of opportunities out there and a lot of different possibilities and that they could be creative in many different ways. But, I sort of see a dilemma, in the sense that my parents certainly let me know that there was a direction, that there were still strong goals, and they let me know that it was important to produce. So there was this feeling that I wanted to please them. I wanted to. As a parent, then, how much do you let kids know that a direction is important; how much pressure do you put on kids to produce? How much do you just hang back and let them do what they want to do? To a certain extent, I'm allowed to be creative and to use my creative strengths in a field that I landed up in because of the pressure and direction of my parents. And so if I didn't feel that pressure and direction, I may have ended up being creative in some other, totally different way, but I think that they opened up and made a nicer life for me directing me into this field, that produces a lot of income for me, that produces a nice, flexible lifestyle, though there are lots of pressures. Maybe it wouldn't have been my own choice, had I not been given any guidance at all.

I hear you saying that there has to be some kind of a balance, kind of, of direction and guidance.

Yeah, there has to be, it has to be a balance and I think that kids have to know that whatever they choose, you're going to love them and support them, and yet I think that it's not so bad letting them know that you do have high aspirations for them.

What advice would you give to mentors who work with highly creative kids?

A good mentor is somebody whom you feel is taking an interest in you personally. It's important to know that there is somebody who is taking an interest in you personally. My mentors were also a number of different people who I watched, not necessarily people that actually took an interest in me. I mean, there were some people who did that, like the judge that I worked for, and then there were a number of people that I learned a lot from just by watching them.

Okay [laughing].

If you could design a time capsule, Cathy, that represented you as a creative person, what would you include in the time capsule? Maybe five items?

I think I'd have to put pictures of my kids in there [both laughing]. Although they definitely are, in and of their own way, their own creative beings. [Long pause.] This is hard, but . . . [long pause] there's an article in the St. Paul paper about me and my husband as rainmakers [laughing] and I don't know if I would put that in. I could put in a *vitae*, a *curriculum vitae* or a resume. Of all the publications and boards that I've been appointed to and I've been on a number of Supreme Court task forces. So I think a resume of all that, that would be one thing. I would put in photos of my parents, who were my inspiration, and a photo of my brother, who I am very close to also. I might also include some of my poetry, photographs, and letters that I have written to family.

SUMMARY

Cathy Gorlin has been very successful in her career. She works at maintaining a balance in her career between her job as an attorney and her role as a mother and wife. Her mother has always been a strong role model all through her life, and Cathy is now reflecting back to her children the unconditional love that her mother gave to her. She is now using her creative skills of listening/communication and problem finding/solving not only in her law practice, but with her children. Cathy is a "Torrance Kid" who learned the value of finding a great teacher while "knowing, understanding, taking pride in, practicing, developing, and exploiting her greatest strengths."

thirteen

TED SCHWARZROCK

ENTREPRENEUR "IN OVERDRIVE," CEO OF A MEDICAL-PRODUCTS COMPANY

"You might be someone different than who the heck your parents are!"—Ted (1998)

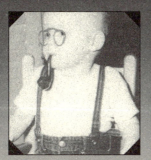

Ted Schwarzrock, circa 1958

A very successful student in the longitudinal study, in terms of career, is Ted Schwarzrock. He took a different path to become a chief executive officer (CEO) of a medical-products company in the health care sector. Ted's case study is an example of a very creative and intelligent person who had the courage to question the professors he encountered at medical school. His parents repeatedly told him that he wanted to become a physician and he *almost* believed them. His most miserable five years were spent at medical school, but that experience enabled him to become a very effective sales representative and ultimately CEO of a medical-products company. Ted was able to use his knowledge of the medical field, creativity, and exemplary people skills to design and develop successful businesses.

Along his professional and personal journey, Ted's career illustrates the importance of accepting yourself for who you are and reflects the following dynamic career influences:

- Know, understand, take pride in, practice, develop, exploit, and enjoy your greatest strengths
- Don't be afraid to fall in love with something and pursue it with intensity
- Learn to free yourself from the expectations of others and to walk away from the games they impose on you. Free yourself to play your own game
- Do what you love and can do well.

SCHOOL YEARS

Ted was a middle child in a family of three. His parents were professionals: his father was a dentist, and his mother had a doctorate in speech pathology. As a young student at University Elementary School, he was assessed by a variety of creativity and intelligence tests during the period from 1958 to 1962 while he attended grades 3 through 6. His creativity tests showed that he was above average in

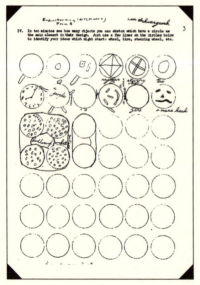

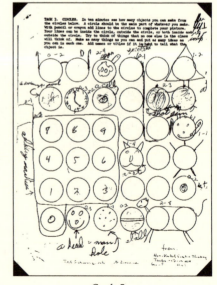

Grade 4 *Grade 5*

both his creative potential and intelligence. His creativity scores showed relative strengths in the factors of fluency, flexibility, and elaboration, with creative strengths such as richness of imagery, unusual visual perspective, movement, and synthesis of diverse elements. The two illustrations on the previous page from the "circles test" show Ted's ability to synthesize objects into meaningful products.

Ted indicated in grade 5 that he usually ranked "right near the top of his class" according to his academic marks. In this same grade, Ted said that he planned "to go to college" and that his parents also had similar expectations of him. One of Ted's best friends during grade 6 was Jim Koehler, who helped him learn college-level algebra. Jim's father was a professor of mathematics, and the boys would do math at Jim's home for "the fun of it." Dr. Koehler would mark their algebra!

FIRST FOLLOW-UP

At the time of the 22-year follow-up in 1980, Ted was 29 years of age, married but did not have children, and was working as a sales representative based in Minneapolis, with Cobe Laboratories, Inc., which is located in the West. This company sold medical equipment for the monitoring of cardiovascular and arterial pressure. Ted reversed the trend of declining sales. His effectiveness as a sales manager prompted his promotion to eastern regional manager. In less than two years, Ted led the country in percent increase in sales of specialized medical equipment. He worked as a salesman with Pepsi Cola of Minnesota from March 1978 to December 1978. His impressive sales record led to an award of "Salesman of the Month" by Pepsi Cola. Prior to this, he worked for the Universal Parcel Service as a tractor-truck driver. At this time, Ted's career ambition was to find a position in management in either marketing or as general manager. In March 1979 he took a training seminar by Xerox in Professional Selling Skills I and II. Ted obtained a Bachelor of Medical Science degree, majoring in psychology, from the University of Minnesota in June 1975.

He then attended the graduate medical school at the University of Minnesota, receiving several scholarships. He completed three-and-a-half years of medical education: two years of basic science courses, and one year of psychiatry concentration. He did not complete graduate school, due to not meeting the standards of National Board Exams.

In high school, Ted's achievements were being elected to the student council and performing in a play. Since graduating from high

Ted, from the university yearbook

school, he had been elected to three positions of leadership in his college dorm. Ted's score for quality of creative achievement at this time was 4.0 out of 10.0. This score was considerably below average for the group of case studies. Ted's interests and hobbies at that time were jogging, weight lifting, hockey, and refereeing hockey.

His greatest spur for continued achievement was self-satisfaction and making money. His greatest obstacle to continued achievement was frustration with the traditional means of establishing competency (i.e., diplomas, degrees, etc.) rather than demonstrated ability. He felt able to handle responsibilities in the business world faster than his superiors recognized it.

At this time in Ted's life he had a mentor at graduate school, being the associate dean of the medical school. He supported Ted during rough times and added perspective during good times. This relationship ended when Ted left graduate school. During the next decade, Ted's career image was to hold a position with major responsibility in management, marketing, or sales. Would he succeed?

MIDDLE TO LATE CAREER

In the 1998 follow-up questionnaire, Ted had just retired, but was involved in the setting up of three new companies—just for fun! He had indeed fulfilled his ambition of having a major role in management, marketing, or sales. Since the 1980 follow-up, Ted had worked as national sales manager and vice-president sales and marketing, national sales director, vice-president sales and marketing, regional vice-president, and vice-president in six separate medical equipment and products companies—and succeeding in all of their mission statements. His last company, in which he was vice-president, sales and marketing, made $55 million in revenue its first year and was bought out one year later for $595 million. He was now financially independent and desired to spend more time with his wife and three children.

Ted and family

Ted's score for creative public achievements was 9.0 out of 10.0—very high compared to most others in case studies, and in relation to his score of 4.0 in the 1980 follow-up. He had started up, and funded, three companies. Needless to say, he had done a tremendous amount of work of in-service training for workers and co-workers; developed and applied policies; and regularly created advertising ideas and original educational materials.

Ted with current interests

Ted had "found" himself since medical school and was doing what he loved to do. His greatest strengths are exemplary people skills; seeing opportunities that others don't see; and making things happen. He was able to execute business opportunities with diverse groups of people. Ted's behavior reflected the slogan, *Dream, Dare, and Do!*

INTERVIEW ON JULY 15, 1998

This interview with Ted Schwarzrock was conducted in Minneapolis. Ted reflected on the early influences on his creativity; his career path and transitions; creative accomplishments; and finally, general comments on creativity. His own words relate his experiences best.

EARLY INFLUENCES ON CREATIVITY

At what age were you first aware of your creativity?

Wow! [GWM laughing.] I don't know exactly. I'm going to guess—third grade or something like that, and I think that the reason that the whole concept even came into existence for me was being pulled out for these little exams—Dr. Torrance's tests. But I don't think it's a concept that I spent much time thinking about until, probably, in my 40s and trying to do some assessment of why I'm where I'm at, what's going on for me, why is it that sometimes I don't seem to fit. That's when I really started to come around to the fact that I see things some people don't see. It comes to bear in a business sense for me.

Do you have any idea how creativity showed itself at that early stage?

An incident I remember was that a person was talking about a fire truck and asked me, "What could you do with this toy to make it different and better?" I came up with a couple of suggestions. What I remember is how the psychologists reacted. I can't even tell you what the heck the suggestion was I came up with, but I remember their response to some of the ideas I came up with.

Working in business, I've been in a situation literally hundreds and hundreds of times where I see connections and ways to make things work that other people didn't see. I'm very used to people saying, "What the hell are you talking about?" That's just par for the course.

At elementary-school age, can you think of what influence your schooling had on your creative ability?

I think that University Elementary School had some really gifted teachers who were terribly committed to kids. I think that positive environment was probably really the strong thing. I compare what I think I remember about it to what I see my kids going through today with some of the teachers they get. I think overall it was above average in terms of being positive, nurturing, accepting of ideas compared to lots of schools today.

My friend at the time was Jim Koehler. His dad was a math professor. We used to sit out on the back porch of University Elementary School and work on math that probably was high school- or college-level algebra. He'd bring worksheets from home [GWM laughing] that his dad made up and we'd be doing this algebra. It would be sent home, his dad would correct it, and send it back the next day. [GWM laughing.] There were just some really rich ideas that not only were flowing around with teachers but I mean the kids came from enriched home environments.

Can you think of some specific incidents then at that time that enabled your creativity to develop?

Not specifically. Again I think that being with this group of special children and the dedicated teachers helped.

Was there any influence at an elementary age which you now recognize as having had an impact on your subsequent career or chosen field of work?

I don't think it's likely I can point to one specific thing. I would go back and say during those years an awful lot of good things were going on. In terms of just building very strong skills that were brought to bear by teachers who I think were there for reasons other than just, "I want a job." I think that was one of the attractions of University Elementary School. They had people that were interested in something beyond just "I'm feeding, clothing and housing my family." There was something special going on there, interest and a dedication, too. I mean intellectual curiosity was encouraged. We would be asked to stop and reflect about day-to-day things.

What would you say was the most important lesson that you learned with regard to your creativity at that stage?

Again, I think it was just that there was something good and different going on at University Elementary School.

How would your peers have described you at that time?

Hmm! [GWM laughing.] I don't know.

Jim [Koehler] and others, what would they have said about you then?

I don't know. I think, it's all general stuff that was probably true about most of the kids. They all were bright and motivated and a nice bunch of kids to be around. I can't remember a problem kid like the ones I see my kids have today.

I was pretty quiet. I think I was reasonably bright and a nice guy. But I'm sure they would have said that I was really quiet.

CAREER PATHS AND TRANSITIONS

What is your present job?

Presently, I'm retired. Although my wife would laugh and say, "What are you going to do around the house? You're never here [laughing]." But I'm working with a couple of very small start-up medical companies here in Minneapolis/St. Paul. I am helping them to pull the business together, get funded, and raise some money at ground level. The titles that go along with that are chairman of the board, and CEO, and president.

Well, those are impressive titles!

Very impressive titles! But we're talking about small businesses. [GWM laughing.] It doesn't mean much.

Are you able to apply your creativity to what you're doing now?

Yeah, I can economically afford to just step back and say, "Well, if there's no paycheck, that doesn't matter. I can do this anyway." I like doing it for money, but I can do it just for the fun of it. I think you actually can make a lot more money doing it that way. You have to be in a position where you don't need to worry about it on a week-to-week basis.

That's what I'm doing right now. But that just started last August, so it's just a lot of fun right now. It's working out well;

it's been a big adjustment, more wrestling with myself than I thought. It's hard to remove a work ethic that says I'm supposed to get up in the morning, shave, put on a tie and be in an office by eight o'clock. What is fun for me is seeing how much of a habit that was as opposed to something that was really necessary [both laughing]. Here all these years, I've been fooling myself.

What other jobs have you had before your semi-retirement?

I would break post-education experience into two categories. Ever since I was old enough to understand English, my mother and father told me I wanted to be a physician. Being a good white Anglo-Saxon Protestant boy, I went ahead and took the Medical College Admissions Test (MCAT), applied to medical school, and got in. Surprise, surprise! It was the most miserable five years of my life! I'm sure there are still people at the university who lost hair or turned gray because of my presence within that system. [GWM laughing.] In a way, medical school was really preprogrammed and I don't think anybody meant ill. It was just that my mom and dad both came from environments where they had little. I wouldn't call them disadvantaged, but they looked at a medical degree as an ultimate achievement. They were trying to make sure I had my head pointed in the right direction. Unfortunately, they missed one thing that's important—that is, you have to figure out who the heck you are and go be that person. You might be somebody different than who the heck your folks are or want you to be.

I had an intellectual ability to pull off the grades—the MCAT scores were so high that nationally I was at the top. The opening line out of this guy's mouth for an interview here at the University of Minnesota was, "Why have you been f 'ing off?" His point was simply that my board scores were in like the top one percent nationally and my grades were Bs. So to him, that's f 'ing off.

Yet now with the advantage of 30 years of perspective, what I probably should have said to him was, "Well, that might be what you expect, but for me, that's just fine."

There are a lot of things that I like doing that aren't in the classroom. I've learned what I want to learn in the classroom and most importantly, I'm learning how to learn without a classroom. I'll be able to take that with me as opposed to the grade, which I'm not sure would be useful. That was the difficulty the medical school administration had with me during the time that I was there. They'd be hauling me in to ask me why wasn't I doing more of something and I'd say, "Well, why do you expect me to memorize the Krebs cycle when I can open it up, page 485 in my biochemistry book and it's there." I mean, why do I need to know that. I can find the goddamn thing. What is the point of trying to grind and memorize it?

They looked at my behavior as an affront to their authority, which might have had something to do with my style. I looked at it as stupidity. A lot of other kids felt the same way. In fact, they had more kids drop out in the first quarter than they are used to losing in the entire four years of medical school. By the time the four years were up, they had lost one-sixth of the class, which had never happened before. They actually changed their admission requirements subsequent to that whole experience. I wasn't the only smart-ass in the group. They changed to looking for somebody that was academically more proven. A person who had some flexibility in things like grades and extracurricular stuff and they kind of narrowed that focus. They wanted to have somebody that was more applied, that had proven themselves as somebody that would be more applied and probably question things a little less. Now good–bad, who knows, but I wasn't the only guy standing around saying, "Why exactly are we doing this?" They used to say things to me like "Do you want to become a physician?" And I'd say, "How the hell do I know until I get there? If this is what being a physician is, i.e., being in school, I don't want to do that. This isn't any fun; this isn't what I came here for. I came to work with people and help people. I want to make money." Those were the three things that I would keep telling them. To me, practicing medicine wasn't much related to any of that stuff you studied in a classroom. But is that being a physician; is that practicing medicine? They'd send us on rotations with doctors in clinics; it didn't look like it to me. I'd just stand there saying, until I get a chance to practice medicine, I cannot honestly answer your question, "Do I want to be a physician?" I can tell you what I think. I can tell you what my perceptions are but I have to do it. They didn't like any of those answers. [GWM laughing.] I understand their position. I was a real curve ball to them. Some of my feelings had to do with being bright and being creative but I also think a bigger piece of it had to do with the rebellious guy that I was and to some extent still am. I'm frequently reminded that I have a style where occasionally I just piss-off people in authority. I'm sure there are other issues that relate to why that's going on and then you put some creativity to work on that task of pissing-off authority and you come up with some very volatile things. I'm still not sure it was a fatal sin but nonetheless, there was an awful lot of kids asking really tough questions that the medical establishment wasn't real happy dealing with. Actually, it was a real growing experience for them. So I left medical school and of course, all the money I borrowed to go to school resulted in my becoming a bad credit risk. Everybody said, "The guy's going to the dogs." [GWM laughing.] So I sat down and thought about what I like to do. I like working with people and had good people skills, liked to make money, so I worked at it. I got a job selling and did very well at it. I talked my way into a job selling medical products at a level that I found out, entry-level sales guys just don't normally get. There is just no way in hell that I should have successfully negotiated my way through an entire interview process and got hired. But I did and turned it into a career. I went up the corporate ladder very fast to sales management, to national sales management, to VP sales and marketing, and to domestic and international sales. I worked for a company as a general manager and kind of in a real big rush got to be the president, got to be the big guy and got to make all this money. I was kind of just in overdrive. [GWM laughing.] I don't know whether that relates to being in control, secure, but all those are hot issues for me. The big deal is being in control. What I have done in the last ten or fifteen years has really been health-care-related, sales and marketing, general manager, and then starting six medical companies. Most of them have been successful in recognizable ways.

When you made changes in your working life, was there anyone whom you relied on for support and advice?

That's been an issue for me for at least ten years—the idea that I would really benefit from being able to hook up with somebody in that classic mentor–mentee relationship. It has not happened but there have been a couple of times in the last ten or fifteen years when I thought it might. I really just continuously have been looking for that person and most of the time when I thought I'd found somebody, what I figured out was, and God this sounds arrogant, that in about thirty-eight minutes, I knew more than they did. I was better at making judgments than they were and I had eclipsed them. Eclipsed what I could learn from them, not that I couldn't learn human goodness and judgment and things like that from somebody, but I mean in terms of being able to constantly go back for a long-term relationship, it's just really hard for me to find somebody that can move at that pace and has the knowledge base that I can tap and not go beyond too quickly. Twice I thought I'd really found some guy that could be a mentor and in one case, the guy retired and moved to Florida and kind of just dropped out. He wasn't sending negative messages like, "Gee whiz, I don't want to talk to you." He was just going to play golf and hang around with his wife. He started a family at that time at age fifty.

The other guy was the one person who I think had the brains to really keep me challenged. The communication was always a one-way street. I always had to call him. I think in the eight years that I've known this guy, he's called me once. I'm looking for a relationship that's got some give and take in it. He likes me a lot—it's just that there's just something not of value about our contact that I'm looking for. He's too busy doing something else or things just don't fit for him. There have been a couple of times when I've thought somebody was going to be able to fulfill that mentor role for me but those periods of time were short.

How are you able to integrate relationships into your working life?

I definitely spend more time with my kids, which I like. That's a whole lot of fun. My seventeen-year-old said to me, "Well, don't you think you've taken enough time off? I think it's time for you to go find a job." [GWM laughing.] And I said, "Well, I don't think so." And he says, "Well, what are you going to do?" I said, "I thought I'd just hang around and bug you. What do you think of that?" He kind of rolled his eyes. Yeah, he's at that age where he wants to know where I'm going and then he goes somewhere else with his friends. He doesn't want to accidentally [laughing] run into his parents anywhere. [GWM laughing.] But no, it's a real boon, I really enjoy it. I like being able to have the flexibility. For an awful lot of years, I just wasn't there and that caused its own unique set of problems that had to be dealt with. I don't think that you ever say, "Well, okay, I've dealt with it." You know what I mean? It's a continuous, ongoing process. My wife and I have a different relationship since I retired. I was off working all the time; now we bump in a little bit to the flip side of that. I'm around the house more and she'll be doing something and I'll say, "Well, you know, why don't you do this?" I want to change things or do this control thing. She'll stop, look at me and say, "Now I've been doing this for twenty-five years. Everything's been fine with it. What the hell are you doing [both laughing] thinking about changing it now? Get out of here! Go do something else. [GWM laughing.] Find something to do. You're bugging me and interrupting my routine here."

CREATIVE ACCOMPLISHMENTS

What do you consider to be your most creative achievement to this point?

There are a couple of things that jump out. One of them that I'm really proud of and yet very quiet about is that I think I have broken the physical and psychological abuse cycle in our family and that was no small task. I had to figure that out myself. I figured out the whys and the wherefores and used enough rational thought where my kids haven't experienced physical abuse. I realize that's one accomplishment of which I am very proud. Also, pulling a relationship together with my wife in which we really have a fun relationship. It's got a lot of depth to it right now. That took a lot of work as well. Business has provided a creative outlet for me. Pulling some of these companies together is an example. We are all alarmed by the number of bacteria showing up that resist antibiotics. We may have pulled together an intellectual property around the way antibiotics turn bacteria off or turn them on and there appears to be no resistant bugs to it. That would be a hell of a thing to pull off and yet be economically viable. It's the kind of thing where you might have a Jim Henson who doesn't die from a bug that's resistant to antibiotics. Or even think about it, treatment for kids in our country and Third World countries. It would be a stunning thing to pull together. We'll see if we can get it going down the road. It's not over with, it's not done but being able to see how to get that thing on the pathway which clearly has not been done yet . . . it's really a kick. Making a lot of money, that's a kick, being able to go do that.

I realized that in the last company I worked, I was very different from the guy who ran it. We didn't have the same business ethics; we didn't operate the same. I thought that I could make a hell of a lot of money if I could just help make it successful for two or three years and then step out. I was there four years, made more money than I thought I was going to make and got out of it. It is still a fairly successful medical company today. He will sit there and operate in an environment that when I was twenty-six or twenty-seven, I would have self-destructed or got fired. But instead I tried to go in there and control my environment. I had to decide which issues I was going to waste bullets on and where I wouldn't. Working in an environment like that is very different.

What do you consider to be your creative attributes?

The biggest idea I go back to is one I've already talked about and it's business situations where I see solutions that other people don't see. This works very well in negotiations of all kinds. It works very well, especially at this real early stage, within little teeny companies where you're missing things that a lot of business executives are used to having; i.e., money in the bank, revenue. They may be used to working in environments where they've got resources to solve problems. So you develop a structure where you can get or trade; something for something. I find a way to get the right people together to get the job done. Personally, it has so much to do with me making a lot of stuff happen and it's just getting the right people connected.

I also think part of that has to do with individual work styles, putting people in the "box" together that are not all the same, yet are they going to get along? This is something I've ended up spending a lot of conscious time trying to develop, that kind of strength or product in the last six years.

What would your close associates say about your strengths?

I think some of that's invisible to most or at least to a lot of people that I have worked with. I think they'd tell you I'm very confident, even to the point of being overconfident. They'd say I'm a very bright guy with good people skills. That's historically a good skill, having great people skills. I have developed tremendous relationships with people who have a history of being very difficult for people to develop relationships with. I have developed connections with doctors—orthopedic surgeons and cardiac surgeons—that spanned years and years. One of the things that kind of smacked me in the head was an incident with one of the engineers at a company that I used to work for. He spent twelve years developing artificial knees with Johnson and Johnson and they are a premier company in that particular product. He needed to hire a knee surgeon. I'm sitting there thinking, "Well, I wonder who he's going to go get, because you figure twelve years in the business, he ought to know exactly who the good guys are." You know what he did? He asked me to find someone. He really didn't know? So I thought, I'm going to test this whole business, see what the hell is going on. And so I said, "You want me to go find out who the heck we should get here and test them?" "YEAH." So, I said, "You've gotta know, after all those years, you've gotta know some people out there." He said, "Well, no, geez, I really don't remember." I think he really didn't. I think he really had just flashed those relationships by for that period of time and that was it. There was no connection with those doctors that went beyond that piece of metal [knee]. When he was out in the field talking to people he didn't connect with them. That just isn't what happens when I get involved with people and I know it. I get to know their families. I might have stayed at their houses. You wind up becoming friends although you always have that little commercial underpinning. [GWM laughing.]

Ted, what influences guide or constrain your creativity?

Well, I think that the biggest constraint is the other aspects of my personality that are the result of a goofy childhood. That doesn't mean I had it tougher than anybody else but I mean, this rebellious side of me, I'm beginning to understand why it's there and what it is a result of. There was an environment that I perceived as being physically abusive. There was enough smacking around going on to where it was a big issue for me as a kid. It drove a lot of the things I did when I was sixteen, seventeen, eighteen, nineteen—in that time frame. Today, there's still components of that, that influence my interaction with people that I don't particularly like. I think sometimes it creates a backdrop or interaction in which I don't fully apply the positive aspects of my personality as much as I might. I'm trying to remember and keep in check a negative piece.

QUESTIONS RELATED TO THE "MANIFESTO FOR CHILDREN"

Would you say that you are in love or passionate about what you're doing now?

It's a great question to ask me right now because I've had a year to think about that question in a very focused and real way as opposed to when I was working full time. The need for a paycheck every other week gets in the way. I think that makes it harder to stop and sometimes say, what am I passionate about and what do I like to do? Yeah, I'd say unequivocally I am. I want to be closer to my kids and understand more about those issues that are going on with them and help them. I also want to be closer to my wife and understand more about our relationship as it develops. But the business piece of taking little teeny-weeny projects that might not even make it in the light of day and a) figure out if they're worth it; and b) try to figure how to get all the resources pulled together to actually kick them up and over the top. Yeah, I enjoy the hell out of that. The number of times I've stopped and said, "This can't really be happening. It's just too much . . . I'm so spoiled it's ridiculous." I'm constantly telling my wife that, or I'll be riding a motorcycle someplace and think, I can't believe I'm actually out here doing this [laughing]. I wish it could happen to everybody.

In what way is your creativity affected by the expectations of others?

Well, that used to be a bigger issue than it is now. I think part of it is just accepting the fact that there is something different that's going on in my head and that doesn't mean I'm better or worse than someone else, but just different. That's fine.

Do you think you're "free to play your own game" and "sing in your own key"?

A lot more than I used to be.

Yeah?

Now I'm not telling you that people would see that. Because I think one of the things that happened at the same time I kind of came around the corner with, "It's okay to be different," and also, it's okay not to show all my cards. There's a time and a place to play it my way and I'm okay one way or the other. There are times when seeing things differently is very, very valuable, and there're times when it's just plain disconcerting. Production people like to come to work Monday through Friday, from eight to five, get the same check every two weeks, come hell or high water. Having somebody like me walk back there and say, "Gosh, why don't we change this sixteen ways from Sunday and maybe we can see if things go up, down or sideways." It's disconcerting to them. You know, to have me walk in and say, "This principal core piece of business that we're focused on here is all f 'ed up. We ought to sell it, move on to something else." There's a time and a place for that kind of stuff. Even though I would tell you that I think I'm probably right more often than I'm wrong, it isn't everywhere. I think just getting some at ease with who the hell I am makes it a lot better, for everybody around me also [both laughing].

What relationship has been most instrumental in helping you to achieve your potential?

Well, I think there have been two of them. One of them probably doesn't fit under anyone's classic definition of a relationship. I'd say one of them would be my relationship with my wife. Especially in the last ten years, there have been a whole lot of good things that have come out of it and being okay with who you are is one of them. One of the things that I think my wife has done a phenomenal job of is helping me get comfortable with who the heck I am. Number two is my relationship with myself and that's the one I would say is not necessarily something that everybody's going to categorize as a relationship. But it has been getting to know myself and who I am, what I am, and why I am this way. I spent a hell of a lot of goddamn time trying to do that in the last ten years. It's been hard work. It's the toughest task I've ever undertaken.

Would you say your wife has been a mentor?

No, but perhaps in a remote sense. I've watched her become very accepting of herself and at the same time, become accepting of me—in some very low-key and very pragmatic ways. She says, "Yeah, it's just the way you are. Why are you arguing about it, this is you." That's just her, that's how she likes to do things or that's what's important to her. There doesn't necessarily have to be a "why." And it's okay. She has just really been amazing about that whole process. She's been very accepting of me.

In what ways do you interact with others to enhance their career or personal lives?

I think there are people that look at me that way. I would say about 1981, I had a boss for a very short time who was a very interesting sales-manager–type personality/mentality. We were a little company and he used to always go through this thing. When he'd call people and if somebody asked him who's calling and what is it regarding, you could hear him afterwards going, "May I tell him who's calling?" It was really, are you f 'ing important enough to talk to him today. If I didn't want to talk to somebody about something on the telephone, I'd tell them. I'd never not take a call even if I didn't know who it was. Of course, if you and I are engaged in some heavy conversation about some work thing, I wouldn't be taking phone calls. But I mean if I'm sitting there working on something and ding, it's George Murphy and I don't know George from Adam, I wouldn't just say take a message just because I didn't want to pick up the phone and talk to him. That turned into never saying no, part of a cardinal rule, never saying no to somebody asking me to get together and have lunch or help him or look at their resume or help him figure out where to get a job or something like that. Now that didn't mean dump everything upside down to meet him. It might be two weeks, but I wouldn't say no to him. I've met a hell of a lot of interesting people doing that. In fact, this antibiotics/clinic thing probably wouldn't have happened if I hadn't talked to him. I'll talk to a brick wall.

Would you describe yourself as more as well rounded, or more able at some things than others?

Oh, more able at some things than others. I think I've got general-manager skills in the work environment—clearly sales and marketing. I actually ran a company for a while because I had to have that job and I got it. I realized this isn't all it's cracked up to be. Now the funny part of that is, I go back to sales and marketing, make a lot of money and stop. What are all the jobs I have today? They're all that, being the head guy job. It's just in a very tiny and small environment. But I think I'm far better at the big picture, getting the pieces to fit together the right way all at the right time, in the right place, going the right direction at the same time. I end up doing most of those job functions, although mind you, if somebody said to me, you have to go out and be a regional sales manager for a medical equipment company, I think I could do a real strong job at that. But it would be hard work to stay focused on that narrow a task.

GENERAL QUESTIONS ON CREATIVITY

What are your goals and aspirations for the future?

Well, this antibiotics/clinic deal that I'm involved in, to really get it shaped up to the point where it can take off and then get out of the way is a goal. There's a brokerage house here in town that does a lot of small, medical stuff, and one of the guys that founded that company and I were talking about a particular start-up and he asked that same question, "Well, what do you want to do?" I said, "Well, you know, I kind of think I'd like to pull a couple of start-ups together and get them so they're off on the tracks and rolling, and then get the hell out of the way." He kind of looked up at me and said, "Boy, that's a refreshing point of view. You know, I wish a lot of CEOs of little companies that start up would realize that you can't use the same skill-set once they're up and flying and especially once they get to be . . . $50, $100 million. It's not the same skill set."

He's a guy that deals with them day in and day out. If they're successful, that's one of the problems they're going to have. Once something really gets going, they've got this egomaniac who's worth a lot of money who doesn't want to get out of the way. He is actually more harm to the corporation than he is helpful at that time. So I want to get a couple of things started and make some more money. If I could keep doing this for ten years, I'd be quite happy.

If you could provide educators with advice for nurturing creativity in kids, what would you share with them?

I think you've gotta have tolerance for more answers than one. [GWM laughing.] I see more of that with teachers that my kids have. I'm sure I don't understand all of the problems that they have as teachers, but they picked the job. We all have problems other people can't see, so goddamn it, figure them out. One of the problems is that some kids may not fit in the system the same way the other ninety percent do, but you'd better be paying attention to them because it doesn't mean they're stupid. My seventeen-year-old son was lined up for Special Ed help. The school people said, "Gee, he has Attention Deficit Disorder [ADD]." They wanted him on meds; they wanted all this kind of stuff. This kid, all by himself, is off taking Microsoft Certification. The instructors are saying, "You're the brightest kid we've ever had. You're better at this than anybody we've ever had. You're better at this than we are!" All he's done is read and do his own thing at home. He's clearly got a gift for computers and how they work and how the software and hardware interacts. Yet the school tells me this kid is ADD. This kid is *not*. I mean, get the hell out of here. One school psychologist in the middle of an evaluation said, "I am not convinced that Nick belongs in an ADD class." He said, "I think this school system just needs to have a whole different way to relate to him. I'm not sure anybody here can figure out how to do that." That's what he said. It was really a sad goddamn message. This is supposed to be a well-funded, very accomplished school district in the state of Minnesota. What the hell kind of message is that? I'm sitting there thinking as a parent I'll help but I'm not re-teaching him. I expect you to find some answers.

Right!

But goddamn it, you guys have to do this and I think for the most part, they don't get great grades for being able to deal with somebody who looked like he was a little bit out of the mainstream to them. He clearly has unbelievable gifts in a couple of areas. Yet if you asked him about school, he says it has become a game. He can get as good a grade as he wants, but he doesn't really give a shit most of the time. He's gonna do just enough to keep Mom and Dad off his butt and he's gonna link into some career outside of school. I'll bet you before he graduates from high school, he winds up with a full-time job offer to do local-area-network stuff for companies right in town. The tough part for him is gonna be that they're gonna offer him $50,000 per year to go do it. He's gonna be sitting there saying, "Dad, what are you talking about college for?" [GWM laughing.]

You say educators? They've gotta be listening. They've gotta be able to get a message, and it's coming from students who are not developed enough to be able to phrase it ten different ways so you can hear it. It's gonna be a message that comes just once or you get those kids turned off. I still believe an awful lot of kids that are in Special Ed, certainly there are kids who do have really significant basic educational issues, but I think there's just as many that are absolutely gifted—that are just sitting there with a different screen on a different wall. You can't give up on these kids. You know, it's the old cliche, did Albert Einstein graduate from high school? Does anybody know the answer to that question? [Pause.] Do you know?

No, he didn't.

Now he had a whole bunch of degrees that were all honorary afterwards. I don't think he's the only guy.

So you're saying, formal schooling isn't the answer?

I think you've got to teach kids how to learn. I think there certainly are some formal schools that are the answer. If you take

Wharton or Stanford or Harvard, there's clearly something truly excellent going on at those institutions and others that aren't as good. I think the important part is, do you learn how to learn? This goes back to a bias of mine that I have because I was getting beat up in medical school having these guys who were clearly not any smarter than I was, telling me, memorize this stuff. And I was saying, "Well, why? You think I'm gonna absolutely have to know the Krebs cycle looking at a patient in an office somewhere?" If they do, they're sadly mistaken. You know, I'll never practice medicine. I think it's a real issue. Probably my kids have brought it to light. I've got two that fit that. My third absolutely has the other style of getting along in school and gets straight As. She has teachers wrapped around her finger and can manipulate the living shit out of them. She's so smart, it's just plain scary. The world does not know what is running at them yet with her brains and her will. She's gonna run into some contests somewhere that she's gonna lose and it's gonna be an authority issue. She just will not back down on some stuff. She's terribly bright and terribly gifted.

If you could provide parents advice for nurturing creativity in their kids, what would you say?

Well, I think some of that's harder in that I have tremendous respect for the difficulties of daily life for families today. We have a lot of two-paycheck families trying make ends meet and then you're going to say, "Oh, come home and be sensitive to your ten-year-old," whose way of expressing a need for attention is to break something. I mean that's really hard and I really understand that. I really identify. I think if there's any way one parent can be around at least part-time, if not full time, I think that's really important. You can get a lot of good things by substituting after-school childcare and good ones. You get a lot from them, but I think you can't get everything. I don't believe for a second that we have thirty minutes of quality time every night. I like that idea, but that's the beginning, that doesn't replace not being there. Looking at most of my adolescent life, I was alone. I had a car in senior high school that I put eighteen thousand miles on.

If you could provide guidance to mentors now who work with highly creative kids, what would you say to them?

The first thing I always say is pay attention. Be looking for the signal that somebody wants to try to develop a relationship. I think we all owe it to the human race to do those kinds of things, to put something back to make that investment. I think sometimes it's really hard, although I think mentors have it probably easier but I'm guessing because I can't touch that base very effectively from my own experience. But I think they have it a little easier than parents in that situation in that you're not involved day to day and buried in the little minutiae that gets in the way sometimes with some of those bigger ideas. I think, really let the opportunity occur to see somebody at absolutely their best, probably also at their worst, but stay clear of some of the judgments, such as, "Where did you leave your underwear?" or "Did you brush your teeth? Did you make your bed?"—the kind of shit that kids get shoveled their way. Then you can deal with some of the issues because I think if you can do that, then it'd just be a riot. I think it would really be a hell of a lot of fun.

If you could design a time capsule that represented you as a creative person [TS laughing], what would you include in this capsule? Maybe five or ten things.

[Long pause.] I don't know how you'd package some of these things up. I'd try to package one thing up and that would be stopping this physical abuse thing. I'd put that in there.

I would love to be able to put this antibiotic/clinic thing in there. The real accomplishment is going to be that we get it out there where people have access in a commercially usable situation as opposed to some toy in a lab.

I think probably pictures of my wife and kids, I'd put those in there for sure.

I'd like to find a way to package up whatever contributions I've made to the human race. A way to say he added this to the lives of fellow human beings that was positive and good.

SUMMARY

Ted had a tough time ridding himself of the expectations that his parents held for him—to be a medical doctor. Sinetar (1998) stated that "most of us spend adulthood dancing to tunes our parents composed." She says that "these scores spun out in childhood can run our lives." However, his career journey in medical school led him to use his strengths to work as an exemplary salesperson in the medical field and, ultimately, to establish his own medical-equipment companies. His medical training undoubtedly complemented and contributed to his business acumen. He realized what doctors and hospitals needed in order to provide some of the necessary health services for people.

Ted also realized that a successful business venture involves people that have differing points of view. He has learned the skills of interdependence and gladly shared them with his colleagues and workers. Ted has been able to apply his creativity and intellectual ability to his work in order to enjoy his greatest strengths. Others depend upon him for his leadership, creative strengths, and strategic vision.

Ted is still moving along on his journey, but has moved his "gear shift" from "overdrive" to "drive" as he has become more understanding of himself and appreciative of those around him.

fourteen

FRITZ REEKER

"A TOP LAWYER IN MINNESOTA"

"Fate plays such a significant role in my life"—Fritz (1998)

Fritz Reeker, circa 1962

Fritz Reeker is the only student in the sample that has had a mentor for 38 years—his grade four teacher, Rod Myers!

SCHOOL YEARS

Friedrich Arthur Reeker is the eldest of three children and only boy in his family. He has two sisters, Pam and Karen. His father taught German at a local high school, while his mother was a homemaker with two masters degrees. As a young student at University Elementary School he was assessed by a variety of creativity and intelligence tests over a three- or four-year period while in grades 3 through 6.

His creativity results showed that he scored about average. He experienced a definite slump in fourth grade in spite of having Rod Myers as a teacher. He did, however, demonstrate creative strengths in the following areas: synthesis of diverse elements, movement and action, expression of emotions, resistance to premature closure, unusual visualization, breaking boundaries, and richness of imagery and fantasy. Fritz's intelligence was well above average and he consistently performed in the top one-third of a very high achieving group of children. His best subject was mathematics; Fritz developed a rapid strategy to calculate batting averages and would astound fellow students and adults with this ability.

His admiration for his grade 4 teacher Rod Myers (now Dr. Myers) was evident in this response to the following question from the *Learning by Imitation* checklist: "Of all the people in the world, name the ones you would most like to be": "1. President Kennedy, 2. Mr. Myers, 3. Me." Wayne Kirk, one of Fritz's teachers, indicated two characteristics that best described Fritz in grade 6: "1. Shows leadership with a plan in mind, and 2. eager to learn and explore." Fritz clearly remembers Mr. Myers telling the class at the end of fourth grade that in ten years he would send each of them a postcard that would read, "It's up to you." He never forgot the thought! Fritz for one, took charge of his own learning. In elementary school Fritz thought he might be a chemist or a sports player when he grew up.

According to Rod Myers,[1] Fritz was a model student. He was serious and conscientious. Because he had good native intelligence, he did well in all subjects and likely placed in the upper quarter of the class, which had several scholastic stars. Rod Myers indicated that ". . . most teachers would love to have several Fritz Reekers in their class." Myers would not have predicted that Fritz would become a lawyer, but was not surprised. He would have guessed at that time that medicine or teaching might be his career path.

FIRST FOLLOW-UP

At the time of the 22-year follow-up in 1980, Fritz was 28 years of age, married, and was an attorney-at-law in civil practice. He had completed his B.A. (cum laude) in English from Carleton College, Northfield, Minnesota, in 1973 (including a quarter at London University), and attended the School of Law at the University of Minnesota, graduating with his J.D. degree in 1976. Fritz had demonstrated his strong academic achievement again and was awarded two prizes: the Aliss Foundation Scholarship for Academic Achievement, and the Highest Honors for Political Science Senior Project. At the same time he was a member of the undefeated varsity tennis team and was school chess champion. Fritz had worked as a tennis professional at Richfield Tennis Center during the summers of 1970 through 1977, and in 1973 and 1974 at Lilydale in Minneapolis.

Since high school graduation he listed his three most creative achievements as follows:

1. Marriage
2. Creation of a law practice
3. Development of a backhand top-spin lob.

Fritz's score on the 1980 quality of creative achievement index was 4.0 out of 10, which was below average for the case-study group.

His career ambition at this time was to establish and maintain an enjoyable and helpful law practice. The greatest obstacle to continued achievement in his mind was fate. He said that the primary frustration is "probably that fifty percent or so of life that human actions do not control. I suppose this frustration only manifests itself when things take a nasty turn for no apparent reason." He indicated that his wife gave him assistance and support. Although Fritz did not report any particularly creative accomplishment at this time, he did indicate the following as an illustration of how he best displays his creativity on a day-to-day basis: "I recall courtroom tactics designed to make it appear that I was giving something up when I was really getting what I wanted." He rated his current lifestyle as very satisfying. When asked what he would choose to do in the next ten years, he said, half-jokingly, "I would escape to a warm climate and practice law."

MIDDLE TO LATE CAREER

In the 1998 follow-up questionnaire, Fritz was still working as an attorney-at-law, with a specialization in trial law, in Minneapolis. He was now 47 years of age, married, and father to a 14-year-old daughter, Carla. Although he has reported few personal and public manifestations of creative achievements, he is considered to be a top lawyer in the state of Minnesota. He has succeeded in his career since the

Fritz, circa 1998

1980 follow-up. He was cited in the *Minnesota Law and Politics Magazine* as a "super lawyer."[2] The article cites his academic preparation and his involvement with petitioners in workers' compensation litigation. Fritz's notion about the influence of fate on our lives is reflected in his remark in this article: "When you practice in this line of work for two decades you see so many people injured and ill and even killed, and you have some idea of the general unfairness of the world, and that lawyers can help to do something about it."

Fritz indicated that he is not exactly in love with his work; however, he's had "moments of affection." His greatest strengths are intellectual honesty, a solid education, athletic past, financial practicality, narrow philanthropy, and a good night's sleep! He cites collecting books and playing golf as interests and hobbies.

He clearly states that Rod Myers, his grade 4 teacher, is his longstanding mentor of 38 years. Myers taught him how to catch a forward pass keeping one foot on the ground in grade 4 and today provides support and comments on his various activities. Regarding using the skills of interdependence, Fritz clearly said that a successful marriage relies on these skills. His wife has been disabled for five years and they have both had to make adaptations. Today, Fritz can be counted on to maintain the addresses of all students who attended classes with him at University Elementary School in Minneapolis. He has been instrumental in organizing two class reunions during the past few years.

INTERVIEW ON JULY 8, 1998

This interview with Fritz Reeker was conducted in his Minneapolis law office on July 8, 1998. Fritz reflected on the early influences on his creativity; his career path and transitions; creative accomplishments; and finally, general comments on creativity. His own words tell his thoughts and experiences best.

EARLY INFLUENCES ON CREATIVITY

At what age do you feel you were first aware of being creative?

[Pause.] I don't think that I ever was. I don't think I ever gave it a thought at all.

All right. When Dr. Torrance was involved, back in the fifties, were you at University Elementary School?

I was.

Right. Did you feel at that time at all that you were creative or maybe you were able to kind of apply some of your skills in different ways then?

[Long pause.] No, I don't think so. I think I was interested in academics, generally. Reading, I did a lot of reading and I was interested in athletics. And I had a vague idea that creativity was an interest of some of my teachers, but I didn't regard myself in that way at the time.

Okay.

Would you say now, in the elementary years, that there were some influences in the school that helped in your athletics, for example, or your interest in that area? Were you able to sort of apply any creative skills that you could think of?

Well, I remember Rod Myers was teaching some things on the football field [both laughing] . . .

All right.

I don't know if that's intellectual creativity or not [GWM laughing], based on what I can see, it probably isn't. I guess I really never gave that a thought as to my being creative or applying creative kinds of considerations, although I suspect I probably did. I didn't regard myself that way.

So no one has said to you that we feel, Fritz, that you are fairly creative and these are the kinds of signs that indicate that creativity?

No, no, not that I recall, no.

You mentioned in your questionnaire that Mr. Myers used to throw you that pass, and told you to keep one foot on the ground.

You've got these memorized. [GWM laughing.] I remember that very clearly.

So there must have been a relationship, certainly, that you developed with Rod Myers at that time.

Yes, right away.

And I would think that you would regard him, probably, as a mentor.

It would be true.

Because you've maintained that relationship, I think you mentioned, thirty-eight years.

Thirty-eight years or so, that's correct.

Were there any specific incidents, Fritz, that can you remember in your childhood which enabled that creativity to develop? It could have been at school or in your home environment, in your community.

[Pause.] Well, again we're using creativity and we're assuming a fact of which I've not been aware, so it's difficult for me to . . .

To relate to that?

To answer that question under those circumstances. I did a little writing when I got a little older and I, you know, I guess I made up games, that kind of thing. But all kids do that, I guess I never really considered myself exceptional in that sense either.

I'm just looking at the definition of creativity and let me just read it to you, to see if that makes some sense to you. This is the way that Dr. Torrance has defined creativity.

Okay.

"Creativity is the production of something new, or unusual, as the result of the processes of sensing difficulties or problems, gaps in knowledge, missing elements, something askew, making guesses and then formulating hypotheses about those deficiencies, evaluating and testing these guesses and hypotheses, and possibly revising and retesting them and

finally, communicating the results." I've said quite a bit there, but that's how he defines creativity and he has developed a test to get at those various components of creativity. When he and Rod Myers were working with you and others in the class, they were involved in developing the tests; they were called the "Minnesota Tests of Creativity" at that time.

Right.

And they've now become the "Torrance Tests of Creative Thinking." They're on the market and people who are actively translating them into some thirty-five different languages use them. They're used by people doing research on creativity and some schools use them to identify kids that have high creative potential for gifted programs and that sort of thing. So that's the beginning and that's how he defined creativity. Quite broad—not like producing a painting or something that people think of as a form of creativity.

Oh, all right. Well, if there were to be a broader definition of that nature, I suppose that a lot of the analyses that I've gone through in the elementary years involved that kind of process.

Yes, certainly. I just wanted to mention that so that you had that understanding.

Okay.

We cannot say to kids in school that you are creative and these are skills that you are demonstrating. I suppose, someone mentioned to me at another interview that it may be good if we do tell kids that they are creative, that they have creative potential. I think it's important to say "potential" because if they don't use it, of course, then it's a waste, isn't it?

I guess. [GWM laughing.]

It's like intelligence. You don't typically tell kids that they're intelligent or what their score is on intelligence tests, because if people don't apply that intelligence, then what use is it?

Let me ask this question then, Fritz, how would your peers or friends at that time have described you at school?

Well, as a good student, good athlete, got along with people. I would say that's the way people probably would have described me.

Okay. Let's move into your present job then.

CAREER PATHS AND TRANSITIONS

What are you presently doing?

I'm an attorney.

And do you think you apply the skills of creativity, as we've talked about it, in this job?

Oh, I think so, I think, under the definition that you read to me, that would be the case, yes.

Have you had other jobs, other than this one?

Do you want me to go back to age 11 or [GWM laughing] how far do you want to go back?

Oh, not too far back . . . maybe the last twenty years or so.

I have been practicing law for twenty years.

Okay. Prior to that then, Fritz.

Okay, well, immediately prior to that, I was a tennis professional. And before that, I was in college, in fact, I turned professional with the U.S.P.T.A. in 1973, but I taught tennis from 1970 to 1978 in the summer and for one full year between college and law school.

Oh, okay.

Do you feel that you applied any skills of creativity in that job?

I suppose. Tennis is a difficult sport and I used a warm-up pattern whereby I analyzed the skills of the opponent and kind of the geometry of the situation, and as soon as I spotted a weakness, I didn't let that player practice that shot anymore during warm-up, for instance. And then I just used a geometric approach to hitting the ball so that I calculated the angle at which the ball was likely to return and I was able to cover up my own weaknesses that way. I suppose that involves some kind of category that you're talking about.

I would think so, yes. You were solving the problem. A lot of creativity has to do with solving problems, whatever they might be to the individual.

When you made changes in your working life was there anyone whom you relied on for support and advice?

Oh, I was writing pretty regularly to Rod Myers back in the 60s, but I think that I, to some extent, my career path was sort of haphazard. I scored well in something and decided to do it, and here I am. One way to look at it, I guess. [GWM laughing.] You fall into things to a certain extent and I certainly did.

Yes. Yet it sounds like you relied on Rod Myers for some of your direction, I suppose, or some ideas from him as to what you should do.

Well, I would say that he has never told me, "don't do this" or "don't do that," but he always seemed to put the best possible light on whatever it was that I had decided to do and that was encouraging. And I would say, I'm going to either medical school or law school and I remember once he wrote me a letter saying, "well, you know, in a law program, you could do a lot of things other than practice law, if you decide not to do that." So he was always able to handle just about any situation, I think, and that was helpful to me, because I hadn't gone through it [laughing] yet.

Right.

Didn't know what I was doing.

Sure.

So it helped to have someone who was encouraging but I wouldn't say he ever said "don't do that." I don't think he ever did that.

I don't know whether mentors who you look to for support and ideas should do that.

I guess.

That sounds more like our parents, in a way [both laughing].

Fritz, how are you able to integrate relationships, as a parent, a partner, as someone's child, for example, into your working life?

[Pause.] Well, I guess I find it a little more difficult now that my daughter's a teenager, to try to balance what I'm supposed to be doing at work as against what I'm supposed to be doing at home. My wife is disabled as well and that makes things even more difficult; from a physical standpoint, she's not there.

Right. I see.

So, I have to try to figure out who my daughter is and what she needs and try to be there for whatever it is that she's needing at a particular stage in her life where she changes so fast [laughing], that that's not easy to do.

Yes.

In terms of my other relationships, I try to be in contact with my friends, even if they are distant, at least once a year. I play golf with people going all the way back to the time I was eight years old.

Oh, I see.

So it's kind of a satisfactory situation over all. From a social standpoint, it's not so satisfactory, because my wife's situation is such that it makes things more difficult.

CREATIVE ACCOMPLISHMENTS

What do you consider to be your most creative accomplishment or achievement at this stage, this age?

Well, you want me to use the broader definition than the one that I was using when you first began talking.

Yes—I think so.

Well, I've handled thirty-six-hundred-odd cases now. And in some instances, well, under some instances, I wish I'd done things differently. But I guess there've been, there've been cases that I'm happy to have been able to follow through over a couple of years to some success, things that have gone to the Supreme Court and come back down and I've been successful. I've won some, won some awards through the course of time. Those are somewhat subjective, you know. I don't think those to be gospel, but I'm better to have them, I guess, than not.

Yes.

At this stage in my career. I guess probably having experienced twenty years of practicing law, I have to say the law because I can't remember the other stuff very well [both laughing]. I guess it would have to be that.

In what areas of your life do you feel most able to be creative now? [FR laughing.] Or in what area of your life, I suppose?

The nature of dealing with people. Sometimes it's an academic discipline in which I'm involved but for the most part, I'm dealing with people and people who have lots of problems, not just the problem they're presenting to me, but all kinds of other problems.

Yes.

And so to deal with each individual in a manner that allows the best possible result, I guess requires a certain amount of, I suppose it's creativity, I don't know. The ways of a teenage daughter are quite a challenge too. I mean, I suppose, I don't know how good I am [both laughing].

In any of them?

Yes.

Boy!

That's for sure.

Working with people.

Yes.

When you think of your own attributes and your own skills, what do you consider to be your creative attributes?

[Pause.] I'm not sure I understand the question.

Well, you mentioned earlier that your creative skills show when dealing with people. Do you feel that you're a problem solver, for example, or are you able to get at the issue fairly quickly and easily? That's what I mean by your creative skills or attributes. I just wondered how you see them.

Well, I guess my philosophy has been that I try to analyze the situation as best I can and then be honest about it. Lawyers are supposed to be advocating positions, but my experience has been that the people with whom I'm dealing aren't idiots and if I begin to take positions that, well, are zealous to some extent, are also somewhat skewed in the wrong direction, that develops a . . . you develop a reputation for being excessive in your positions and . . . So I try to strike a balance I guess, that's intellectual honesty or something, that I try to maintain over the course of time.

Do you think your associates would say the same kind of things about you? How would they describe your creative attributes?

Depends on the associate, you know, I mean, I'm dealing with maybe a hundred defense lawyers on average within a year and a couple of them probably don't like me much. For the most part, I get along well with people and they would probably say that I'm a pretty good trial lawyer. I don't know that they can get inside of my mind very well to see what I'm doing.

What influences guide or constrain your creativity?

[Pause.] Well, again I think intellectual honesty probably is important because you don't say something that you don't believe, just because it sounds good—just because you think it might work out better because in the long term, it doesn't. I guess that would be the guiding principle that I would consider it to be. And it's not a universal thing with lawyers either. A lot of people are not that way . . . are advocating positions that sound a little silly and the judge sees that silliness and the next time the judge sees that person he or she remembers. [GWM laughing.]

GENERAL QUESTIONS ON CREATIVITY

What are your goals and aspirations for the future

[Pause.] You know it's funny to say, I guess I view my life as being, in some ways, extraordinarily fortunate, and in other ways, extraordinarily unfortunate. With the death of my father when I was young and my mother when I was almost as young, I thought that was a little bit on the unfair side. And with my wife becoming disabled at such a young age now, I don't know anyone with that combination of problems. With the things that I've done, been able to do, I don't want this to come out wrong, but being able to continue with athletics and academics and the professional things that I've been able to do, I've pretty much accomplished what I want to accomplish and I know that might not sound right, but I'm forty-seven years old, I've made the money I wanted to make and more, I've gotten the honors that I wanted to make and more. I have the material possessions; I'm not that interested in material possessions.

Right.

We lead a pretty modest lifestyle. So what am I supposed to want? I can't think of anything in particular. I guess what I'd really like to see is to have a little luck in some of those other areas, and not having any major tragedies occur. I know that's a negative way of looking at things, but I'm a little skittish about that, so I guess avoiding major problems [both laughing] is probably my first goal. I'll probably continue doing this for a number of years, until my daughter's out of college and if I can just kind of maintain a reasonable level of personal and professional comfort, I'll be very pleased. And so I don't want to be president [both laughing].

If you could provide educators advice for nurturing creativity in kids, what would you share with them?

[Long pause.]

I think that you had a fairly supportive and rich kind of environment, at least at the elementary level, with people like Myers. Now what would you say to educators to help them nurture creative potential in kids?

Well, I believe, as you've indicated, that the teachers I had in grade school—and I had a tremendous number of good teachers also in high school and college—I think the quality of the individuals with whom one is associated is probably the single most important determining factor for that. I haven't given a lot of thought to what specific attribute is necessary to make a good teacher great, but I guess enthusiasm for the work, I mean, intelligence and maybe liking kids a little better is helpful. So I couldn't teach, because I'm not sure I want to be around a whole bunch of kids all year 'round. But if the teacher were able to combine those three things, I think that would be a start. I think there are a lot of intangible kinds of things that I don't really understand.

You put it very well, Fritz. It's not easy to articulate.

John McPhee wrote a book called *The Headmaster* twenty years or so ago, describing the headmaster of an eastern prep school, and there was this little tiny guy and he started out with 12 students and as an interim teacher; they were unruly students, they were kids who were having a little trouble [both laughing] controlling themselves and one day, he walked into a room where there had been all kinds of problems and he told the people to quiet down and—bam!—they quieted down. And it was at that stage that he had some idea that he could do this, that he could work successfully with kids.

If you could provide parents some advice for nurturing creativity in kids, what would you say to them?

[Long pause.] Well, I suppose you play to the strength. Find the strength, and find the interest and play to it and don't suffocate it. I see so many so-called children's activities that are really not children's activities at all, but are apparently for the purpose of continuing the childhood of the adult. I was fortunate not to have people push me that way. Now, if somebody had made me go to baseball practice every day, I'm not sure I would have liked it so much.

Right!

So find it, nurture it and don't suffocate it. I think that would be my advice.

What advice would you give to people who work with highly creative kids?

[Long pause.] I think that somehow you have to modify behavior without appearing to modify it. Because children are children, and they're not finished products at age seven or eleven or seventeen, and yet the potential is there in all of them, I suspect, for some kind of work, play that is very creative, and yet kids are so attuned to strong beliefs, right or wrong. And so if it's possible to somehow mould behavior without seeming to, I guess that would be the way [laughing]. Good luck! [Both laughing.]

That's a tough one [laughing]!

Ah, yes!

This is the last question that I want to ask. If you could design a time capsule that represented you as a creative individual, what would you include in the time capsule? Say, five items that would represent Fritz Reeker.

Going all the way back to whenever I want?

Whenever you want.

So you want five items, do you? Okay, I'm not sure this is what you want, but I guess to balance things out a little bit the first one would probably be a system that I developed for doing quick mathematical calculations. I'm not a mathematician, by any stretch of the imagination, but my arithmetic abilities when I was young were very quick. And I developed that system so that I could calculate baseball batting averages.

Ah, ha! Okay.

The second thing would probably be a picture of tennis, a tennis picture. The third would be a scientific paper that I published when I was twenty. The fourth would probably be a Supreme Court case I had about permanent total disability. And the last one would probably be a picture of my wife and daughter. I guess if I had five, that would be it.

Building your creative upbringing. [Both laughing.]

Oh, we'll see, that's a work in progress.

SUMMARY

Fritz Reeker has been very successful in his career as a lawyer and is one of the best examples of the "Torrance Kids" who has been significantly influenced by an enduring mentor. He had great difficulty thinking that he was creative until he heard the broad process definition that Paul Torrance formulated in the late 1950s and which is reflected in his tests. Although he scored in the average range for creative potential, his academic performance was always in the top third or quarter of his class. He excelled in college and law school and is considered to be a "top lawyer" in Minnesota.

Fritz identified with his grade 4 teacher Rod Myers, who eventually became his life-long mentor. He has had other people who have supported and encouraged him as well. He mentions that his parents helped him greatly, but they were deceased by the time he was 21 years of age. His wife, also, has been very helpful over the course of time—just by being the opposite to him in terms of personality. However, Rod Myers has been a "signpost" for Fritz since grade 4. His mentor puts a lot of effort into the questions that Fritz has asked him over the years. He conveys to Fritz that he is capable and can succeed in many areas of life. Encouragement and affirmation are key ingredients of their relationship. Fritz feels a great deal of gratefulness toward Dr. Myers.

Like so many bright individuals who are successful in their careers, Fritz struggles with the balance between work and personal life. The support from his spouse and continued mentoring by Rod Myers has made the difference and enabled him to succeed in life with all its vicissitudes.

NOTES

1. Personal communication from Rod Myers to Garnet Millar, November 29, 1999, in possession of the author.

2. *Minnesota Law and Politics Magazine.* (August 1998). "Super Lawyers! Our Brand New Survey of Minnesota's Top Lawyers."

fifteen

ALEX ADAMS

A MEDICAL RESEARCHER
(PULMONARY DISEASES)

"My job is to ask questions and design studies to answer medical problems"—Alex (1998)

Alex Adams, circa 1958

Alexander Bernard Adams is a good example of a person in the longitudinal study who scored in the average range creatively as a student in elementary school but fell in love with an area of work while being supported by strong parents and a mentor. He has succeeded in his work and family life due to factors that were difficult to predict from his creative potential in his early development.

SCHOOL YEARS

Alex Adams was an only child raised in a suburb of Minneapolis. His father was a professor of geography at the University of Minnesota, and his mother was a homemaker and librarian with two master's degrees. Alex attended Sydney Pratt Elementary School and participated in the creativity test development by Dr. Torrance and his associates during the 1958–1964 period. Alex was involved in this during the fourth, fifth, and sixth grades (1958–1960). His creativity was estimated to be average at that time, but his intelligence score was in the superior range. He ranked in the top quarter of his class consistently. When asked in grade 6 what he wanted to be when he grew up, Alex stated that he wanted to be either a "politician or astronomer."

FIRST FOLLOW-UP

At the time of the first follow-up, Alex was 29 years of age and married, with one child. He was enrolled as a part-time student at the University of Minnesota in the Master of Science program, specializing in biostatistics and epidemiology. This branch of medicine deals, according to *Webster's College Dictionary*, with the incidence and prevalence of diseases in large populations and with the detection and source and cause of epidemics. He was teaching full time at the St. Paul Technical Vocational Institute, where he taught respiratory therapy.

Since high school, Alex had completed his Bachelor of Science degree from the University of Minnesota, majoring in biology. He had held several full-time jobs since high school: pizza deliverer (1967–1970); respiratory therapist (Universal Hospital Services and St. Mary's Hospital) (1970–1975); and then instructor of respiratory therapy at St. Paul Technical Vocational Institute. Alex also held several part-time positions related to his teaching area. He provided respiratory-therapy services to the Metropolitan Medical Center (1971–1972) and to Bethlehem Hospital (1977–1980). He acted as an instructor in first aid from 1977 through 1980 for the Red Cross; in cardiopulmonary resuscitation (CPR) from 1975 through 1980 for the Heart Association; and taught the Quit Smoking Program during 1978 through 1980 for the Cancer Society. He held certificates of instruction from the Red Cross, the Heart Association, and the Cancer Society. In 1980 Alex worked at St. Paul Technical Vocational Institute, providing clinical instruction in respirators, oxygen devices, CPR, aerosol therapy, chest physiotherapy, arterial blood sampling, and testing pulmonary functioning.

His career ambition was to continue with his education with an aim of computerizing retrospective analyses of all medical-therapy procedures and medication administration. This information would ultimately alter procedures to improve the effectiveness of respiratory therapy. This work related to Alex's interest in pursuing biostatistics. He did indicate that he interrupted his education since high school to live for 18 months in Spain, where he worked as a carpenter. He did it, he said, to "mature." His interests in 1980 revolved around playing chess, camping, computers, writing and editing, and travel.

In high school Alex had achieved the status of "scholar-athlete" of the senior class. Since graduating from high school, Alex indicated the following creative achievements:

- published three articles in a scientific journal
- received an award for a professional paper
- edited a professional magazine
- created original educational materials
- conducted many in-service sessions for co-workers
- suggested many modifications for policies that were adopted by co-workers.

Alex also had been involved politically in his field of specialization. He was past delegate and is currently president of the state Society for Respiratory Therapy.

His three most creative achievements since high school graduation are:

- completed three scientific papers that were published in a national journal
- developed an accredited respiratory therapy program
- developed a state journal for respiratory therapy.

Alex had a mentor at this period in his life: a professor of zoology who influenced him in three ways:

- introduced him to a system of organization of medical information
- provided positive feedback to his ideas
- displayed an effective teaching style that he still uses.

Alex's career image for the next ten years was reported as follows:

- to complete and publish four projects that he had started
- to complete his Master of Science degree
- to direct an educational program.

Alex, circa 1998

MIDDLE TO LATE CAREER

In the 1998 follow-up questionnaire, Alex was working as a medical researcher in his field of pulmonary disease at the Regions Hospital. He had completed his Master of Science degree, specializing in epidemiology, at the University of Minnesota. Alex was now 50 years of age, and he and his wife had had another child since the last follow-up in 1980. His score for creative public achievements was 8.0 out of 10.0—high, compared to others in the study group. He had published 30 articles and had written two books. In addition, he had conducted many in-service sessions for co-workers and had made several presentations at professional conferences. Also, he had received recognition for leadership and had been elected to office several times in his professional organization.

Alex indicated that he is "in love with his work" and that his greatest strength is finding solutions to research challenges. He has had the benefit of mentors who displayed enthusiasm for his work and showed him how to access information. Alex feels that in the past eight to ten years he has had the opportunities to do what he loves and can do well.

INTERVIEW ON JULY 7, 1998

This interview with Alex Adams was conducted in Minneapolis in my hotel room. Alex reflected on the early influences on his creativity; his career path and transitions; creative accomplishments; and finally, general comments on creativity. His own words communicate his experiences best.

EARLY INFLUENCES ON CREATIVITY

At what age were you when you first were aware of your creativity?

[Pause.] Oh boy! Probably somewhere between seven and ten. I didn't necessarily think of it as creativity.

How did this show itself in your mind?

It's something I can see in my son. I suppose it's just very much imaginative play and seeing patterns in things. I can coalesce or see patterns in either activities or concepts or words. I can see it in my children.

At elementary-school age, what influence did your schooling have on your creative ability? How do you feel it helped you see patterns and so on, as you already explained?

Oh, I probably agree with what we were talking about earlier. I don't think that schooling did much to foster my creativity.

Was there anything then in your schooling that you think helped you along the way, in understanding, as you mentioned, seeing patterns, and so on, more so than other kids, was there anything in the school or was there a teacher maybe that you think made a difference?

There were certainly some teachers I remember that were very encouraging. I can't say exactly what they did but there were periods of time where they'd have said, "Take this time to go through the encyclopedia and just roam through it." I think everybody has mentors. I remember activities in the class and some projects that were open-ended. The teacher chose to do open-minded activities. I doubt that it was in the school curriculum, that it was what needed to be taught at that time. There were definitely three or four teachers that were very helpful. One was Mr. Lang. He was the fifth and sixth grade teacher. I would say he was quite influential.

Just to follow that a little more, Alex, what specific incidents can you remember in your childhood which enabled your creativity to develop? These may not necessarily be just at school, but just in your childhood.

I had parents that were really pretty open. My dad was a professor and my mother was a librarian with a couple of master degrees. They would encourage me and they didn't necessarily push me. They set the example for me.

So they were a model for you?

I think so, yeah. They read constantly. They traveled often and they just encouraged me to be observant as they were.

Can you say more about your parents?

Well, my father was in a strict discipline, geography and statistics and the Soviet Union. Those were his three specialties. But my mother was a philosophy major, French-literature major, and eventually she became a librarian. She read constantly and was probably the one that was a little more creative. Nevertheless, I think it doesn't do a lot of good to be creative unless you can sit down and be disciplined about something that you're interested in. You can't just be too flighty about it. You need to take an idea, define it, and then pursue it.

What were the skills or qualities, behaviors of your parents that you remember that influenced you then?

Encouragement to read and their modeling of reading influenced me. They had a variety of interests. My dad was very much of a generalist and he knew something about everything [GWM laughing]—that was sort of his nature. He was a very good conversationalist and it didn't matter whether it was literature, another culture, or politics. He really was considered very intelligent by almost everybody because of the breadth of his knowledge. He taught me that you are capable of learning many things.

You mentioned that your mother seemed maybe more of a mentor type for you.

Yeah, she was.

Say more about that.

My mother is more of a philosopher, more of an artist. She was creative. She continues to travel constantly. Even now at her age she's always into new projects. She has either joined a new group such as a hiking club or she's taking a course. She's now with a group of university professor women who go to weekly lectures and take on new projects. She has been involved with Elder Hostel and she has gone to collect information on bears in the north woods. [GWM laughing.] She would be there for two weeks.

What age would she be now?

She's seventy now.

That's a good age!

It is an age when many people would be settling down and staying close to home.

What would you say was the most important lesson you learned with regard to your creativity at that young age that we're talking about now?

I would say that it's really important not to be discouraged and to be enthusiastic about your work. That's the way I've been approaching my job, which allows me to be creative.

And our last questions on that period of time of your life would be, how would your peers, the people around you at that time, have described you?

Probably, pretty much as a nerd. [GWM laughing.] I was relatively studious and I took learning very seriously. I did real well in school and I was not very active socially. I became more so later. I didn't act out. I didn't get in trouble. I guess you would say that's not how someone who is considered creative would be described.

CAREER PATHS AND TRANSITIONS

First of all, explain your present job. What do you do presently?

I'm a research associate in pulmonary disease. So I work on accomplishing, developing, completing, measuring, and writing studies of important questions, mostly in the area of mechanical ventilation for lung-injured patients. That's our primary area. We do some modeling, though, of the lungs and develop different interventions. These could be things related to the position of the patient or whether the gas flows into patterns.

Who are the associates that you work with, basically?

Dr. John Marini is the leader of our group, and the team is Dr. Nahum, Dr. Shapiro. They're all professionals.

I see. Is that the Minneapolis or the Minnesota hospital?

No—well, it's an affiliate; so Dr. Marini is a full professor in medicine but he's assigned to an affiliate hospital.

Okay. So you're at the University of Minnesota?

I'm not a faculty employee. I work over at Regions Hospital for this group and I see that their studies are conducted. The doctors provide the ideas and I see that they are pursued further as medical studies.

How do you apply creativity to your work?

We'll discuss an idea in a meeting and we'll say, "Well, how are we going to develop a study for this?" Our lab is considered to be in the top four-to-six labs in the world in our specialized field.

So it's really your job then to push the ideas forward and to make them into a research study, in a sense; you follow that through?

Yes, I consider these people to be very creative.

Have you had other jobs prior to this?

Oh yes. I was in management for six years, that was financially rewarding but I was extremely unhappy. I very much liked working with other people, but it was too large a group of people— sixty to eighty people in management. We were dealing with a lot of important problems. There was no opportunity to do anything other than to see that the place ran well.

Were you able to apply creativity in those jobs?

I don't think so. No, I just needed to see the place function well.

So it was more certainly politics that would play a big part in that kind of work.

Oh, yeah, definitely. I mean, prior to that, I was a supervisor in another department but in another hospital. That was not too bad because we developed new services. They were services that were going to monitor patients. They would get equipment to measure parameters that hadn't been measured before. That was sort of exciting. Before that I taught for several years, which was the best job I had other than what I'm doing now.

Was that at the college level?

Yeah, yeah, it was technical-college level.

What area did you teach?

I taught respiratory care. There was no discipline of respiratory care when I was in college. It has developed as an occupation but I practiced it before it was really well defined. I made money in this area while I went to college and then later I taught it.

What major changes/transitions have you experienced in your working life?

I'm very grateful and fortunate to have been able to work in several areas. Most people don't get that opportunity. I found the change from practicing allied health and respiratory care to teaching was a major transition. Another major transition was going into management and the belief that it is important to make a lot of money.

What caused these transitions that you've described?

Just a lot of unusual circumstances at the time, opportunities, and possibly misguided interests, and then, in some cases, a bit of luck. In general, the other things that you have to do, which I did on the way, was to keep learning.

Well, when you made changes in your working life, was there anyone whom you relied on for support and advice?

Actually, I wish I could say, yes, but not very often. Perhaps my mother, but she wasn't that much of a career-guidance person. She just left those decisions up to me. There are a few people who've been good friends, but not just one person.

Can you remember what they did that was helpful to you during those times?

Well, in a couple of cases they were physicians, and in a couple of cases they were other teachers. It's not some sort of pattern that I can think of. In one sentence, it was timed right and they just said, "Well of course, you should do that. That's an opportunity that you'll probably enjoy." They knew me well enough. For example, moving into management, a physician who was a good friend said, "You know, we would like you to work here." He would add what you'd done, we like your enthusiasm, etcetera. In another case, there were a couple of people who said, "Well, you've always wanted to go into research. Why did you get a graduate degree? You're working in management, with a degree in epidemiology which doesn't make sense. Go towards what you were planning."

How are you able to integrate relationships, like as a parent or as a partner or as somebody's child, into your working life?

Well, I have a best friend that I run with every day or every other day. He's a member of the group at work. While we run, we discuss all the ideas and studies. My work is not work to me, it is what I do and care about. He cares about what I do and he has a lot of interest in what we do in the lab. I don't work at this friendship; it's a natural relationship that we have.

CREATIVE ACCOMPLISHMENTS

What do you consider to be your most creative achievement at this point?

Well, I suppose it's what is closest to you at the time. There's a study that I did in '86, repeated in '92 and I'll replicate in the future. It's the only study on ventilator patients and it happens to be in Minnesota. My colleagues are encouraging me to conduct the study on a national level. Although in '86, I didn't think of it as important, but now I have three sets of data. I can show what is happening to long-term ventilator patients: who they are, where they are, what their problems are, and how they're changing. The study was just accepted and will be printed as the lead article in a professional journal. I consider that my best and most important accomplishment. I also wrote a chapter for a book, but I didn't necessarily think it was creative because a lot of it was coordinated with other writers. The chapter I wrote was titled, "The Pulmonary Function of the Ventilator Patient." One thing that really confuses me is that when I was younger and in high school, I really couldn't write well. I had no idea why I couldn't put together sentences very well. It was when I was in late college when it really clicked and now I think I can write pretty well. I have several publications now. I'm complimented often about my contributions to the literature.

In what area of your life are you most able to be creative?

I enjoy playing with kids. With my little boy, that's all we do. I have a boy who is six. We take little figures and have them talk to each other or organize a group of them and have them go on a hike. He's just getting to where that really isn't that much fun for him anymore.

What do you consider to be your creative attributes?

Well, I can think of two things. I am able to take bits of information from several sources and coalesce them in order to make sense out of them. Secondly, I can define a problem and create a study to find out more about it.

What would your close associates say about your creative attributes?

I can usually have my colleagues working on three or four projects at a time. In the lab, they would describe me as the one who's energized and has three or four things going at any given time. I don't need to be told what to do.

What influences guide or constrain your creativity?

I'm not constrained very much. I'm guided by the general direction the lab needs to take. Our field is pulmonary research and I need to keep that in mind and realize we're going to have to stay on mechanical ventilation. We can't look at heart disease; we need to stay right on mechanical ventilation. Being in that area may seem constraining to some who come into the lab, because many of these people and training fellows will come from general medicine. They'll see us as being interested only in pulmonary care. You need to become single-minded. I actually think this was a problem with my father. He was considered to be knowledgeable in many areas, but not an expert in one. He was interested in everything and could discuss everything. But you really have to choose your area of interest and pursue it intensely.

QUESTIONS RELATED TO THE "MANIFESTO FOR CHILDREN"

When did you fall in love with your work?

I fell in love with my present work not more than six months to a year into it. I had to create the setting because I was pretty much working for a person who was a controlling individual who tried to have me do things in a specific way and would be hypercritical. I was second-guessed and told I was going in the wrong direction. That person was someone you had to convince to be a little more open. Eventually the person did became a little more open. After a year in the job I realized that this was fun work. Within two or three years our lab started to realize some real success with the work we were doing.

In what ways do you pursue your passion for your lab work?

Well, I just do it all the time. [GWM laughing.] Yeah. The time I spend at it is never enough. I often need to be told to come home. Not that I don't want to come home [GWM laughing], I want to go home too. I'll continue working at home or I'll read more at home; it's just something I like to do. I'm happy doing my work and I do it as much and as often as I can.

What are your greatest strengths?

[Pause.] Well, probably the ability to get these projects going—generating the study and the ability to get other people interested in them. We have several visiting fellows from four countries with us right now. One is from Japan, two from Spain, and one from Turkey. Because of the attention our lab has generated worldwide, we've had people from Chile, Australia, Greece, England, and Japan. We've built friendships and have gone to study with people in other countries.

In what ways is your creativity affected by the expectations of others?

Oh, they expect a lot of me. That's why Dr. Marini can come in and say, "I've been thinking about this, what do you think? Well, great, why don't we try to measure it this way or that way?" So, it's expected of me and what they know I'll be able to do. I can sit down with three or four of the doctors and really affect their thinking. They can just be totally open-ended, talking about concepts, and they can just bounce them off each other. They know full well they will get me engaged.

Would you say that you are "free to play your own game" or "sing in your own key" in your work?

Yeah, I would. There's not too much I would do differently. I've been successful at it and there's probably more expected of me. We have several studies that are queued up that need to be explored.

What relationship in your work has been most instrumental in helping you to achieve your potential?

Probably the relationship with Dr. Marini. He's the director of the group. He's the one who has the ideas and the resources. He encourages me to keep the lab going in a meaningful direction.

Would you say that he's a bit of a mentor for you?

You certainly could say that, but it's not really the right term. His role is to be a mentor for the fellows. I'm more somebody who's a colleague or a collaborator.

When you say "fellow," what do you mean?

Pulmonary fellow. These are physicians in their third year of pulmonary training. They've already completed their residency for internal medicine. They're already internists, and now are taking another specialty, which is pulmonary medicine.

What qualities or skills do you see that Dr. Marini has that others might emulate?

Well, there are two or three things that really make him exceptional. He's probably the best writer and speaker in the area of pulmonary care. He's continually asked to write chapters and editorials about the lungs. He has a way of captivating the audience. I've seen three thousand to six thousand people crowd into a room, just to hear him pull together the current state of ventilators or some aspect of it. In other respects, he's not that great at certain things, but nobody's good at everything. Those are two areas that he excels. The third area is really what makes him unusual. He's extremely good at connecting things up and generating ideas from little snippets from this or that. I would consider him to be highly creative because he generates ideas for the fellows and myself to start projects. Then we begin with the expectation that we can put them on paper or speak about them in a similar manner. We may not actually have those skills, but then he can speak about them, write about them, and help us become better at writing or more at ease when presenting the results.

What do you feel towards him and what do you think the other fellows feel towards him?

Well, there's a great admiration and a high degree of respect. Because the written word is so powerful, people call up and can't believe that he isn't running the university. [GWM laughing.] It just amazes me, the kind of respect that he generates. They think so much of him.

In what ways do you interact with others to enhance their career/personal lives?

Well, this is a highly competitive field. The fellows really need to publish and have only a year or two to do so. They will either succeed at it and go into academic medicine or they will go into private practice. I work with them on their studies to help them with every aspect of it. They write up their project and I may end up writing about a project that they have dropped or didn't have time to write up. The fellows have to propose a study, find or obtain the necessary resources, conduct the study, and generate the data. Then they make the measurements, analyze it statistically, and write it up completely so it can be submitted for publication. These are people that are all highly accomplished and very competitive. These are the people with whom I'm working.

In what ways do you allow others to interact with you to enhance your life?

I certainly learn from the people who come through the lab. As I've mentioned, they are in training and are from all over the world.

Would you describe yourself as well rounded, or more able at some things than others?

I guess being well rounded is more characteristic of my father, but people ask me a lot of questions like, where can you go rent a car, or what do you think of this political issue. I'm up at 4:45 A.M. watching the news, and I'm constantly channel surfing, just like most crazy Americans. [GWM laughing.] I try to keep up with most things. I like to get a good deal. I like to find out where the best rental car is, where I can get the best trip price, or what the hot stuff is in Washington. If that's well rounded, I try to be. And I think most people look at me as someone you can ask about anything. They'll probably get a very strong opinion, but they like to ask me. [GWM laughing.]

Okay. So you would describe yourself as more well rounded, rather than single minded?

I think on the surface I would appear to be someone who's interested in pulmonary physiology or pulmonary medicine. I'm not a physician so I don't have to keep up on all areas of medicine.

GENERAL QUESTIONS ON CREATIVITY

What are your goals and aspirations for the future?

Right now I'm editing a large second book, but there's a third book in the area of pulmonary function that I want to write—that's a goal I have. There are several studies that we have completed that have valuable information. My goal is to do more writing. I need about three to six months to complete it.

If you could provide educators advice for nurturing creativity in children, what would you share with them?

I guess I would suggest they try to nurture the creative students by identifying them and giving them positive feedback when they demonstrate creative thinking or behavior.

If you could provide parents with advice for nurturing creativity in their children, what would you share with them?

Well, I sure wouldn't want to fall into the group of people saying don't discipline children, let them do what they want. That's what I've heard for two or three decades and I still hear it. I think children need to be in a relationship that fosters encouragement. There's no substitute for that.

I've witnessed so many people who were properly disciplined at the right time and they were creative as well. That's extremely necessary, when the time comes you're going to be able to stay on task.

If you could provide guidance to mentors working with highly creative kids, what would you share with them?

I don't know why that would be too different from the advice for parents.

It's a very similar question, I think, and I agree with you. I don't know if there is much difference that you would say. This is the last question I want to ask, Alex.

If you could design a time capsule that represented you as a creative person, what would you include in this capsule? Say five to ten items that would represent Alex Adams as a creative person. What would be in that time capsule to be opened sometime in the future?

I would put my book on respiratory care of pulmonary patients, drawings done by my son Zack, and a couple of yearbooks of the fellows who studied in our lab to represent our work.

SUMMARY

Alex Adams has been very successful in his work as a medical researcher, due in large part to factors that have influenced his creative behavior. Alex fell "in love" early in his career with an area—respiratory therapy—and was able to pursue it with intensity. He also had minor mentors who encouraged him along his career journey. They provided not only strong emotional support, but also directed his work technically. His work also calls upon his ability to use his skills in interdependence. He must work with and rely on many professionals to find problems and then go about designing research to solve them. It is likely that Alex Adams will continue to contribute to his special field of interest, cardiopulmonary care, in one of the top laboratories in the world.

sixteen

DAVID KWIAT

MANDATED TO EXPLORE CREATIVITY

"Creativity was something reinforced at University Elementary School—and I appreciate the weight in which that value was presented to us"—David (1980)

David Kwiat, circa 1960

David M. Kwiat is an example of a student who "fell in love" with his area of interest—acting—at an early age and then pursued it with intensity throughout his career. He also had mentors: his father, a university professor; and Rod Myers, who encouraged and supported his passion. David vividly recalls the strong influence of the latter, one of his elementary-school teachers. He stated that "Rod E. Myers, my fourth grade teacher at University Elementary School, had a tremendous influence on so many of us. He *always* encouraged and challenged us and I will always be indebted to him. He once came up to me while I was sitting at my desk/chair and whispered in my ear, 'Never lose your creativity!' I have from that point on attempted to meet Mr. Myers' mandate and challenge—truly."

SCHOOL YEARS

David Kwiat is the younger of two children. He has an older sister, Judith. His father was a professor of American studies at the University of Minnesota, while his mother had four years of college education and elected to be a homemaker. However, his mother held various teaching positions such as adjunct faculty member teaching freshman composition at the university. As a student at University Elementary School in Minneapolis, David was assessed by a variety of creativity and intelligence tests over a four-year period while attending grades 2 through 5 (1958–1962).

He consistently scored in the average range on his creativity tests. David showed the following creative strengths: originality, resistance to premature closure, expression of emotions, movement and action, expressive titles, unusual visual perspective, breaking boundaries, humor, richness of imagery, fantasy, and putting things in context. David's intelligence scores were well above average.

Rod Myers, his fourth-grade teacher, indicated recently (1999) that David tried very hard and improved greatly during that year. His schoolwork was not on a par with that of his advanced classmates. His eagerness to learn shone through all of his activities at school. He also indicated that the other students would have identified David as being "creative." Apparently, he sang original songs each week in a talent program. David was animated and winning when he sang folksongs that he composed. Whereas he struggled somewhat in doing regular schoolwork, David bloomed during talent shows and creative dramatics.

Regarding a future career, at age ten Myers[1] predicted that he would be a musician—that he came an actor didn't surprise his teacher. At this time David's future career image was that he wanted to go to college and become either a teacher or a doctor. In reflecting upon this early period of his schooling, David recollected the following incident in elementary school that encouraged his creativity: "Mr. Myers, my fourth-grade teacher at University Elementary, often encouraged me to write songs—or rather, make up songs—and then sing them for the class. I think Mr. Myers was *extremely* influential in developing my creative skills."

David had apparently found his niche in elementary school where he fell in love with acting and drama and began a pursuit of it with intensity—affirmed by his fellow students and teachers.

FIRST FOLLOW-UP

At the time of the 22-year follow-up in 1980, David was 29 years of age, single, and was acting professionally. He had completed his Bachelor of Arts degree (summa cum laude) in theater arts from the University of Minnesota in 1973. He then studied at Florida State University, earning his Master of Fine Arts degree at the Asolo Conservatory of Acting in 1976. David had demonstrated exemplary acting ability and was awarded the following honors and distinctions: Outstanding Actor Award, University of Minnesota Theater Department, 1973; and graduate assistantship at the Asolo Conservatory, Sarasota, Florida from 1974 to 1976.

During this period since high school he had been involved in writing and acting. In fact, he authored the script and performed as a one-person show, *John Barrymore: Confessions of an Actor*. He performed the one-person show at the Edinburgh Festival in Scotland; King's Head Theatre in London; and throughout the United States in 1976 and 1977. The reviews of David's *John Barrymore* were extremely positive. The BBC Radio (November 2, 1977) called it "a brilliant polished performance." B. A. Young of the *London Financial Times* (Tuesday, October 25, 1977) wrote the following review of the monologue:

Confessions of an Actor

It is a monologue representing John Barrymore in his decline, remembering in his dressing room the good times and the bad times in his life while they hold the curtain for his late, and intoxicated entrance. He calls to mind the San Francisco earthquake, his first satisfying performance (in Galsworthy's *Justice*), the troubles he has had with wives and other women. He talks about the hell of long runs, of audiences, of Hollywood. Now, he says, he is no better than an old, bedraggled prostitute.

David Kwiat, who has written the script for himself, has a striking resemblance to Barrymore in profile, and a voice of warmth and variety. I found his performance all that it ought to be, more than an imitation, an amalgam of Barrymore and himself. The material has been gathered; largely I take it from Gene Fowler's biography, over the last two years.

During this time he performed in many stage plays in a number of different theater companies, such as Peppermint Tent Children's Theater (Minneapolis); University of Minnesota; University of Minnesota Showboat; Friar's Dinner Theater (Minneapolis); Chimera Theater (St. Paul); Minnesota Opera Company (Minneapolis); University of Delaware (Newark); Theater L'Homme Dieu (Alexandria, MN);

Timberlake Playhouse (Mt. Carroll, IL); University of Santa Clara (Santa Clara, CA); Chanhassen Dinner Theater (Chanhassen, MN); Arizona Theater Company (Tucson); Actors Theater (St. Paul); and the Asolo State Theater (Sarasota). He played a variety of roles in plays or shows such as *Hamlet, Pinocchio, The Odd Couple, King Lear, Don Juan, Much Ado About Nothing,* and *Pygmalion.*

David was deeply involved in acting. When asked about his current interests and hobbies, unrelated to his career, he stated: "Have none, theater is my vocation and avocation." He listed his three most creative achievements since high school as follows:

1. Wrote and performed a one-man show on John Barrymore
2. Wrote a full-length play
3. Learned to "clean-up my lateral 's' distortion."

He cited self-doubt and fear of failure as his greatest obstacles to continued achievement. At this time of his life, David still relied on his father for assistance and encouragement and also said that the chairman of the department of theater was a mentor to him.

When asked to describe an incident that best illustrates the creativity that he displays in his daily life, he stated:

> As an actor working in a repertory theater, I am called upon daily to use creative skills. Between the director and the cast we often will interpolate the script we are working on with additional vocal responses, change words to suit our audiences, etcetera. These decisions are often a compromise between director and actor.

His creative achievement score at this time was 7.0 out of a possible 10. This was higher than the average for the case-study group.

In 1980 David again stated that both Rod Myers and University Elementary School had been instrumental in developing his creative skills and enabling him to fall "in love" and pursue his area of passion—acting. He indicated that his career ambition in the next ten years would be repertory acting. He rated his current lifestyle between "somewhat satisfying" and "very satisfying" four on a five-point scale. What was the primary frustration in his life at this point? He stated succinctly: "In theater, one can never 'rest on laurels'—you are always at start point zero—always proving yourself."

David, New World School of the Arts, endowed chair

MIDDLE TO LATE CAREER

In the 1998 follow-up questionnaire, David was still working as an actor but had taken on additional responsibilities as a teacher and professor of acting. He had joined the faculty of Miami's New World School of the Arts in 1989 as a professor in the theater division. His courses of instruction include acting, improvisational theater, voice, and diction. He works with high school and college students specializing in theater and acting. This appointment enables David to continue his own acting and performing. Since the last follow-up in 1980, he has been involved in a tremendous number of plays with wide versatility in character roles, and has added to his repertoire, conducting intensive workshops, directing plays, commercial work/industrial film work on camera, as well as "voice-overs" and television theater.

His acting ability has been recognized by a number of honors and distinctions including:

- Selected to be part of a delegation of theater artists accompanying George C. White, president of the Eugene O'Neill Theater Center, to visit theaters and theater artists in Moscow and Tiblisi in the Soviet Union, 1984
- Nominated as Best Actor by the South Florida Entertainment Writers' Association (Carbonell Award), 1995
- Receipt of the Peter Masiko, Jr./Miami Jai Alai Endowed Teaching Chair, 1996–1999
- Receipt of the National Institute for Staff and Organizational Development Excellence Award, University of Texas at Austin, 1997.

- Nominated as Best Actor by the South Florida Entertainment Writers' Association (Carbonell Award), 1997
- Winner of the Pint Size Play Contest with *Backwards Looking*, Florida Studio Theater, Sarasota, 1992
- *Who's Who in America, 2000.*

David in Three Hotels, *January 1997*

In addition to his acting and teaching, David had time to write 75 poems, some of which have been published. With his permission,[2] I am reprinting below one of his poems, "Flash Point," that was published in 1996.[3]

"Flash Point"

With each life
a new language is born.
Arbitrary symbols and random sounds
search for new patterns of meaning and intent.
All is recorded in
what someday will become
disputed sources of fact and fiction.
The passage of time crimps room
for additional tiers of new editions;
and most certainly
every time a person dies,
there is a library
found burning.

In January of 2000 David indicated that a collection of his poetry ti-tled *Travelers in Residence* would be presented at a Miami theater. The theater showcased six Miami playwrights in February. Three actors presented approximately 30 of his poems. He indicated by correspondence that the poetry reading and performance was well received.

In an article[4] written by David in 1992, he describes what he learned from a workshop in London for actors. The teachers in that workshop often introduced the word "courage" as a prerequisite for acting. They emphasized the fact that it takes "courage" to give yourself to the role that you are portraying. We know that to be a creative person, even though it may be uncomfortable, takes courage to be "in a minority of one."

David's creative achievement score in 1998 was 9.0 out of a possible 10. This score is well above the average for the case studies, and higher than his score of 7.0 in 1980. As indicated earlier, he had written a great deal and performed a tremendous number of plays—45 roles in ten years. In response to listing personal creative achievements, David wrote that "for the past 8 1/2 years, I have been learning how to be a theater instructor. This seems to be a process of perpetual 'skills acquisitions,' i.e., psychologist, mentor, coach, recruiter, adjudicator, etc." His response to "falling in love with his work" is illuminating: "As an actor, I have always loved my profession. As a teacher, it took a few years to gain the confidence which afforded me the opportunity to 'relax' and enjoy the day-to-day challenges of teaching."

Expectations were always high for David by his parents and teachers. He has certainly proceeded in a very unique, individual style despite the ephemeral, allusive nature of theater. He admits that his father was extremely helpful to him in his career. "He took it upon himself to shape my aesthetic sensibilities," says David. He did that through discussions, travel, seeing plays together, help with homework, plays he wrote, and so on. His father invested heavily in him. Now David feels a need to give back to his audiences and students. He has, up to this point in his career, lived out that mandate whispered so adroitly in his ear by his fourth-grade teacher: "Never lose your creativity!"

INTERVIEW ON AUGUST 12, 1998

The interview with David was conducted by telephone in his home in Miami. He reflected on the early influences on his creativity; his career path and transitions; creative accomplishments; and finally general comments on creativity. His own words tell his thoughts and experiences best.

EARLY INFLUENCES ON CREATIVITY

At what age would you say you were first aware of your creativity?

It was heavily influenced by my fourth grade teacher, who was Rod Myers. He was an incredible influence on a number of us and . . .

In what role actually?

Well, he was an extraordinary teacher and role model. . . . I am in touch with a good five or six people from high school and a few from the elementary school, who were actually in class with him. We get together every once in a while and reminisce. I can name three or four people in that class who I'm still pretty closely in touch with almost on a yearly basis. We all have vivid memories of Mr. Myers's class. Sometimes things become a haze and a mishmash, second, third, fourth grade. You may remember the name of the teacher, but specific incidents sometimes become a blur, but he was such a profound influence on so many of us that we all have many specific memories of him. It was like a mandate from him for us to explore our creativity and to become aware of it. He really tried to do that for a number of us and I know he certainly did it for me. I remember him once literally whispering in my ear, "Never lose your creativity." So it seemed like a mission on his part, in terms of fostering that for us and to help develop it. He helped develop it by encouraging us to put on skits, to sing songs, to make up songs. I do specifically remember how we would have recess time to rehearse as it were, then come back and perform for the rest of the class.

So he was just a really big influence. I would definitely say that fourth grade was the time when creativity was reinforced and fostered, cultivated and rewarded for the endeavor.

Yes. Can you think of some other incidents that come quickly to mind regarding that fourth year?

I can specifically remember singing, "Hang Down Your Head, Tom Dooley" with another student. It was kind of like a Western scenario and we created a skit around the fact that he was hanged.

I remember another time, I, in a very impromptu way, made up a song, and obviously Mr. Myers was really impressed with it because he brought out the old Wollensack tape recorder, reel-to-reel, and I froze up and I couldn't reproduce what I had done so freely. I remember there was also a person who came into our class in fourth grade who maybe came once a week or every other week and he was someone who would do theater games with us.

I remember him being very artsy looking, wearing a turtle-neck. So that was my first brush with what somebody kind of arty looks like. We played theater games with this person. Those are pretty much the specifics that I remember of creativity, at a specific point.

David, are there other influences that you can think of, at an elementary-school age, which you now recognize as having had an impact on your career?

Well, my father has been a tremendous impact on me. He always cultivated a sense of aesthetics and he did it in a number of different ways. Jumping two years ahead, when I would have been in sixth grade, we lived in Austria for a year. My father was a professor of American studies and one year received a Fulbright Scholarship, which allowed us the opportunity to live in Innsbrück for a year. I remember we went to Florence on a vacation and a really vivid memory that I have of how he could do something really, really creative in a fun way. We went into these incredible galleries and he played a game where he would say, "Pick your favorite painting and your second favorite painting in each room" and then we would confer as to which they were and invariably my first would be his second or his second would be my first. It was a fun game; where now as an adult I realize what he did . . . really cultivate a sense of aesthetics.

So that was a vivid memory. Also, we went to see theater at the University of Minnesota—a theater called Showboat, something that I ended up working on myself. I remember that was a dream, to someday be one of the actors on that Showboat. The boat sits on the Mississippi and they would have a tugboat push it down to around St. Paul and in previous years, to other cities and towns along the Mississippi. So that was a dream, to one day be an actor on the boat. I don't really remember when that happened, but it was early on.

Were there other early influences that you can remember that had an impact on your creative ability?

Well, I remember seeing *Peter Pan* at the University of Minnesota, and the director of that show, Dr. Frank M. Whiting, was the chair at the University of Minnesota. He later became a mentor of mine. Seeing that first play was a really vivid experience, something very magical. I remember seeing a play that the University High School kids did, *Rip van Winkle*. In fact, I talked to one of the actors two years ago who had been in *Rip van Winkle* and is now on Broadway. I told him I remembered how the set fell down around him and how he kept on going. He couldn't believe that anybody was there to have seen that. I think I was in fourth grade when I saw that high school production.

I did not dwell on wanting to be an actor in elementary school, but once I got into seventh grade and they asked at home room which club I would like, French Club, Journalism Club, and then they came up with Drama Club and it was just like a light going off in my head or a bell going off, going "Boing!" I said to myself, "That's something, yeah, I would like to be in a play." It was as simple and as clear as that. It was just that I found a place for myself.

And was that about grade five or six, . . . junior high?

That was seventh grade.

David, what were some of the qualities or skills that you remember from people like Rod Myers, and I suppose, your father—the two mentors that you mentioned?

They had a strong presence—and I may be talking in a vocabulary used in theater, but that's pretty much my world. I would say they had a strong presence. They seemed larger than life. They seemed very committed and seemed to have a mission. They seemed sometimes even evangelistic, you know, in terms of having a mission that had to be met and had to be answered for. I also recall them being very strict yet fair. I remember one time playing football with Mr. Myers during recess. I mean this guy gave 110 percent all the time. He was playing tag football with us. I never saw myself as an athlete at that time, but I think I made some kind of a play, which probably meant I caught the ball and was feeling really, really good about the fact that I was an athlete. Then we lost the ball and I felt really like a team player, so I must've been moaning or whining about it because I remember him being really, really tough, and saying, "Don't be a sore loser." He had such a strong influence on us in so many ways, because he was basically teaching us how to be good human beings. And from what I gathered at that moment, being a good human being isn't somebody who's going to moan or gripe because they lost the ball.

Yes, yes [laughing].

And so that's a really strong memory. I have other memories of his examples that were so vivid and clear. For example, things like, if somebody's on a tricycle and there's fire coming from their shirt, does that mean that they're moving quickly, like a jet. What makes something propel forward? That's a pretty sophisticated concept. What is jet propulsion? Just because somebody's on a tricycle and they have flames coming from their back, does that mean they would be moving forward quickly? I remember him once asking, "Where does the water in the sea come from?" The examples were many. He asked once if a politician promised to put lemonade in every drinking fountain, would you vote for that person? [GWM laughing.]

So he brought it down to the level of the kids, did he?

Yeah, and they were vivid, so it's easy, forty-some years later, to remember these examples. They were vivid. And he also created a sense of competition. Rather than a spelling bee, he had a math bee where to get to the head of the class, you had to be able to do a math equation. I didn't have a chance. I was never good at math, but a few of the students really were incredibly bright and really good at math. There was a ferocious competition taking place.

I remember another memory, in terms of teaching us to be good human beings. One of the students in our class had a father who was a professional photographer. So as a secret we were going to have him take a class picture and present it to Mr. Myers as a gift. So we're all very excited that we're keeping it from him, a lot of giggling going on, and somehow, someone had convinced him to leave the classroom and he came back in because there was no control in the room. It just made it even better because ultimately, he was going to find out who was involved for his benefit to get a class picture. But he seemed to be vivid in his examples, strict, and really committed.

A strong presence—a notion that really strikes a bell with me.

Oh, yeah.

And their impact on you.

Definitely. I remember the Oxford pants that he wore and we all looked up to him. I remember he invited us over to his home once so as a class, we actually went to his home. I can't remember that happening with any other teacher. His commitment was so clear and as a teacher now I see this also with other teachers, that when you give, you give of yourself. I respect that so much and it doesn't go unnoticed.

What would you say was the most important lesson that you learned with regard to your creativity at this age that we're talking about?

The important lesson about creativity, well. . . . The most important lesson probably was when Mr. Myers whispered in your ear, "Never lose your creativity!" [GWM laughing] and it was like an order; it was like a mandate. It was really bizarre [GWM laughing] because you know, he was so impassioned to say that. It was something that had a profound effect on my life that someone would go out of his or her way, that a teacher would go out of his way—going above and beyond the call of duty.

So if there was any lesson in fourth grade, it was the lesson, "Never lose your creativity!"

And it seems like kids have such a creative openness and, as we become adults, we lose that openness. We see that with kids on a daily basis, whether it's the supermarket or wherever, we see them doing things that, as adults, we wouldn't dare do anymore. Yet there is something wonderful about it. As a teacher today I'm always asking my students to go back to a four-or-five-year-old state of being in terms of finding that playfulness.

How would your friends or your peers have described you at that time?

That's a tough one. How would they have described me? I think they would have described me as someone who was a follower, as someone who was relatively quiet. They would describe me as someone with average intelligence. I think they would describe me as being not very athletic.

Let's move on now and think of your career and some of the transition points.

CAREER PATHS AND TRANSITIONS

Could you tell me about your present job?

For the past nine years, I've been living in Miami, Florida, where I am a professor at New World School of the Arts. It's a really interesting program, which deals with teaching ninth-grade students through seniors in college. It's the high school magnet program for the performing arts and it also is a college program that offers a Bachelor of Fine Arts degree from the University of Florida, although all the training takes place in Miami. So I'm a professor of acting. I teach eleventh-grade acting and I teach a forum class on Fridays—for an hour. It is a free-form class—team-building exercises and sensitivity exercises. They may watch a video of a performer—a very open-ended class; acting is very specific curriculum. Then at a college level, I teach freshmen improvisation. So it's nontextual theater games and exercises. I have kind of a five-dollar word for it—noncerebral immediate interaction—and it's basically trying to go straight for an action rather than censoring it through the brain. And then I teach scene study for college freshmen, which is how to analyze a text, how to do scene work, how to do a six-minute scene. I teach college seniors a course called the "senior project class." They have to create a one-person show for their senior project, which is anywhere from twenty minutes minimum to forty-five minutes maximum. They create their own show and perform it. They're really the only person on the stage. It allows them to be unbelievably creative when they create their own show. The other half of the senior project class is teaching senior research, which is basically trying to market yourself. We go to New York for a week in February to meet agents; see shows; meet producers; and generally acquaint them with New York. We have a large group of alumni performing there right now.

Sounds extremely exciting!

I feel really fortunate because I enjoy teaching high school level and at the college level. They provide different challenges. In the morning, I teach college; in the afternoon, I teach high school, pretty much on a daily basis throughout the year.

This seems like a trite question, but . . . how do you apply [laughing] creativity to your work?

Okay, it's . . .

You can see what I mean by being trite because I think what you do is creative.

No, I understand what you mean. The thing I've learned and the thing that I'm always saying to my students is that I have tremendous respect for the obvious. The obvious eludes me all the time, and I really try to teach them to have a really healthy respect for the obvious, so the question that you asked is obvious . . . but it's really important.

And you know, on the face of it, you go, "What kind of question is that?" but really, it's an important question. The way to creativity is by staying open.

And it's trying to say "yes" to things rather than saying "no." "No" comes from fear and "yes" means that you are ready to explore and be open. And if you're ready to explore and ready to be open, then you're going to be available to creativity, rather than having preconceived barriers that are going to shut out stimuli.

Have you had other jobs? And if so, how have you applied creativity to them, David?

I really haven't had any other jobs. I've basically been an actor, and a teacher. I've done other activities but I really haven't had any other jobs. When I was fifteen or sixteen, I worked in an office during the summer. In college I worked in the library. But since the age of fifteen, in the summertime, I've worked in a theater somewhere. I basically have been an actor, a director, and a teacher. I have a hobby of writing poetry.

And I notice you've published a few of them.

Yeah, a few of them.

David, what major transitions have you experienced in your working life?

Well, the most obvious transition was becoming a full-time actor, then becoming a teacher. I wouldn't really call that a career change. Although I still act a lot.

The first transition occurred in 1989, when I became a full-time teacher. I didn't act as much. I acted with my students at school. In the last three-and-a-half or so years I've been acting more in the professional community at the same time while teaching. I would say becoming a teacher and having the identity of a teacher rather than being an actor was a huge shift for me.

What caused that?

Well, a number of things caused it. I think I was getting frustrated with making $20,000 a year. I've never really considered myself to be a materialistic type of person. I think our family values are such that we enjoyed travel and eating in restaurants. My parents and my sister enjoyed books a lot more than I did.

I was really tired of just making $20,000 a year, though I was very fortunate to work three-quarters of the year, because I worked with Actors Theater of St. Paul, usually from September through May, sometimes through June, and I would do summer theater or teach at a governor's school in Virginia, which got me interested in teaching. In '87, '88 and '89 that was a month-long experience. I worked with talented kids in Virginia. They would come to Radford University in the Blue Ridge Mountains. That experience got me interested in teaching. I really enjoyed it a lot and thought, "Wow, it's fun for a month. It might be fun to do it all the time." And so, after my second summer in Virginia, I went back to Actors Theater of St. Paul and told my artistic director that I was actively going to be looking for a teaching job. So I finally landed a job with the New World School of Arts in Florida. I think I applied to eighty or ninety schools.

I remember back in the mid-eighties, the medium income of our audience was about sixty thousand dollars a year. Basically, when it's all said and done only about two or three percent of the population goes to live theater and I felt like I was pretty much in a vacuum, that I wasn't really part of the real world. I don't know whether being a teacher gives [laughing] you more of the real world or not, but I do appreciate and enjoy interacting with kids. The diversity of the college is amazing. It truly is a melting pot and I find that very satisfying. So I think there were several factors that really came into play. I think I wanted to make more money. I felt that as an artist in America I was not really appreciated. I felt that teaching gave me a higher sense of satisfaction and accomplishment. I also think there was a huge psychological factor in the fact that my father and mother had been teachers. I think I openly rebelled against wanting to be a teacher. I wanted to be anything but what they were. I think I reached that age of maturity [at] about thirty-six or thirty-eight, that I didn't feel I had anything to prove from not wanting to be a teacher. In fact, I remember when I had the interview, the principal of the school said, "Well, what makes you think that you can teach? You've been an actor all your life and now you want to become a teacher." And I just looked her in the eye and without thinking twice, I said, "Well, I'm a born teacher. Both my parents were teachers and so I'm a teacher, too."

And that was a pretty revealing statement to myself. And it could've come off as being cocky as it was a pretty hard sell at the moment when she asked me that question.

I think there were a number of factors as to why I became a teacher rather than an actor. I really like trying to juggle both.

When you made that transition, was there anyone whom you relied on for support and advice at that time?

I remember talking to a close friend of mine during a long talk walking around a lake about the possibility of shifting careers. I'm sure I talked with my father a lot about it too, but to a large extent, it was really self-initiated and a self-propelled kind of activity.

How are you able to integrate relationships into your working life?

I'm always amazed at the people with families, kids, and jobs. I just look at people with just tremendous admiration and wonder, how do they do it?

And they keep it all going [laughing].

Yeah, yeah. There are a couple of things that surprised me. I don't know how they are able to keep it all going, and I also don't know how people literally can afford a family.

I don't know how people do it. So there are a lot of things I'm not very skilled at. I would say that I have not been successful in maintaining an intimate, significant relationship. I think I'm very successful at maintaining long friendships. In fact, most of my friends see me as someone who is deeply committed to sustaining friendships and people are amazed at how far back my roots go. I just spent a week in Phoenix with someone who I consider has been my best friend for the past twenty-five years.

I'm very proud of my commitment to a number of relationships and as far as having a significant other, I've been unsuccessful at that.

Let me just switch our thinking here to creative accomplishments now.

CREATIVE ACCOMPLISHMENTS

What would you consider to be your most creative accomplishment?

I would say acting is the biggest accomplishment in terms of creativity. I think the poetry I write is, or it may be, in terms of, if we're getting right down to semantics, that's the most creative because an actor is an interpretative art. We interpret the material that someone else created.

So, perhaps in terms of creativity, writing poetry is more creative than the acting. My self-image, how I view myself, how I see myself, is that of an actor and a teacher. So I would say on a day-to-day basis, where my creativity comes out is being an actor. In terms of the very specific accomplishments, I created a one-person show called *John Barrymore: Confessions of an Actor*, which I wrote in graduate school when I was about twenty-five. I still do the show . . .

And I've been doing it through the years and it has served me tremendously well throughout the years in terms of getting a foot in a lot of different doors. I've performed it at the Edinburgh Festival, in London, and then coming back to the States, with that kind of credit, it opened up some doors, possibilities. Whenever I can, I do the show. I did it as recently as April for a couple of weeks. So I do it every few years. That's a pretty creative endeavor because I created the show and I act it.

So in summary I would say creating a one-person show is an accomplishment. I would say writing the poetry that I've written is considered a creative accomplishment. In terms of teaching, I really enjoy it because I find that it's a very creative endeavor. The more I teach, the more I create my own vocabulary and my own analogies.

What do you consider to be your creative attributes?

I have a very expressive face. That's what people seem to notice initially, and respond to. I have a very malleable, expressive, energized face. I would basically say a heightened level of energy also, that captures people's attention.

How would your close associates describe your creative attributes?

I think they would say pretty much the same. I think they would say I am essentially fair and personable, able to do different kinds and styles of theater. They would describe me pretty much the way I did, though I think they would probably add versatility.

What influences guide or constrain your creativity?

Okay. I'm an actor in a show and I have a director. And sometimes directors like to enhance your creativity and sometimes it's stifled.

I think a good dose of respect is really important to guide your creativity. If I feel someone is patronizing, condescending, or doesn't have trust that I'll be able to do the job, it becomes a sort of self-fulfilling prophecy, in terms of not being able to accomplish something. I would say the biggest boon to creativity is people who give you the confidence and trust that you can be creative.

The biggest constraint to creativity is people who communicate that you're not able to do it. I can give you a really simple example. Sometimes I'll work with a director who tries to steal your initiative by showing you how to act. Why don't they just do the play?

GENERAL QUESTIONS ON CREATIVITY

What would you say would be your creative goals and aspirations for the future?

My creative goals are to stay open, to keep exploring. I have a really hard time knowing what I'm going to do five years from now or ten years from now. I just want to be open to and receptive to the possibilities. I've been a teacher at the same school for nine years; I don't know whether I'm going to stay here or not, but my feeling is I probably will, simply because I don't see anybody knocking down my door to hire me anywhere else. My aspirations are pretty much to do the same thing. Every year I have to do a self-assessment. One of the first questions is, "What are your goals for next year?" I hate the question. I always say goals for next year are not unlike previous years.

My goals are to continue to act. My father certainly encouraged me to be a writer, but I don't see myself as a writer. Yet when I do write, I find it extremely gratifying. And so I don't know whether that is something I will do more of or not [laughing].

If you could provide educators with advice for nurturing creativity in students, what would you share with them?

I think there's more creativity that happens within a structure, within a boundary, than if you don't have any kind of boundaries or structure. I think absolute freedom is really frightening for young people. That is something I've learned in my first couple of years of teaching and so I think if you can create a boundary, like a frame on a picture, then the students know what the limits are. Then give them the opportunity to really express themselves within the confines of a specific boundary.

Don't change the rules in the middle of the activity. Don't say,

"Oh, oh, you can't draw that kind of picture." So I think you have to create a boundary, a framework, for comfort level and a security; much as they don't think they want a structure, I think structure is really, really important. For all people, probably.

If you were to provide advice to parents for nurturing creativity in their children, what would you share with them?

I think you have to use reverse psychology [laughing], in a major way. I think if you're going to protest too much about wanting something, then children are going to do the exact opposite.

Whether it's having alcohol in the home or giving somebody the ability to extend beyond their curfew, it goes back to respect. And if you are willing to give and share a healthy respect, then it's palpable. I just never understood a parent screaming at kids, "You'd better not come in after midnight." What's going to happen? That person's going to test that parent, and make sure that they come after midnight.

If you could design a time capsule that represented you as a creative person, what would you include in the capsule? Say five to ten items?

With the time capsule being for a creative person, it would include a tape of the Barrymore show that I have done. There would probably be a photo album of good reviews of my shows. It would have a big collection of all seventy-five of the poems that I've written. As a teacher, I may have my lesson plans or course syllabi and a portfolio of my handouts.

SUMMARY

David is clearly an artist—in the field of acting. He has been a prolific actor up to this point in his career. His goal is to stay open and be receptive to possibilities in the future. David wants to try directing and aspires to continue teaching and acting. He is driven by high expectations inspired by his father and by the mandate given to him in fourth grade by his teacher: "Never lose your creativity!" He is an excellent example of an individual who had the courage to fall in love with something (acting) and pursue it with intensity.

In an article called "Theater: Kwiat's Way,"[5] David reveals some elements of his success. He stresses that in order to grow artistically, an actor must be versatile and diverse in an acting company in order to constantly challenge oneself. He states that "there's no room for complacency." David confesses that he is "driven" and admits that he arrives at a first rehearsal with the script fully memorized. He says it gives him more freedom. Few people in any profession share his level of commitment. In fact, he rarely takes a vacation. He is constantly looking for additional opportunities, such as directing and teaching—two crucial endeavors for him. David says that "people have given me a lot and it's time for the sponge to be wrung out." It's the "Kwiat Way."

NOTES

1. Personal communication from Rod Myers to Garnet Millar, November 29, 1999, in possession of the author.

2. Personal e-mail communication from David M. Kwiat granting permission to include "Flash Point" in this book, January 10, 2000.

3. D. M. Kwiat. (1996, spring/summer). "Flash Point." *Spectrum*, vol. 8, no. 1.

4. D. M. Kwiat. (1992, winter). "Over Here. Stage Write." *Royal National Theatre Education*.

5. J. Lewis. (1988, September). "Theater: Kwiat's Way." *Twin Cities*, pp. 37–38.

seventeen

FREDERICK PUZAK

AN UNCONVENTIONAL THINKER

"I like to blaze new trails. I'm simply a broad-based problem solver"—Fred (1998)

Fred Puzak, circa 1958

Fred Puzak is a good example of an individual who "fell in love with something" and pursued it with intensity. He was able to find his own great teacher or mentor who helped him along his career journey. High intelligence and a desire for adventure and thinking "out-side-of-the-box" helped him achieve his goals.

SCHOOL YEARS

Frederick Nicholas Puzak is the eldest of three sons. His father was involved in real estate; he always used Fred, as a teenager and later as a college student, to help run the family business. Fred was involved in the longitudinal study, beginning in grade 1, at University Elementary School, and continued in the study even when he switched schools at the end of grade 4 to Pratt Elementary School, for grades 5 and 6. His creativity scores were consistently above average. Fred did not experience the fourth-grade slump. He demonstrated creative strengths in the following areas: resistance to premature closure; expression of feeling; putting things in context; movement; unusual visualization; breaking boundaries; humor; richness and colorfulness of imagery; and fantasy. Fred's intelligence was in the superior range, and he consistently performed academically in the top quarter of a very high-achieving group of children.

FIRST FOLLOW-UP

After attending Marshall Junior High School in Minneapolis, Fred was offered an academic scholarship in 1968 to attend Phillips Academy High School in Andover, Massachusetts. Fred, having received honors, graduated from Phillips Academy in 1971, and was granted a math award for his exemplary academic work at this special high school. While there, Fred had a mentor who became a role model and provided him with spiritual and intellectual inspiration. His mentor was a humanities scholar and professor of photography.

After graduating from Andover in 1971, Fred indicated that he had taken a year's "sabbatical" before entering college, to pursue something completely different from or unrelated to his "academia." He took this break and decided "to retire at 18" so that he could travel to thirty-nine countries on six continents on various trips, which added up to more than six months and continued during his college years, before graduating in 1976. He decided that life was too short to rely solely on institutional education and had wanted to pursue his current interests of photography, wilderness adventure, and the search for ancient monuments in a global context. He also had fantasized about making a major career change at this time and starting up his own charter sail and diving operation. In high school, Fred had exhibited his sculpture and photography in a regional show and had been elected to student government. Since then, he had held numerous slide shows of his photography and had organized his own business. Fred also had experience in creating building environments; namely, interiors and landscapes.

In 1980, at the time of the 22-year follow-up, Fred was 26 years of age, single, and working with an architectural firm in Minneapolis. He had completed his Bachelor of Science (BS) degree in 1977 in the School of Architecture at the University of Minnesota, and had enrolled as a student in the Master of Arts program in architecture and urban design at the university. He did not complete graduate school at this time because he found interesting employment with large firms in the Minneapolis area. He assisted these large architectural firms with contract administration and troubleshooting during construction. He worked in a variety of roles, such as supervisor of specific building projects; as field representative of larger architectural firms; and eventually ran his own business as a builder/investor.

Fred cited the following as career ambitions in his questionnaire in 1980:

- enjoy life
- stay healthy
- find love and understanding
- have freedom and flexibility
- experience variety
- seek enlightenment
- avoid desk work
- "see the world"
- move to Hawaii.

His score for quality of creative achievements was 7.0 out of 10.0, which was above the average for the case studies.

Since high school, Fred reported a number of creative achievements; namely,

- held various "slide shows" of photographs
- designed and developed his own business
- created advertising ideas
- suggested modifications of existing practices and policies as a builder to superiors and co-workers.

His greatest spur for continual achievement was fun and curiosity. He described his current lifestyle as ranging from not very satisfying to very satisfying, depending upon the specific aspect. He stated several frustrations with his current lifestyle: 1) as the oldest son, much was expected of him by his father to help run the family business; 2) lack of organization; and 3) being a slow reader.

Finally, in 1980 Fred indicated in humorous fashion his future career image for the next ten years:

- walk in space
- improve global access to the world's resources
- pursue, attain, and profess cosmic enlightenment
- stop war and destruction
- contact extraterrestrial life
- fall unequivocally in love.

Fred, circa 1998

MIDDLE TO LATE CAREER

In the 1998 follow-up questionnaire, Fred had been working as a self-employed designer and builder since the last follow-up. He had "fallen unequivocally in love," had recently married, and was living in a suburb near Minneapolis. Fred was now 46 years of age and successful in the creative reuse of historic buildings for providing affordable housing. His quality-of-creative-achievement score was 7.0 out of a possible 10.0, which was the same as his score in 1980. The average for the 18 individuals in the case-study group is 5.4. Fred had several personal creative achievements such as designing his own home and garden, and had designed and constructed unique buildings.

Fred indicated that he was "in love with his work," and had been since he was a teenager. He continues to balance his career by in-

---

volvement in hobbies such as adventure travel, sailing, and photography. The most creative thing he has done in his hobbies is to travel to remote parts of the world to photograph disappearing ethnic groups and historic, ancient architecture. He stated that his greatest strength is an ability to solve problems, whether they are mathematical, design, or survival/repair. To pursue his greatest strengths, Fred seeks new adventure, risks capital, travels extensively, and has sailed the Caribbean on-and-off for seven years. He has enjoyed the mentorship of two individuals for nearly 20 years. These persons provided direction and inspiration in a number of different areas: art, architecture, photography, and humanity.

School never provided the excitement and inspiration about life that he found in other ways. He indicated that school for him was merely a socialization process and didn't encourage independence. Fred said that the skills that other people expect from him now are mostly as a spouse/provider and employer. He has yet to become a mentor to others, except in his role as an employer.

INTERVIEW ON JULY 10, 1998

This interview with Fred Puzak was conducted in his home-office on July 10, 1998. Fred reflected on the early influences on his creativity; his career path and transitions; his creative accomplishments; and finally general comments on creativity. His own words reveal his thinking about creativity and his life journey.

EARLY INFLUENCES ON CREATIVITY

Can you think about what age you might have been when you were first aware of your creativity or your resourcefulness?

[Pause.] Well, probably not until I was a teenager, when I started fixing things.

How did that show itself? Like you mentioned fixing things—what sorts of things did you work at?

Well, I guess it relates to things my dad taught me, how to fix lamps, or electrical cords, or bikes. I had an interest in Thomas Edison, the inventor. That was my idea of creativity, someone who could invent things.

So I always had a little bit of an interest in electricity and chemistry and that type of thing, though I've never invented anything [both laughing].

Your father, then, was sort of a help to you at that time?

Well, yeah, he got me going, I think. But it was probably as a teenager that I became creative on my own. I started building these things but I didn't really have a creative life as a kid. Other than fixing things, the only other things I remember doing were the sculptures and other projects that were assigned in school. But I always enjoyed sculpture in school.

So the arts program—you enjoyed the art program generally in school?

Yes, the modest program that was presented.

The next question I wanted to ask is: What influence did your schooling have, you think, on your creative ability that you've been talking about?

High school I would say was influential in that. I attended a topnotch high school, Phillips Academy in Andover, Massachusetts, and they had a great facility, some nice programs, and I was able to learn photography and sculpture. I always had an interest in sculpture and the Andover program was the best program I was introduced to until the college years. I received a scholarship to go to tenth, eleventh, and twelfth grades. They recruited people from around the country.

What type of scholarship?

It was a financial scholarship, just to offset the costs of travel and tuition.

Was that something you applied for or did they seek students out?

They actually offered it to me as an incentive to round out their student body, geographical distribution, and that type of thing.

Can you think, Fred, of some specific incidents in your childhood which enabled your creativity to develop? Anything back then in your home or in your school environment?

I would say my dad taught me to fix things, and certain professors had opened my mind to photography. I had a great photography teacher, Steve Perrin, who was also a humanities fellow. As a child, nothing comes to my mind immediately. The University

Elementary School: I remember it being very stimulating, but I can't say it enabled my creativity to develop.

Were there certain teachers that stood out that you remember?

There again, well, they were all good.

But oftentimes, you know, there's a teacher that's more like a signpost, who was really helping you—helping you in your education.

Yeah, but that wasn't at the elementary level. Fred Lang in fifth and sixth grades was good. In junior high, I don't really remember anybody as inspiring, until I got into senior high and went out East. Then there were some exceptional minds there who were really inspiring.

Was there any influence at that elementary-school age, at that elementary-school time, I guess, which you now recognize as having had an impact on your career or chosen field of work?

No, actually. Elementary [school] was pretty generic from what I can remember. That was right up until college. I never really focused on a career; even in my college education, and architecture was almost a default because I didn't want to focus on one thing. To me, architecture represented a broad liberalized education that melded liberal arts and science. So because I couldn't choose a career path, I went into architecture.

Can you think of the qualities or the skills, the behaviors that Fred Lang, your teacher in grades 5 and 6, exemplified for you?

Well, I just remember him as being a friend. You know, taking time out, and helping me; just being interested in teaching. Maybe I was just closer to him as a person than with some of the other teachers. That was when I switched from University School to Pratt.

Oh, you made a switch there?

I switched between fourth and fifth grades. So fifth and sixth grades were my first years at Pratt. And I just remember him being a good teacher.

I know what you're saying, just, yeah. And understanding you as a student and spending time with you.

Well, I was one of the top students in the class and Pratt was a public school and it had kids from the housing project down the street and there were a couple of guys in the class who were really disruptive. I just remember asking him, well, why do we have to spend half an hour disciplining two individuals while the rest of the class is waiting to learn? And maybe that was why he just spent a little extra time with me on certain projects or whatever.

What would you say was the most important lesson, if you can think of that, that you learned with regard to your skills, your creativity at that age?

I learned that being creative and fixing things was key to self-reliance. For example, by knowing how to fix my bike, I knew I would never be stranded and I could venture out further. In that sense, self-reliance has been the key to my success. Self-reliance defines my persona.

How would your friends at that time have described you?

Well, I'm a pretty good athlete. I was popular, a good athlete, and a good student. I remember my dad used to say I needed more self-control [both laughing]. But that was the teacher; that was Fred Lang. He was just trying to get me to have a little more self-control. [GWM laughing.] But yeah, I got along well with kids at our school.

And you played all kinds of sports pretty much?

Yeah, you know, the regular—baseball, basketball, tennis, and football. At Marshall Junior High, I was elected president of the junior school council. I was pretty popular then.

CAREER PATHS AND TRANSITIONS

What is your present job, Fred?

Well, it's hard to define: I'm a self-employed investor with a background in architecture-construction management, real estate development.

Are you able to apply creativity to your work?

Oh, all the time. Right now, I'm getting into real estate. I'm always designing things. Remodeling—we do a fair amount of remodeling work to improve real estate I have invested in. And I run a crew and I do the design work and then supervise the execution.

Right. So there's a lot of, as you say, freedom to . . .

Well, a lot of troubleshooting, too. When you don't build from the ground up you run into problems, and so there's a lot of troubleshooting in that type of work which I consider creative problem solving.

Have you had other jobs before this one?

Well, I've been self-employed since '81; for the three years prior to that, I worked with architectural firms here in Minneapolis. And through them got more into the construction-management end of architecture.

Were you able to be very creative with those kinds of jobs?

Those two jobs weren't very creative jobs. They were office jobs. They weren't very creative jobs. That's probably why I left.

The nice thing about working for firms like that is I worked on projects with greater scale. The first firm I worked for, the job I was assigned to was the largest construction project in the area; it was a ten million dollar addition to the Dakota County Votech and I was there every day, I was the owners' and architects' representative in the field. And that was a big poured-concrete project—it was six football fields in size—and for a young man, it was a lot of responsibility; it was interesting.

But I was basically a liaison for the owners and the architecture firm; I was their man in the field. The second job I had with Miller Hanson was somewhat office-related but then I hated to be behind a desk all the time. So they got me out in the field doing the pay requests. We were doing fourteen-story high-rise-type buildings. My firm did most of the public housing in the state at that time, and government-funded housing. So they gave me the principal-of-the-firm's airplane and would fly me around with routine requests and job inspections every two weeks. Which was fun. I got to work on huge projects, like I've never worked on since. But I wouldn't really call it a creative job.

What major changes or transitions have you experienced in your working life?

Well, I've gone from working for a salary—a wage—to being an investor, an entrepreneur, a risk-taker, and a venture capitalist in a way. So there hasn't always been a dependable flow of income.

There've been years when I've lost money and, you know, it hasn't been easy. That's the difference between having a steady paycheck and going out on your own.

What caused you to make that transition from a secure income to being on your own?

Well, I saw the potential for making more money than twelve dollars an hour. In 1981, I was only making twenty-six thousand dollars a year, yet signing my name to millions of dollars in construction projects. I felt I was a liability hedge for the owners of the company. And I thought, well, I could be doing this on my own. We did a certain amount of renovation work—you know, certain projects were adaptive re-use of older structures for housing—and I learned a few things there. In 1981, I bought an old brownstone building in downtown Minneapolis and started renovating it for my own account.

I see. Was it a project-on-the-side kind of thing?

Well, no, I left the firm. My new business was full time—you know, it was eighty hours a week. That's full time. I wanted to make more money [laughing] I guess, basically. And be my own boss.

When you made these changes in your working life, was there anyone whom you relied on for support and advice?

[Pause.] Well, if I could back up, even before I got into this life, I had a mentor, Al Hoffmeyer, who was an architect and a friend of my dad's. Always, I guess he was the one who encouraged me to get in, to study architecture, and I knew him as a teenager and as a college student, and after that. I actually worked with him briefly, so he was probably the person most influential in building my career.

Maybe the fact that my dad was always self-employed influenced me. He's a real estate salesperson. He's got an MBA from Harvard and he's a graduate of Carleton College. He worked briefly for the state of Minnesota and General Mills, and then branched off on his own late in the fifties. I guess he's probably influenced me as much as anybody. That's pretty typical, I think.

Let me ask you this question: How are you able to integrate relationships into your working life? Yeah, I'm thinking of, you know, as a parent, as a partner, as somebody's child, that kind of thing. Are you able to integrate that into your working life?

Being self-employed enables me to take time off when needed to be with family or friends, or to help family. For example, I spent several "work" days helping my mother move from our family homestead into a new condo. I spent numerous hours working on design ideas for my brother's new house. I'm able to balance work and other commitments easier than if I had a full-time job.

My wife and I both have our own careers, but since we both work at home, we can discuss projects we're working on, share ideas. We have lunch together, often, yet we get our work done, too. Our work and personal lives are highly integrated.

Right. Like today, for example, you had, I assume, some free time in order to see me, which I appreciate.

Well, I set aside a block of time, but I do have site inspections to make this afternoon, and I have my office out of the house here, so I do my phone work and book work here, which allows me a lot of flexibility.

CREATIVE ACCOMPLISHMENTS

What do you consider to be, at this stage, your most creative achievement?

One of the things that I did that influenced me or I feel proud of is spending six months traveling in Southeast Asia. That would have been in 1975. I basically set my career aside to travel and photograph ancient architecture and to experience Indonesian and Thai and other Southeast Asian cultures, which may or may not be creative, but I got a lot of great photographs.

I've never had a show of those photographs, but donated many to the library of the School of Architecture. And it's not just the photographs that I consider the creative part, it's the whole experience and the whole act of leaving everything behind and dropping out of college for two quarters. Well, I left college, but I didn't feel like I was losing education.

Right.

It was just another chapter in my education.

You were enhancing it actually.

It took a lot of strength to do that and it was an accomplishment.

I would consider it that. Because it obviously has influenced the way you think about what you do now in your life here in Minnesota and obviously the architecture that you had seen and photographed would help you in your thinking about your work.

Yes and no. I mean, some of that stuff was mind-boggling, like trying to understand ancient people and what they thought was important. As far as creativity goes, sometimes just the small things, like making a part for a transmission on a sailboat is a creative achievement. I was working on a sailboat once in Bayfield, Wisconsin. It had a British—what do you call it, British Standard of measurement? It wasn't metric and it wasn't SAE. We couldn't buy a part to fix the transmission. So I made a part. And we got it to work and we enjoyed the boat the rest of the summer. So, that was creative.

In what area of your life are you most able to be creative now?

Well, now is in design and spatial relations and the use of space and form, mostly because adaptive re-use of existing spaces is what I've been doing.

Now what do you consider to be your creative attributes?

Well, I've always had a good sense of navigation and a good sense of space. I was probably born with that: a strong mechanical aptitude, the ability to visualize a great photo—light, color, and composition—and an appreciation for beauty and uniqueness.

When you say navigation, what do you mean . . . a good sense of navigation?

Well, I mean, I have an intuitive feel for where I am and . . .

Where you're going.

Yeah, well, it's not just being good with maps, it sort of relates back to the flow of spaces and the spaces around you on a . . . on a building level, that's what I've been doing.

How would your close associates describe your creative attributes?

Well, I've had compliments about the designs I've done. As far as troubleshooting in the field, well, they all turn to me for solutions to what might be mundane technical problems, which we usually find a way to fix and adapt as a solution to a problem in the building. I'm able to "think outside the box" and devise creative solutions. I find new ways of doing things. I like to blaze new trails; but maybe that's just because that's what I'm doing. I don't know if that's necessarily my best attribute. Well, on the other hand, business-wise, I mean, I'm really good with numbers and being able to analyze projects from a financial standpoint. I always was very good with math. And probably could have had a career in it.

Accounting type of thing?

Well, no, even more esoteric than that. Five quarters of calculus with a minor in computer sciences. If I'd kept at that, I was actually writing computer programs on how to do interactive computer graphics. That was back in 1973. I had to get permission from the School of Architecture to even get credit for the project; the concept was ahead of its time in 1973. It wasn't even a course; it was just an independent study project. I was developing a program that allowed you to draw with a light pen and rotate three-dimensional objects and I dropped it. . . . In a span of six months, I could have had a nice program, if I had followed through that career. Look at where the software industry is today. It's come a long way in twenty-five years. Now everything's computer aided, designed, CAD CAM. So I was on the cutting edge of it then . . . but I kind of missed the boat.

In your work, what influences guide or constrain your creativity?

When renovating or building, I have to think of who will use the building, what their needs are, what they will pay for rent, etcetera. You have to design for your market in order to be successful. As far as developing real estate, the biggest constraints are political [both laughing]. But who can control that?

You just have to find out, know what it is, and try to work with it, right?

Right. I just basically avoid politics. [GWM laughing.] Don't have the stomach for it.

What about finances? Would there be any financial constraints, I suppose?

Well, you have to work within the times. Right now money's easy, lending is easy, but when I set off on my own in '81, we were paying twenty-one percent interest, two points over prime, and I was on short-term lending and that was a big constraint. I don't know if it constrains creativity or enhances it out of necessity.

QUESTIONS RELATED TO THE "MANIFESTO FOR CHILDREN"

Would you say that you are in love or passionate about your work?

I love it, yeah. I'm passionate about the design end of it. I love to build. Yeah, I mean, that's why I stuck with it. I guess it would be nice to be working on larger projects. But . . . I'm not unhappy with what I'm doing.

In what ways is your creativity affected by the expectations of others?

Well, none really, because I run my own business and you know, everything starts and stops here. I guess I could say maybe there's been a marriage partnership; you know, my wife is sort of an influence as to how we build our new life together. In designing renovations, I do need to satisfy the market, such as the needs of tenants. That dictates the number of rooms, etcetera, as well as how much to invest in the project.

Would it be fair to say that you're "free to play your own game" or to "sing in your own key"?

Well, yes and no. Yes, because I'm my own boss; no, because I would be doing more building without the physical constraints, if there wasn't so much politics. In Minnesota, if you don't play the political game, you can't get the good development projects. And sometimes you can't get the approvals to build what you want on your own land. So that's frustrating.

What relationship has been most instrumental in helping you to achieve your potential?

There have been certain mentors along the way. Well . . . well, yeah. I guess, starting with my high school photography teacher, Steve Perrin, who was more than just a photography teacher—he opened my mind to the humanities and to a way of life. Then Al Hoffmeyer, in architecture. Can't forget my dad—he's always influenced me: to be true to myself, be my own man. I guess overall, it'd probably be my dad—in the big picture.

What were some of the general qualities or skills that these mentors had?

Well, Mr. Perrin was a really bright guy. Perrin, Hoffmeyer, and my dad—they had a common bond, they were all a little bit counterculture . . . not really mainstream. They were free-thinkers—yeah, independent thinkers—but all extremely bright people.

What did you feel for these mentors? Did you have any feeling for them?

Well, yeah, I did and still have deep love and respect and admiration and gratitude.

In what ways now do you interact with others to enhance their career or personal lives?

I do what I can to help my closest associates, along with my brothers. I'm always helping them with their design projects—and one brother in particular, I guess he looks up to me for guidance in design and construction. But no, I haven't really taken any professionals under my wing [both laughing].

Fred, would you describe yourself more as well rounded, or more able at some things than others?

Well, I'm fairly well rounded, but less able at certain things than others. You know, I'm not a brain surgeon. I haven't entered a very specific field of study. I've not been published or specialized. I'm simply a broad-based problem solver.

GENERAL QUESTIONS ON CREATIVITY

What are your creative goals and aspirations for the future?

[Pause.] Well, my aspiration right now is to raise a family. I recently married and don't have any kids. Professionally, I guess I really don't have a lot of professional goals right now. I would like someday to do a show of photography. I always wanted to do that—I just haven't focused on doing that. I've always hoped that I could do that someday.

If you could provide educators advice for nurturing creativity in kids, what would you share with them?

Well, from a personal point of view, the people who had the most influence on me were friends. And that came naturally; I mean, you can't just say I'm going to be *that* person's friend. Maybe we had a chemistry. Yes, so I guess the advice would be to find a kid you have the best chemistry with, and that's just going to come naturally, I guess. If you can influence him, try and make the most of it.

Let me ask the same type of question for parents. What would you say to parents as to nurturing creativity in their kids?

From a parent's point of view, I guess the answer is: always encourage your kids to challenge their minds and to think things through—that would be it.

Trying to not settle on anything and be scattered about then.

That's one of my problems, too, like when you're trying to design something, you just sort of, you have to make choices that sometimes eliminate other great solutions. But . . . as far as being creative, I guess you have to keep your mind open to all this stuff and continually analyze and look at all the solutions. Choose one. Hopefully it's the right one [both laughing].

What guidance would you suggest to mentors who work with creative kids, what would you share with them?

Trusting and, obviously, be liked, but that doesn't always come easily. You have to show interest in the kids.

If you could design a time capsule, to be put in one of your buildings that you're designing, that would represent you as a creative person, what would you include in that time capsule? Maybe five items.

[*Fred added the following paragraph after he read the transcript for verification of information, April 12, 1999.*] Assuming you are not looking for *symbolic* tokens, I would include actual photographs or color slides, possibly in compact digital format to facilitate their storage. I would include photos taken while traveling to remote places in over sixty countries on six continents, which might communicate my quest for knowledge and understanding outside of "the mold." Secondly, I would include photos of my own products, such as my favorite drawings, sculptures, and several architectural designs actually constructed. Perhaps I could include a digitized video "walk-through" of several spaces I have designed and built. Hardest of all would be to find a way to communicate or document my ability to troubleshoot or problem solve, which often manifests itself in the mundane aspects of day-to-day life, as well as during the occasional misadventure. Finally, I might include a copy of my 1972 letter to the U.S. Government Draft Board, which expressed in a nutshell a creative alternative to war, which earned me status as a "conscientious objector."

SUMMARY

Although Fred scored in the above-average range as far as creativity is considered, he has succeeded very well in his work due to strong scholastic attainment, being in love with his work, and benefiting from having a number of mentors along his career journey. Fred related well with his fifth- and sixth-grade teacher, Fred Lang, and considered his teacher Steve Perrin, at Phillips Academy, a mentor. Mr. Perrin introduced Fred to the worlds of sculpture and photography, which have been enduring interests for him. In fact, photography has been Fred's dominant hobby and on his world travels enables him to capture on film ancient civilizations and buildings. Also, Fred's father and a family architect friend have been enduring mentors to him. For Fred, they represent independent thinking and the courage to challenge the culture of the status quo. He is also "in love" with his work of designing and building homes. He is well known among his colleagues for his ability to solve problems and is sought out for help in that area. Fred knows, understands, takes pride in, practices, develops, uses, exploits, and enjoys his greatest strengths.

eighteen

ANN LUMRY

A "PLAYFUL AND GUTSY" PSYCHOLOGIST

"I want to figure out how to balance a family, marriage, and profession"—Ann (1980)

Ann Lumry, circa 1958

Ann Lumry is a "Torrance Kid" who demonstrated high creativity in elementary school, and illustrates as an adult other factors that continue to support her creative behavior. For example, as a psychologist in private practice, she is doing what she loves and does well; she has learned the skills of interdependence and shares them gladly with those around her; she has learned to free herself from the expectations of others and to walk away from the games they try to impose on her; and she has encountered mentors who have helped her along her career and life journey. She has worked hard at maintaining a healthy balance between her work and family responsibilities and obligations.

Information and details are presented about Ann's school years, questionnaire results (1980 and 1998), a recent interview, and a brief summary of major events that have influenced her life as a creative individual.

SCHOOL YEARS

Ann was assessed on a variety of creativity tests while she attended grade 6 at University Elementary School. She was involved in exploratory studies on creativity that Dr. Torrance and his associates from the University of Minnesota were developing. Her estimated creativity quotient at that time was in the superior range, with a number of identified creative strengths: originality, expression of feelings, putting things in context, movement and action, synthesis, unusual visual perception, breaking boundaries, humor, richness and colorfulness of imagery, and fantasy.

Ann is a middle child with two brothers. Her parents were professional people: her father was a professor of chemistry, and her mother a clinical psychologist. During elementary school, she experienced six months in Denmark and Germany with her family while her father took a sabbatical leave. In Denmark, she learned to read a great deal and to assert herself as a child despite the language barrier. In Ann's words, "When I was in Denmark, we did not have a TV. There was nothing to do, so I started reading a lot." In grade 6, Ann indicated that she read 12 to 15 hours a week on her own, and read about 13 books per month.

Ann recalls an incident in elementary school that may have had an influence on her career journey. She remembers being singled out by her first-grade teacher because of a poem she had written. Most of her "creative" activities took place outside of school. She was a lead dancer in *The Nutcracker* in first grade.

FIRST FOLLOW-UP

The first follow-up with the elementary students was conducted by Dr. Torrance 22 years after testing them at University Elementary School. At the time, Ann was still living in Minneapolis. She had married and was now 26 years of age. Her husband had earned a Ph.D. degree in biochemistry. The two enjoyed cooking creatively.

In high school, Ann reported a number of creative achievements, such as involvement in a high school play; election to student office; and special recognition for leadership. She also was a member of a semiprofessional modern-dance company that toured the state of Minnesota.

Since high school, Ann had been a student continuously from 1967 to 1978, including an internship and part-time employment as a psychologist. She graduated from the University of Minnesota with a Bachelor of Arts degree (summa cum laude) in psychology (1971), and with a Ph.D. degree (1978) in clinical psychology and behavior genetics. While in graduate school, Ann received three academic awards and assistantships: a Behavior Genetics Training Grant, a Veteran's Administration Traineeship, and a teaching assistantship.

Before moving to her private practice in 1984, Ann worked full time in several hospitals. She was a psychology intern at the Hennepin County Medical Center (1974–1975), a psychology associate at Veteran's Administration Hospital (1975–1976), and a staff psychologist at St. Paul Ramsay Medical Center (1977–1984). Her work at this latter institution involved diagnosis, assessment, and treatment of psychiatric patients. Her research focus was on the disorders of mood, including recurrent depression. During Ann's graduate-school program she switched from a purely academic focus to a clinical, people-oriented program. She had several hobbies and interests at this time of her life: tennis, "power" volleyball, jogging, dance, cooking, and volunteerism in political campaigns.

Since high school, Ann reported the following achievements:

- presented a professional paper
- received a research grant
- performed a lead role in dance
- conducted in-service seminars and developed policies for co-workers.

Her score for creative achievements was 6.0 out of 10.0, which was average for the individuals in the case-study group.

In 1980 she described her three most creative achievements since high school as 1) writing a Ph.D. dissertation; 2) her current job—a tricky melding of research and service, plus coping with diverse staff; and 3) development as a psychotherapist.

At this time in her life Ann had a person whom she considered to be a mentor. He was her professor, Irving Gottesman, who recognized her potential and facilitated her career work and research interest.

Ann stated that her greatest spur to continued achievement was her husband and her recognition of her role as a "model" for other women, particularly clients. Her greatest obstacles to continued success were: a lack of time; heavy work/service load; and a residual "burn-out" feeling from the dissertation.

Ann indicated that her Swedish-born husband supports her in every way possible. He has encouraged her through graduate school and automatically assumed responsibility for housework. He has encouraged her to move forward to reach her professional goals and was willing to reduce his workload to share in child care. The primary frustration in Ann's life in 1980 was working within the rigid medical health-care system, which required more than 100 percent job commitment. During the next ten years Ann was looking forward to the challenge of having children and figuring out how to *balance* a family, marriage, and profession. She had a desire to explore the area of art history and learn a foreign language.

In 1980 Ann was at a decisive point in her career. She was feeling being uncomfortably pulled in several directions. She began asking questions of herself: "Should I forge a nationally respected research career?" "Should I develop excellence as a psychotherapist/clinician?" "Should I delegate employment interests to a smaller role entitled 'job' and put my energies into as-yet undefined areas?" She was feeling a lack of confidence in her skills and talents, and a general lack of enthusiasm. She was also feeling that she had no real creative outlets other than the challenge of "diagnostic puzzles" presented by her clients. She longed to return to dance or painting to fill the void. Ann was at a real crossroads in her career and expecting her first child!

MIDDLE TO LATE CAREER

In the 1998 follow-up, Ann was working as a private psychologist and was a busy mother of two children. Her husband was a chief executive officer of a small biotechnical company. Ann had indeed made a choice. She decided to leave the hospital job that required so much personal commitment and did not foster her growth, and now was involved in marriage/relational counseling practice along with four other colleagues. This enabled her to have more time to spend balancing work, marriage, and family life. Ann is able to apply her creativity to her work, family, and leisure pursuits (including gardening).

In public creative achievements, Ann scored 3.5 out of 10.0, below average for the case-study group. Her score for creative achievement

Ann, circa 1998

was 6.0 in 1980. Ann had decided that publishing articles and the like was not her priority. She had published and co-authored a number of professional articles, made presentations at professional meetings, and conducted in-service sessions for her co-workers. She stated that it is a creative achievement to leave a traditional job, be married to an entrepreneur, and try to balance that "roller-coaster ride." Ann's personal creative achievements have increased since the last follow-up. She helped design and develop a garden for people in a crisis home. (See the end of Ann's case study for a newspaper article that describes this initiative.) She calls herself "a born-again gardener." She became involved again in dance and in 1992 played a major role in a fully staged modern dance, which was performed at the University of Wisconsin. She has also taken an interest in teaching the "Junior Great Books" to students in her daughter's school. Ann feels passionate about her work as a psychotherapist and loves working with relational issues: couples, individuals, and groups. Her shift from working with trauma survivors and depression to working with couples has invigorated herself and enhanced her career.

Ann's hobbies are gardening, cooking, reading, and sports. The most creative aspects of her hobbies are presentation of her cooking in an appealing way; garden design; and mothering (the challenge of being the best mother she can be!). Her greatest strengths are being:

- artistic
- persistent
- creative
- passionate

- intuitive
- loyal
- integrative.

She has had a minor mentor, who was a social worker and "grand-mother" of her profession. The lady was a "powerhouse," even into her eighties. She was a role model for Ann. Ann also took a course on Women in Leadership in 1982 that gave her the strategies and courage to leave her hospital position and begin to work for herself in private practice.

INTERVIEW ON JULY 6, 1998

This interview with Ann Lumry was conducted in her office in St. Paul, in which she reflected on the early influences on her creativity; her career path and transitions; creative accomplishments; and final-ly, some general comments on creativity. Her own words tell her story best. (*Note:* The bracketed information was added by Ann after she read the transcript for verification of information, January 13, 1999.)

EARLY INFLUENCES ON CREATIVITY

At what age were you first aware of your creativity?

I was probably about three or four, thinking back. My mother en-rolled me in a dance class. I remember the colored scarves that we danced with.

At elementary-school age what influence did your schooling have on your creative ability?

I don't remember very much about kindergarten through grade 4 in terms of the school setting. I remember more about the home-setting. What stands out in my mind is my family traveled to Denmark; we stayed there for six months and then to Germany for three, but I remember the schooling there far more vividly.

Can you say some more about that?

Well, going to a country not knowing the language, and becom-ing a girl scout and trying to memorize the girl scout motto [laughing], and then going to an international school, and so it was a small classroom and I remember vividly the fellow who sat next to me was the son of some friends of my parents and how he would do watercolors of the botanical flowers on a report, so that was kind of just one of many examples. [So that was just one of many examples of seeing possibilities that had never occurred to me in elementary school in Minneapolis.]

What brought you to Denmark?

My father was a professor of biophysical chemistry and he was on sabbatical. And so we lived, I think six months in Denmark and then, I don't remember how long, maybe three months in Germany. So that was very vivid for me, going to a German school and not knowing any German.

[I think that I learned how to be more flexible and to trust my own resources, and to give things my best shot even when I wasn't fluent in the language. It was challenging every day just to take the train to school in Denmark, or to play with children in Germany who knew little English. I also remember being hungry for books in English, and reading anything and everything, including George Orwell and *On the Beach*, a book about nuclear catastrophe. Those experiences, coupled with witnessing the beginning of the wall dividing East and West Germany, were very powerful in terms of being able to think about the world outside of the Midwest. I also toured many museums, the Roman ruins, Stonehenge, and other sites that helped give me a sense of history and art that no textbook ever captured.]

Then I was involved with dance. Pretty much from an early age and in dance productions at the Walker Arts Center here. We would perform for other children.

[Dance was both an opportunity to perform, but also express myself nonverbally. Apparently I made an impact on others, as my good friend, Marie Winckler, whom I met in seventh grade at University High School, recognized me when meeting me for the first time in seventh grade as the duck from *Peter and the Wolf*. I performed the role in second grade. Performing probably gave me some confidence, and the support to try out new ideas and ways of being in the world that weren't very available to children in the early 1950s.]

What specific incidents can you remember back then, in your childhood, which enabled your creativity to develop? You mentioned certainly the travel, I suppose, and the dance, but are there any other specific incidents you can think about that you think really helped you free yourself to use your creativity?

[I think my parents both valued creativity—both in their professions, and in the experiences they exposed us to. My father has a great deal of intellectual passion, tends not to accept the status quo, and really pushed us to challenge ourselves. He is still active at seventy-eight, trying to get people to rewrite physical chemistry textbooks to incorporate his ideas, and is working on a web page which will include protein structures. My mother was in graduate school working on her doctorate during my elementary-school years, and many of her materials, like the block design test (a subtest of the Wechsler Intelligence Scales), were readily accessible for us to play with. She was prolific in exploring the impact of war experiences on veterans.]

In what field?

Psychology. She studied the effect of alcoholism on neurological functions, and she would have things scattered around, in terms of materials that she used, like the block design. So I think it was a sense that you could go for whatever you wanted and stick with it. And that was supported as well as reading. I read every single book on the shelf of fairy tales in the bookmobile. Just kind of consuming whatever it was that most interested you. That was really fostered. We didn't have a television early on and so we filled up the time with other things.

Was there any influence at an elementary-school age, which you now recognize as having had an impact on your subsequent career in psychology or, I guess, psychotherapy?

Well, I wanted to be an archaeologist when I was in sixth grade. Of course, I don't see it as being very different from what I do now. It's more with the human psyche, kind of digging with people through the dark of their past or whatever, but that was my fascination because we had also visited Rome and that's what I had passion for, and still do, . . . is different cultures and how people figured things out, and how they did things two thousand years ago and. . . . So I think it was really the travel in terms of shaping my career. I can't think of any other specific thing, elementary schoolwise. I think my fifth-grade teacher wanted us to write a poem a week and I think that shattered my [both laughing] inclination to write poetry. It had a negative effect.

What were the qualities or skills or behaviors even of some of the people that influenced you. You mentioned your father and your mother, but what were some of the qualities of those people that were important to you at that time?

[One of the important people who influenced me in high school was Nancy Hauser, a dancer. I was in her dance company, which was unusual since I was about four years younger than the other members of the troupe. This was the mid-sixties and people involved in the arts were more "counterculture" than people I typically was exposed to. Nancy spoke out against the Vietnam War when I didn't even know there was a war going on. She was married to a sculptor, and she brought live musicians into the studio, including her sons who played the guitar. I remember doing an improvisation in the courtyard of the architecture building at the university to a live jazz band for the architecture students, and that was simply exhilarating. Nancy's passion for the arts and zest were infectious. I think those two traits are pretty important to fostering creativity and the freedom to keep exploring. We did many improvisations, starting with lying quietly, and just noticing our breathing. The movement would emerge out of that experience. These experiences are pretty available in the nineties but were pretty unique then.]

Nancy Hauser was a very important model and support person. She really helped me to have a belief in myself, being elevated to doing something even my friends didn't know much about. So also, you know you worked really, really hard to get something that you wanted in movement and dance. It's not just learning in that kind of rational linear way.

It's experimenting . . . feeling free to do it.

Right, right. And getting into your body in a kinesthetic sort of way. She was very important. I cannot think of any particular high school teacher. Well, actually that's not true. I had one, my eleventh-grade teacher in English. She really encouraged me to read what I wanted, separate from the class. I did my own because I was a good reader, and that wasn't unusual for the time, in terms of people going off in the direction they wanted. So I think I read most of Faulkner one year and my essays certainly looked like it because I would have a sentence that would go on for two pages [both laughing]. So she was very important, I would guess. I know to this day when I'm working with the kids in my daughter's school, I really think back to her, wanting them to have someone who would influence them and have a passion about literature. And then I had a science teacher, and I can't remember who it would be, who had a greenhouse on top of the building and he let me go up there and I know my father gave me some—what was the name of the acid that was supposed to make plants grow faster? So I would keep fooling around up in the greenhouse.

That still is one of your hobbies, I understand.

Somewhat. Right! Right! And I was, until my first year in graduate school, . . . I wasn't sure if I would go more in the direction of the hard science, so I did not have a passion for gardening at that age.

But some of the beginnings were there.

Well, apparently so [both laughing].

If you think about it . . .

Apparently so.

Ann, how would your peers at that time have described you?

Well, I think I was sort of a separate person. I remember I was not a cheerleader. I had my passion in my dance, and so that was a circle of friends, and then I had my circle of friends in the school, but I, . . . I probably would have been described by some, as they told me, as more reserved or withdrawn, and others, as friendly and pleasant.

CAREER PATHS AND TRANSITIONS

Tell me a little bit about your present job.

I'm a psychologist, doctoral level, licensed for both marriage and family therapy and psychology. At present, I really am working primarily with couples and relational issues, and that's evolved over the years. About five years ago I started doing some more training in the area of working with couples, so that's really shaped my practice to the present.

How do you apply creativity to your work?

I think it's integral to what I do every day, in terms of sitting down with a couple and each time "clearing the plate," to be present to what's going on, both individually, what their issues are, and their histories and patterns, and then what's going on in the relationship. Basically I use myself to sort out and intuit what's going on and what would be a helpful way to work with the couple. So that there is less defensiveness, less disconnection, and more connection.

Have you had other jobs and, if so, were you able to work creatively while in those jobs?

I spent seven years in hospital settings—well, eight years in hospital settings after graduate school, and I think that everything I have done as a psychologist requires some creativity, in terms of taking in the data, whether it's from my interview or my own experiences with people or using psychometric tests, and then sorting out and making recommendations based on my assessment. So I think that requires creativity. When I was at the St. Paul Ramsay Medical Center for seven years, I was affiliated with several long-term follow-up studies of the affective disorders. I developed ideas for grant proposals and data analysis and that kind of thing. I left there having worn too many hats, trying to be a clinician and trying to be a researcher and an educator. I was in charge of training for psychology and it was too much, especially when I was having children. I had to focus.

That was a transition point for you there, wasn't it, from the hospital to your private work?

Right, right, very much so.

What precipitated that?

Well, that was a setting, which as you can probably imagine, was like most medical centers, going through a great deal of transition and I had a lot of dissatisfaction about how I was being treated. I was one of the only women when I came to the hospital. There was one male psychologist and between the two of us, we built up the department into something between ten and fifteen folks. I would go into an area, physical rehab or the seniors clinic, for example, and become a presence, develop sort of the demonstration project that there was a need, and then they would hire someone.

So I did all kinds of things within that system, but as more people came on, the salaries weren't always equitable. I didn't think the system always worked in a very ethical manner, . . . professional manner. Many medical systems don't. They had a reshuffling and I really began to think about moving to a new position. And then I took a course from Arvone Fraser, who is the wife of our previous congressman here in Minnesota. She is a dynamite woman. The course was on women and leadership. That was in '82. It was a fascinating class and that helped me make the move out!

I see, okay. That was a big impetus?

That was. It really gave me the confidence to take the risk to go into private practice. I had two very good friends who really encouraged me, and [so I joined this practice that I am with now. We are a group of five women, all doctoral-level psychologists, and all committed to finding a good balance between our work lives and our families].

How are you able to integrate relationships, like a parent and so on, as a partner, a marriage partner, into your working life?

Well, I found first the setting. I am in charge of my own schedule so I set my own hours. I decide when I want to work. My daughter has a soccer game tonight and I know I often work later Mondays seeing couples and I'm not doing that in the summers. I'm in charge and I want to see her soccer game, so I go.

And then I have a partner who is also committed to supporting me and to supporting the kids and so we do a lot of trade offs. My daughter's going to be alone part of the day, so he's going home at lunch to see how she's doing and . . .

So you really work at the balance?

We do, and this is a whole community, this practice of mine, where we all support each other. That is, I think, pretty unique that we've been together, I think. Some of them have been here sixteen, seventeen years, and I've been here fourteen now. And that's just pretty unique.

And I think it takes a fair amount of creativity on the part of all of us to make this practice a community and a supportive one. And one where we can challenge each other as well, in terms of
. . .

. . . to keep growing.

Exactly. And we each have our own area of interest and expertise. [We meet weekly to discuss cases so that provides a richness and continuity to the whole developmental process that is a part of seasoning as a therapist. An integral part of this process is knowing oneself, so we also talk about what is going on in our personal lives. Maybe some of my most challenging and creative work has been in this area so tritely called "personal growth." It takes courage, intentionality, and self-awareness to plumb the depths of what Jung called the "shadow self."]

So I think part of the secret to my being able to do this in a way that's very workable is the folks that I work with. [I think it is a very committed and creative group, pioneering for ourselves how to make our way with consensual decision-making, and accommodating different needs and dreams. An example of this is] Evelyn, our office manager—she's almost eighty-one. She's been here almost since Day One. She came on board in her sixties and she's now retiring.

At age eighty! That's amazing!

[Well, it's a first for all of us. Another person I mentioned in my questionnaire who was important in my professional evolution as a therapist was Minna Shapiro. I was in a consultation group with her over a period of eight years. She is in her mid-eighties now, another role model that you can practice and be creative and productive as long as you want to.]

CREATIVE ACCOMPLISHMENTS

What do you consider to be your most creative achievement at this point in your life?

I think it is the work I do on a daily basis. It is built on everything that I have done up to this point. It is about being as effective as I can be, as a therapist or in my relationships with friends and family. I don't want to separate the two. I think sustaining a relationship with anyone takes a great deal of hard work, creativity, and humbleness.

I could say, well, this is a garden, or there's a journal article, or my winning the recipe contest, all those kinds of things, but I think that that's not the everyday important thing.

In what area of your life are you most able, at this point, to be creative?

I think in my work, and now in my garden. I don't have as much time for such things [both laughing]. But, and I think it's not just my work as a therapist, but also to think about my relationships with people, be it my children or my husband or my friends. But that's, you know, kind of stretching, and we talk a lot about relationships and a lot about taking risks and being fully available in that relationship.

What do you consider to be your creative attributes?

[Creative attributes. I think persistence—sort of a stubbornness. I think I have a passion for learning and lots of curiosity. My daughter teases me that I am always wanting to take a class. Tops on the list are studying Italian, and Italian cooking, in Italy, of course. When I don't have to be so invested in my work, I have a long list of things I'd like to do. Another attribute is being able to put things that are seemingly unrelated together. I have a whole set of visuals that I have pulled together to help couples develop greater awareness of themselves and of the complex dance that is their relationship. I like to think about different learning styles, not just my own, which tends to be visual, to help people learn in the ways they best learn. My goal is to use different modalities to help people shift their worldview, to let go of old habits and beliefs, and open to new possibilities. An example of this is bringing a bottle of molasses to the Junior Great Books class that I taught to fifth graders. It was a powerful way to help them understand what the word "treacle" meant in *Alice in Wonderland*. Other creative attributes? I guess I'm pretty intuitive, and I like to go the extra mile, learn a little more, push the envelope a little more just to see what is there. My style when it comes to gardening or cooking or planning something is to read different books or visit gardens or notice the possibilities around me, and create my own ideas from there. I don't tend to follow recipes, but I get good ideas from those starting points. I also tend to tolerate frustration pretty well, so that if I'm stymied the first time around, I let out a holler—literally or figuratively—and try again. And lastly, I'd say I'm pretty playful and gutsy.]

You talked about your associates here. How would they describe your creative abilities or skills?

[I'm guessing my colleagues would mention similar abilities, especially my ability to pull together ideas into a new way of conceptualizing something. In addition, they would be complimentary about my baking and cooking, celebrate my use of color in gardening, laugh affectionately about my dancing spirit, and talk about my generosity in gifting others with what I know and things I make. One of my colleagues always thinks of me when she pulls out her Christmas decorations and finds a small decorated tree that I made for her to go with her color scheme.]

What influences do you think, Ann, guide or constrain your creativity?

Well, I think that's part of what's constraining me right now, is needing to invest as much as I am in my work life, because I'm the primary breadwinner right now. My husband has his own start-up company and that's not so financially secure. I think that's one of the ways I'm creative, is to support him in his venture. So that my energy is really flowing mostly towards work kinds of things and so there's less time for me, in terms of my own spiritual life, in terms of my own hobbies, pursuing, doing all the kinds of things that I would dearly love to do. So I think it's the time issue and just the reality of being the adult and the primary breadwinner. That makes it hard for me to develop other types of interests. I don't dance now, for example—that's missing from my life. So those are kind of important parts of me that are just kind of lying fallow for now.

Right. But you use the term "fallow," which means it can be or will be developed.

Oh, no question! [I was in a dance production that my friend Marie Winckler choreographed about eight years ago. As an over-forty dancer, I was thrilled there was so much movement left in my body, but also respectful of my need to be more careful with it. Even though I'm not as resilient as I used to be, I'm proud to tell you that I can still do cartwheels. I feel the most alive when I am moving.]

QUESTIONS RELATED TO THE "MANIFESTO FOR CHILDREN"

Would you say that you're in love with your work?

I think so. I have a lot of passion and dedication, and I think that comes across to couples and to the people I work with. And then to go the mile if I don't get something, I consult, I have several people I pay for consultation, I read. I have a stack of things next to my side of the bed to read that's very tall.

That you work at?

Well, I work at it or, I, you know, if I don't understand something, or I want another view on a case, [I'll talk to a colleague, or get a nugget from a continuing-ed class or off the Internet news group I belong to. I'm on a telephone class that meets weekly, twenty to twenty-five therapists around the country and Canada join together to listen to a presentation, and discuss issues related to working with relational issues].

Oh, I see. When you say telephone class . . .

It's a telephone bridge, nowadays, where you can get together, just everybody dials into the same number at the same time and so I have that kind of ongoing infusion of ideas from people who, . . . we're all trained in the same way of working with couples, we have sort of a similar model, and then we all digest it and challenge it and stand on it, so that's sort of the one primary way I get my intellectual zap, in terms of what I'm doing. So that's a big part of what keeps me interested is all this growing knowledge, continuing to want to know more and to be more effective.

Can you describe your greatest strengths for me?

I think it is just my persistence and my passion and my awareness. I think I'm fairly attuned to people and adept at taking in information and integrating it. You could add flexible and resilient to the list.

In what ways is your creativity affected by the expectations of others?

[I think that coming from a home where the academic world was preeminent, going to a school on a university campus, and setting out on a path to be an academic myself by working in a hospital affiliated with the University of Minnesota limited me in some ways. At times I wish that I hadn't invested so much energy jumping through hoops, and getting my doctorate. There were ways my creativity was fostered in those environments, and ways that it wasn't. In applying for graduate school in a program called "Behavior Genetics" (a minor in genetics, a major in psychology), I was told by one professor that women didn't produce and therefore I wasn't welcome. My major professor had great confidence in me, though, and supported me to add a second program in clinical psychology so that I could pursue my interest in exploring the biology of human psychopathology. My interest in becoming a therapist was nourished only outside of the academic world, and it took some time for me to believe that that was "enough." My father tends to devalue those who don't do research and publish, so it took a certain amount of maturity on my part to step away from him and university mentors to find my own niche. I think the real shift came when I realized that I don't have to write books (i.e., to please someone else) and that's just fine. Now that I'm further down the road, I find myself thinking about writing. Writing to please *me*. I guess that's about feeling more in charge as I get more seasoning.]

Ann, you've answered this one, but let's just think about it a little bit here. Are you "free to play your own game" or "sing in your own key"?

I think in this setting I absolutely am. I don't think or feel that there are any gurus or experts. It's my work, the buck stops here.

What relationship has been most instrumental in helping you to achieve your potential?

[I think my marriage. I met my husband when I was fifteen. He came to this country as an exchange student from Sweden, and then decided to relocate here to go to graduate school. He has supported me in countless ways to explore professionally and personally. When I decided to be in the dance production, he was there. When I undertook to be responsible for the garden of a crisis center for women who were abused, he supported me. When I devoted a considerable amount of time and money to do advanced training in relational therapy, he was enthusiastic. Coming from a different culture where men do child-rearing and housework, he has been a full contributor on the homefront, which opens up more possibilities for me. There isn't much of a debate about that.]

If you were to think of him as a mentor, what obviously do you feel for a mentor?

I don't know. I don't think that most mentors are quite in that ballpark. We can think of some other mentors. I love him with a great deal of passion and sometimes get aggravated, all the kinds of things that go with two people trying to [GWM laughing] bring their two realities into an ongoing relationship.

In what ways do you interact with others to enhance their career or personal lives?

My bread and butter [laughing].

You have talked about this, with your colleagues here and so on. Are there others outside of your work group here that you interact with, to help them, I suppose, grow in different ways?

Well, there is my family, of course. And then children. I have gone into the classroom to be a part of my daughter's life. An example is teaching Junior Great Books.

Where did you teach?

At the elementary school . . . when my daughter was enrolled there.

This would be like an extracurricular, . . . it would be done after school.

Right, right. Another example was taking a group of fifth graders to see Shakespeare's play, *A Midsummer Night's Dream*. We read parts of it, talked about it, and then we went to see the play. That's the kind of thing that I would like to do more of.

Would you describe yourself more as well rounded, or more able at some things than others?

I would say I was more able at some things than others [laughing].

Not really well rounded?

Well, I don't know what "well rounded" means. I mean, I was interested to see the Manifesto and to think that probably, in many ways, all through my kind of schooling, I was well rounded because I could do well at pretty much all the subjects. Obviously, I'm not an artist and I'm not a musician.

GENERAL QUESTIONS ON CREATIVITY

What are your creative goals and aspirations for the future?

Well, I could probably separate that a little bit, in terms of work; it's to continue developing my own skills, and that means my own knowledge of myself. That's always a work in progress. I'd like to get better at what I do, without as much angst. That would be a goal that I've been kind of leading towards and that's where a lot of my energy goes. Goals . . . I think to develop more relationships outside of my work, to bring back more parts of my life. The artistic part doesn't have much space. And the spiritual part doesn't have as much space. I'd like to be better and better at bringing meditation into my life [laughing]. I'm a theoretical person—not applied—and I think that will help. But I think it's to develop gardening, and it's to find a way to bring my interest in cooking back into my life and relationships—they all kind of mold together. And then I'd like to travel; that's certainly one of the primary things I'd like to do. I see myself going off to elder hostels when I'm older.

If you could provide educators advice for nurturing creativity in children, what would you share with them?

Well, I was tempted, just as I got this material from you folks, to send you the article about our new graduation standards in the state of Minnesota, because they don't really want to help kids develop excellence or develop a passion. They've gone back to that well-rounded structure. So I would have them rethink that. There was a very good article written about kids taking advanced-placements classes. If they were to meet the graduation standards, they couldn't be following their passion and emphasizing more focused areas of interest. So I would have them look at what kinds of standards they're applying.

But, you know, my daughter's teachers have been pretty outstanding. I think what I've brought to them is the relational piece, in terms of thinking about some of the kids and their learning styles—like when I've been a volunteer mom in the classroom—to think about all that might be going on for a child. There are some dynamite teachers.

Well, these teachers that I've been very fortunate, or my daughter's been fortunate to have, they're the ones who write curricula. [My daughter's sixth-grade teachers developed a project called *Westward Ho!*, in which the kids learned American history by taking on roles. My daughter was an indentured servant for a while, a friend was assigned the role of a British soldier. I thought that was an outstanding way to really understand the American Revolution.]

So that they had a way of teaching those subjects that are fascinating and took a great deal of thought, in terms of what these kids learned. And they would merge all kinds of subject/content matter around this. So I think we were very fortunate. My son was not as fortunate. [There was more of a mix of children in his grade, the classes were too large, and I think a lot of kids, my son included, got lost. So in his case, I think there were constraints that got in the way of teachers really identifying and fostering his strengths.]

I would ask them that they would start languages much earlier. I mean, we're not in the school system that has afforded that. I think language and music should start earlier, because music helps develop a way of learning and thinking that fosters a lot down the road . . . developing that part of your brain. So I would want more of that, but I have to tell you that I have been quite pleased, by and large. Well, basically for my daughter. With my son, there were a lot of worksheets. I would like them to throw out the worksheets. He needed to have been more hands-on experiences, and he didn't get that.

[The question about offering advice to educators, perhaps. I'd like people to be open to the idea that each of our realities is valid, and even though somebody else's image doesn't match yours, open yourself to knowing more. It's about approaching another's view with curiosity and an intent to learn. And that the creative experience is not just about a product, but often a process.]

Now you work with a lot of parents in your practice. What advice would you give them for nurturing creativity, not with themselves so much, but with their children?

Well, I *do* do a lot of work with people struggling how to be the best parent they can and I think it's not just nurturing creativity, but it's allowing each child to be fully themselves and to be really attuned as a parent for what messages you're giving back to your child. We do a lot of work around each parent knowing what works for them, what was done to support them and what wasn't, subtle and not so subtle, like socialization messages, so that they can really allow their child to follow their own path. And that's a challenge, I think, in our culture, with television. So many messages that come to the kids.

Now if you could provide guidance to what we call "mentors" working with highly creative youngsters, what would you share with them?

I think the primary thing that I do is relational issues—is just sort of a three-part process, which I think is probably the most effective—and that is first, the listening, mirror back what you're hearing, to validate that it makes sense, whatever the idea is, from that person's point of view. And to support that and then continuing to explore what that is and just saying and hearing and validating that it makes sense. "Boy, that's an interesting idea" . . . to create the space for someone to pursue their own path or whatever it is.

But if you could design a time capsule that represented you as a creative person, what would you include in this capsule? Five to ten items?

[My raspberry cookbook that I put together for a charity auction . . . My twelve-year-old daughter's poem about her mom gardening, which catches the essence of that experience for me (see poem "The Garden" at end of Ann's case study), coupled with my dirty garden gloves and a picture that was part of a story about my volunteer "friendship" garden that appeared in the newspaper. . . . A picture of the neighborhood children dressed up and putting on a play in our living room. . . . A picture of a flower arrangement and table setting to reflect the ways I like to bring people together for good food and companionship. . . . A well-worn poster from my office illustrating the challenge of any two people actually communicating heart to heart, coupled with a worksheet I helped to develop. . . . An e-mail I just sent to another therapist about an "idea." . . . The videotape of *Dark Dances*, where I danced the role of the "earthling," coupled with an audiotape of me being silly dancing up a storm with the kids. . . . And the talking stick I was given at a conference where I danced. The conference was on becoming a crone . . . for women in transition as they move through menopause. And lastly, one of my photographs of a river from the north shore of Lake Superior, a place I find a deep connection with my spirituality.

It is interesting to note that my doctoral dissertation and published journal articles didn't make the cut.]

SUMMARY

The case study of Ann Lumry illustrates that creative potential measured in childhood *does* predict creative achievement later in adulthood. However, there are other important factors that may be equally or more significant in supporting creative behavior. Ann's case illustrates a number of these factors:

- knowing, understanding, taking pride in, practicing, developing, exploiting, and enjoying your greatest strengths
- learning to free yourself from the expectations of others and to walk away from the games they impose on you
- finding a great teacher or mentor
- learning the skills of interdependence and sharing them gladly
- doing what you love and can do well.

Ann is able to practice, take pride in, and enjoy her strengths by organizing her work life so that she can pursue other passions, as well as maintain a sense of humor and not sweat the small stuff. She says that it has taken some psychotherapy, but she is on the way to freeing herself from others' expectations and is "playing her own game." She practices the skills of interdependence and gladly shares her talents. She practices with four other doctoral-level psychologists who are women, wives, and mothers. They have had a cooperative system functioning together for 14 years, growing and maturing together professionally. Ann relies on others for a nudge to take risks and "reality testing" to reign in her worry-wart tendencies. Others depend on Ann for her intuitive ability; persistence; perceptiveness; integrity; follow-through; passion; organizational skills; "big-picture thinking"; and people skills. Ann is applying her superior creative skills to her work, marriage, and to her family—a tough but admirable balancing act!

"The Garden"

My mother is sitting outside our house planting many beautiful flowers. She has a hopeful look on her face, determined her garden will grow. She did her work so carefully, planting flowers in the Earth. Her expression looked as if she had seen sun shine after many rainy days.

Her patterned, dirty gloves covered her hands and her clothes were covered in dirt, but yet she continued planting her garden that she has wanted for so many years. She was trying to make our world a bit more beautiful than it already was.

She hummed quietly to herself. She kept looking up at the sky wondering when the sun would come out and shower her flowers with sun light so they could grow. She thought of how beautiful her flowers would be, she could already smell them.

—Emilie Hedlund, age 12

Friendship Garden offers peace, tranquillity to home's residents

By Karen Gail Jostad
Star Tribune Staff Writer

Like many gardens, the one at Cornelia Place in Minneapolis is tended lovingly by its creators, psychologists Bonnie Gray and Ann Lumry.

Their greatest pleasure, though, may be the joy and tranquillity it brings to residents of Cornelia Place, a short-term residence in the Seward neighborhood for women experiencing mental-health crises due to past physical or sexual abuse.

"When you're trying to work through the pain of being severely traumatized as a child, one way is through using words," Gray said. "But it's also helpful to have something that isn't about words — a nonverbal way to grieve, to get grounded or comfort yourself."

How did "Friendship Garden" come about?

First there was the gift of hostas to Cornelia Place from the Sisters of St. Joseph of Carondelet, who were moving out of Holy Spirit Convent. Sister Karen Hilgers is a founding member of Cornelia Place and the order supports it financially.

Then annuals and perennials started arriving — a gift from Vicki Chenoweth of Chenoweth Floral and Greenhouses in New Brighton.

"Vicki has donated almost all the garden stuff," said Judith Oliver, Cornelia's executive director. "It [the garden] is just really wonderful — even for me to see it when I arrive. It's very grounding and healing for the residents."

Rich Kuehne and Joanne and Dick Heiser, Lumry's neighbors in New Brighton, donated wild violets, ferns and hostas.

So, for the past three years, the skillful hands of Gray and Lumry have woven a floral tapestry of irises and tulips in the spring — dahlias, zinnias, lilies, impatiens, begonias and roses in the summer — and mums and asters in the fall.

Garden flourishes

"We started from nothing and had a pretty developed garden when the doors opened in October of '96," said Lumry, who with her husband, Bo Hedlund, "dug out

Helping out

stumps, old asphalt and lots of chunks of things."

"Next year we'll add another section to it," Gray said. "We're going to try to make the back yard feel more like a little courtyard with a couple of chairs in the garden so you can sit."

The idea, she said, is to "provide a sense of comfort, an opportunity to get centered or grounded through the garden, the earth — through something that's beautiful and colorful."

It seems to work.

Said one Cornelia Place resident, "Just looking at the colors in the garden gives me a sense of peace and tranquillity. This beautiful garden nurtures me and restores my hope."

Oliver praised Gray and Lumry and the 50 or so other volunteers who do everything from cook to answer phones to fix plumbing and handle mailings. She also complimented the Seward Neighborhood community.

Psychologist Darwin Hendel, research associate and senior analyst at the University of Minnesota and a Seward resident since 1974, has been on Cornelia's board of directors for about seven months.

"As a new board member, I've

been telling my neighbors and members of the neighborhood about Cornelia Place," Hendel said. "It's something that I think is very much in keeping with the general atmosphere of the Seward community, which is very diverse and accepting."

Hendel can wield a trowel as deftly as his wife, Bonnie Gray, but initially, his primary contribution will be to help set up data bases and follow-up studies to document the effectiveness of the services offered.

Cornelia Place was started after discussion among female therapists, psychologists and social workers about what could be done to help women suffering severe trauma from physical and sexual abuse.

The 24-hour residence is licensed as an adult foster-care facility and as an outpatient mental-health clinic. Clients must be referred by their primary therapist, and Cornelia staff work closely with them.

Residents are asked to contribute toward the cost of overnight care, but "our policy is to not turn away women because of payment difficulties," said Holly Smart, clinical program director.

Cornelia Place staffers are master-level psychologists or licensed social workers. The facility also utilizes interns from area colleges and universities.

Start-up costs were covered by gifts from individual donors and foundations. Last year the residence received an appropriation from the state of Minnesota as a "pilot program providing a unique and valuable service."

"Our staff is underpaid and overworked, but really dedicated," Oliver said. "It's like a calling when you do this kind of work. As far as we know, we're one of a kind in the nation that offers this type of therapy and residence for women."

For more information, call Judith Oliver at 612-728-0480.

— If you know an outstanding volunteer you'd like featured, write to Helping Out, Faith & Values, Star Tribune, 425 Portland Av., Minneapolis, MN 55488.

Star Tribune photo by Richard Sennott
Psychologists Ann Lumry, front, and Bonnie Gray created "Friendship Garden" at Cornelia Place in Minneapolis.

JIM YOUNG

A MULTITALENTED ADVENTURE SEEKER AND BEYONDER

"I am frighteningly well rounded"—Jim (1999)

Jim Young was one of the most precocious and creative children in the study. In fact, his elementary-school teacher exclaimed that he had too much creativity for his own good! Phrases such as "holy terror" and "hard to control" were used to describe him. He is unique in that he came from lower socioeconomic parents who were hard-working and hard-drinking but provided positive and stimulating educational experiences for him. He was brought into the world near the end of their lives. His father died when Jim was 17, leaving his mother and Jim in financial hardship. This made things difficult.

Not only were his psychological test scores very high, which eventually predicted outstanding creative achievements as an adult, but other variables or factors during the 40-year study period such as having a mentor and falling in love with his work were equally important to his achievements and future aspirations.

SCHOOL YEARS

Jim was tested on a variety of measures while he attended elementary school. From grades 2 (1958) through 6 (1963) he was involved in a number of exploratory studies on creativity, and also tests that purported to measure the same creative skills. Dr. Torrance and his graduate students and associates from the Bureau of Educational Research in the College of Education at the University of Minnesota designed this battery of creativity tests. Jim's ability to perform creative tasks in written and figural forms amazed the researchers as well as his teachers. His estimated creativity quotient at that time was 136, while his intelligence quotient was 150. His test protocols and writing samples reveal a strong interest in science, space exploration, fantasy, and adventure. His drawings in grades 2 and 3 reveal his interests and display his exceptional ability.

Grade 2 drawing

Grade 3 drawing

During the early period in elementary school, Jim had future career images to be a writer, an astronaut, and a paleontologist. He studied classical piano for six years. He was constantly drawing dinosaurs—on his books, on his hands, and even on his desk!

At age 2 Jim entered a preschool program at the University of Minnesota and then enrolled in the grade 1 class taught by Mrs. Amadon at University Elementary School. His parents owned and operated a restaurant in Dinkytown, which was adjacent to the campus. Luckily, he encountered teachers who understood his "radical right brain" and channeled his creative impulses in positive ways. Wayne Kirk, his grade 6 teacher, described Jim as imaginative, eager to learn and explore, and inclined to have ideas that are unusual and unconventional. He attributes the synthesis of his radical right brain to Rod Myers (now Dr. Myers), his grade 4 teacher. Myers (1980) recalled the following incident involving Jim (in the article a pseudonym for Jim was used):

> For his first two weeks in a fourth-grade class of gifted children, Mack (Jim Young) drew dinosaurs on his binder, napkins, and the back of his left hand. His teacher attempted to involve Mack (Jim) in the curricular tasks he had set for the class of 25 lively and competitive nine-year olds, but it was useless. Once, after making what he imagined to be a highly motivational introduction in a social-studies unit, the teacher was taken aback to find Mack (Jim) at his elbow, proudly showing his latest version of a brontosaurus on a paper towel. Overcoming an urge to scold Mack (Jim) for completely ignoring the task that was set for the class, the teacher hesitated and mumbled something to the effect that the pencil sketch was a good rendering of a brontosaurus.
>
> Mack (Jim) never did complete the social-studies unit, and he continued to draw dinosaurs and scenes about twenty-first-century space travel. Today he is a successful novelist, specializing in science fiction. Subsequent teachers in elementary and high school had indifferent success in getting this keen-minded youngster to perform "to his capacity" in the classroom—and fortunately, they were also unable to prevent Mack (Jim) from dreaming, drawing, and writing.

Jim reports that he had few friends at this time of his life; in retrospect he has said that "he was a show-off, and no one likes a show-off." Jim understood his sociometric status in grade 5 in his response to the following question: Name three people in your class who start a lot of ideas, which no one accepts? Jim's response was: 1) me; 2) myself; and 3) I. He missed a good deal of school in first and second grades due to illness and found that he was forced to rely on his imagination to be noticed, and it got him into trouble!

In a recent correspondence (1999) with Rod Myers (Jim's fourth-grade teacher), he stated that Jim was famous for his digressing from the course of studies. In Rod's words, "he was a daydreamer, a doodler, and mostly an indifferent scholar. While I was teaching math, he'd draw a lovely dinosaur." Apparently he would distract others. Myers placed a female student to sit near him. Apparently the teacher had success with this strategy; it seemed to have a calm and steadying influence on Jim. Myers indicated that his academic achievement was about average in comparison with a class that was full of very bright children. However, on an absolute basis (i.e., not compared to his classmates) Jim was a good deal above average in all subjects. He was particularly interested in paleontology in the fourth grade. He read very well, and widely.

Myers stated that Jim's creativity manifested itself in drawing and talking. His imagination revealed itself in both endeavors. His mind was very active at all times. Jim had hypotheses about exotic and unusual animals. He wondered and fantasized about space travel. He liked to share his ideas with everyone. Myers's final comment in his 1999 letter was: "Undoubtedly, one of the most imaginative pupils I ever had." Regarding Jim's future career, he thought that he was capable of being a scientist, "but obviously, he could have been a number of things—and has been!"[1]

Wayne Kirk was Jim's sixth-grade teacher. In recent correspondence to me, Kirk stated:

> Probably one of the most interesting students I ever taught. It wasn't until about fifth or sixth grade that he finally, reluctantly agreed that dinosaurs no longer existed. He had been sure that in some remote area of the earth they still existed. Perhaps he was right. Some twenty or so years ago a fish of that era was found off the coast of Africa. He was a wonderful writer and always thinking of the unusual.[2]

Throughout his high school years he continued to find creative outlets in music, the visual arts, drama, writing, and science fiction. While there, he founded the Minnesota Science Fiction Society, its amateur magazine, and its convention, which still continues.

FIRST FOLLOW-UP

Dr. Torrance conducted the first follow-up with the elementary-school students in 1980, 22 years after testing them. At the time, Jim was still living in Minneapolis. His mother had just died and he had just completed his doctoral degree at the University of Minnesota. He worked his way through college and graduate school as a medical illustrator and editor of the magazine for the School of Engineering and played in a band performing rock-and-roll music. Jim had reported that the greatest obstacle to his continued achievement was his family obligations, which were enormously emotionally draining to him. However, since his mother died in January 1980, that "obstacle" had been removed. In 1980 he reported that his three most creative achievements since high school were "1) publishing my first novel *The Face of the Deep* (1979); 2) writing my dissertation; 3) writing and performing music."

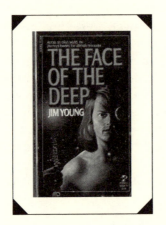 

Jim had reported an inordinate number of public and personal creative achievements. His creative-achievement score for quality rating was 9.0 out of 10, which was well above the average for the case-study group. He founded the first Futures Study course at the General College at the University of Minnesota (1973–1977). The goal was to teach inner-city under-achievers and suburban, gifted high school students creative divergent thinking in a future context. He said that it was one of the greatest pleasures of his life to teach this course.

Jim felt in 1980 that managing to get a dissertation in educational history and philosophy on Utopia Political Theory with special emphasis on Futurism accepted by his committee at the University of Minnesota was a creative achievement in itself! The dissertation, "How Bright the Vision: Social and Educational Structures in Modern Utopian Literature" (1980), discussed the issue of social planning from the viewpoints of three utopists: H.G. Wells, Aldous Huxley, and George Orwell. Jim concluded that the modern theory of utopia construction asserts that there are four components to civilization: human nature, technology, educational systems, and government. Jim had earned enough credits in physics and history to be eligible for undergraduate degrees in those fields, as well as education. It is interesting to note that later in Jim's career, he would work for the U.S. Foreign Service in various countries, assisting them with social planning and policy development. His studies in history would enable him to be well prepared for this work.

In 1980 Jim indicated that Rod Myers, his fourth-grade teacher, had become his mentor and had been an impetus to synthesize his "... radical right brain." He stated that "... fourth grade ended, but his influence has been permanent." Jim concluded the impact of Myers and his elementary-school years by saying: "I hope and have continued to synthesize aspects of the sciences, arts, and humanities, which was in great part what I believe U.E.S. [University Elementary School] was all about."

When asked to recall an incident in elementary school that influenced his career, he wrote the following:

> The most important occurred in my fourth-grade class. A guest lecturer spoke to us about the cold war, concluding his discussion by asserting it was up to my generation to end the conflict. I have worked at that in the arts and social sciences ever since. My first novel, a juvenile adventure, is a kind of parable about the cold war.
>
> A second important moment came in my sixth-grade class; my teacher very much liked an abstract realist painting of the Oedipus cycle that I did outside of class and brought it to school. While I have actually done some professional illustrating in my time, this teacher's comments encouraged my interest in synthesizing the elements of literature and painting; and have continued to draw across universes of discourse like that ever since.

At age 29, Jim described his current lifestyle as "not very satisfying" and recounted the following as his primary frustration in his life: "My schooling has interfered with my intellectual and social development; 1980, however, marks the end to this and I hope for a dramatic improvement, which is to some extent already apparent."

As for the future over the next ten years, Jim forecasted the following, indicating that he would be much freer to "play his own game": "A writer and musician—for me the two are intertwined and some of the writing I intend to do is social research. If I can land a recording contract, I'll be able to develop my own route entirely in financial security." In 1980 Jim stated that because he had to look after his ailing mother during the 1970s his life had been distorted, preventing him from developing socially as he would otherwise have done. He was "free" now, but at a terrible price.

Jim was invited by Dr. Torrance and Dr. Anne Crabbe to give a seminar on future studies and writing science fiction to students involved in the Future Problem-Solving Program during May 1981. He did an excellent job in getting the students to practice creative problem-solving in the context of futures study at the conference. The students were so enthralled with Jim that they followed him to the students' residence building, where he entertained them with his own musical compositions well into the evening. He told Dr. Torrance at that conference that he hoped to enter the U.S. Foreign Service.

George F. Kennan greatly influenced Jim's decision to enter the U.S. Foreign Service. Kennan was a career foreign-service officer. He had been deputy chief of mission at Embassy Moscow during World War II and briefly served as ambassador to Moscow (1952–1953) near the end of the Truman administration. He was also ambassador to Yugoslavia (1961–1963). Kennan is author of the famous article about the containment doctrine published under the pseudonym "X" in *Foreign Affairs*. After retiring, he taught and wrote at the Institute for Advanced Study in Princeton. His memoirs are probably his greatest contribution to thinking about international relations; there are several volumes of his essays, and historical works as well. Jim indicated that what he admires most about Kennan ". . . is that he was able, in the 1940s, to see the evolution of post-communist Europe. No one else equaled that audacity of vision in twentieth-century diplomacy."[3]

Jim, circa 1998

MIDDLE TO LATE CAREER

His response in the 1998 follow-up questionnaire indicated that Jim was working as the political counselor (i.e., head of section) in the U.S. Foreign Service stationed at the U.S. Embassy in Lagos, Nigeria. He had been a principal formulator of the policy for the country, which was in the midst of political strife, moving from a military dictatorship to a democracy. He has done well with the Department of State and has risen in the ranks rapidly. However, he is not completely happy. He said: "I have always loved the nonbureaucratic aspects of the Foreign Service and have managed to tolerate the rest." It is clear that he misses his truly creative outlets—music, art, and writing fiction. Even though he writes reports for the State Department, which may be made into a book, he is not fully able to use his creativity.

Jim moved into the U.S. Foreign Service in 1981 shortly after attending the National Future Problem-Solving Program Bowl in Lincoln, Nebraska. Since 1981 he has spent about equal amounts of time in Africa and Eastern Europe. He has moved up the ranks from consular officer in Frankfurt (Germany) to arms-control officer in Moscow, to his current position as political counselor in the embassy in Lagos. His work in the Foreign Service has exacted a toll. He is divorced, has little time to do much writing, and has no time for music. He expects to retire from the Foreign Service in 2001 and pursue his dream of writing and music. In fact, he plans to attend the University of Southern California (USC) to obtain a Master of Fine Arts degree, and to further network in California. At the same time, he will start writing a series of essays intended to engender a new progressive era. In his words, "U.S. President Bill Clinton and Prime Minister Tony Blair of England both seem to be pointing in that direction, but there doesn't really seem to be anyone out there trying to explain what could be done with health and social security—to name two critical issues." Ambitious goals, to say the least. In 1998, Jim ended a personal letter to Dr. Torrance with this statement: "I've been away from home too long."[4] Jim's quality creative score for public achievements was 8.5 out of 10.0—among the highest in the study. When asked "what do you consider to be the most creative thing(s) that you have done in your hobbies?" he stated that as follows: "I have never given up my dreams of living by my art, though my work for the State Department does not allow much time for it. I suppose publishing my novel *Armed Memory* in 1995 is my most purely creative accomplishment."

INTERVIEW IN FEBRUARY 1999

This interview in 1999 with Jim Young was conducted via mail, because the telephone connection to Nigeria was neither satisfactory nor safe while the country was in the midst of political change. At age 48 Jim reflected on the early influences on his creativity; his career path and transitions; creative accomplishments; and finally some general comments on creativity. His own words tell a cogent story.

EARLY INFLUENCES ON CREATIVITY

At what age were you first aware of your creativity? How did this show itself?

I have always been aware of my creativity. My first love was drawing, followed by sculpting and my work in the plastic arts, including woodworking. Although my memory is far from accurate when it comes to my early childhood, I believe I must have started drawing about the time I started talking (at about age one).

I always loved acting, and did quite a bit of it through college. In fact, I made two comic films in college, each about thirty minutes in length. My parents actively discouraged me from pursuing an acting career, at first by trying to encourage my interest in music.

My parents forced me to study piano. I exhibited some talent at the instrument even though I disliked my first teacher, with whom I studied for two years. At the end of a fourth year of study—in sixth grade, I decided that I wasn't progressing rapidly enough and abandoned serious musical study. I was blessed with a powerful singing voice, and continued to sing in church until my voice started changing at about age thirteen. Just at this time, in early 1964, the Beatles broke on the scene, and that dramatically changed my attitude toward music. I wanted desperately to be in a rock band. And just at about the same time, my parents' lives underwent a trauma: my mother became seriously ill, forcing my parents to sell the family business—a restaurant—and plunging us into financial difficulties. My mother slowly gained ground, but my parents' marriage suffered; had my father not died in April 1968, when I was seventeen, I believe my parents would have divorced. This meant that there was no way I could afford a guitar—the essential rock instrument—and entailed my acting almost like a character in an Edwardian novel who has to "keep up appearances" among a crowd of well-to-do acquaintances.

But it was possible to write under such circumstances, and I decided that I was going to be a writer. I worked on my high school newspaper, and then, at the University of Minnesota, on the college paper. I sold short stories, at first to local magazines, and eventually to national publications. Finally, in 1979, I sold my first novel.

But I didn't abandon music, and as I got into college and had a bit of income, I began playing keyboards with several bands, at first covering songs by others, which you have to do if you're going to work, and then writing some of my own. Towards the late 1970s, one incarnation of this band was surprisingly successful playing the fraternity and college-bar circuit in Minnesota and Wisconsin. We got to the point where we were recording our original music, but failed to get a recording contract. In 1980, all this came to an end: my mother (whom I had to take care of at the last) died, I completed my doctorate, and my girl friend moved to Chicago to start her graduate studies. In mid-1980, we disbanded. I've continued writing music, and I've been in a few amateur bands since then, but I have to have a certain measure of stability in my life and could not find much of it at the bottom of the music industry. Nevertheless music remains the center of my creative life; I need to have music playing when I'm reading or writing for best results. Not always possible in a newsroom or an embassy, I hasten to add.

At elementary-school age, if appropriate to first answer, what influence did your schooling have on your creative ability?

University Elementary School [U.E.S.] was a great influence on my life. If I had gone to a public school, I'm sure my creative impulses would have been suppressed. I would have had a more difficult time making friends in that environment than at U.E.S.— I had one friend who left U.E.S. for a year and subsequently returned, and spent quite a bit of time explaining it to me. That said, I never fit in very well, especially because I was quite sick for extended periods in first and second grades. I'm sure being ill like that forced me to depend on my imagination more than normal— but that was a process that had clearly already begun. After I read quite a bit of Robert Louis Stevenson, and then read about his life when I was about twelve, I began to think that I must be rather like him in a lot of ways.

What specific incidents can you remember in your childhood which enabled your creativity to develop?

I don't remember incidents that enabled my creativity as much as people who did so; three people stand out: my fourth-grade teacher, Robert Myers (with whom I am still in periodic contact), because of his ability to open up the adventurous aspects of learning; and my sixth-grade teacher, Mr. Kirk, who had a similar talent. Both men were able to balance the imaginative with the mundane. Our minister at the First Methodist Church in Dinkytown could also do this, although in a different context. All three of these men occasionally talked about Einstein's theory of relativity, which powerfully drove my imagination. I started reading science fiction passionately at about this time in response to these stimuli.

Was there any influence at elementary-school age which you now recognize as having had an impact on your subsequent career or chosen field of work?

I was always interested in ancient civilizations, which in turn grew into an interest in other cultures. But the real motivation for my interest in foreign affairs came from my high school years and in response to the Vietnam War.

What were the qualities, skills, behaviors of whoever is identified at this age?

As stated, the real motivation came later, and largely in response to momentous events—for instance, the Vietnam War and the Watergate crisis—not a single person or a group of people.

What would you say was the most important lesson you learned with regard to your creativity at this age?

I learned that others are jealous of your talent. If I hadn't come down with pneumonia in both first and second grades, I think my athletic skills would have come more decidedly to the fore; as it was, I was two years behind others, and never really did catch up athletically until I was out of high school. So I was forced to rely on my creative skills, and they got me in trouble as often as not. I was a show-off, and nobody likes one.

How would your peers have described you at the time?

Not very favorably. I only had one or two close friends in elementary school.

CAREER PATHS AND TRANSITIONS

What is your present job?

I am currently the political counselor of the U.S. Embassy in Lagos, Nigeria. I have been a Foreign Service officer since 1981.

How do you apply creativity to this work?

Although the Foreign Service can be quite bureaucratic, it is essential to be creative in developing policy options. In my current position, I am the person who has originated a good deal of U.S. policy toward Nigeria, which Washington must digest and approve before implementing. The key is to develop a range of options, along the lines of Ludwig van Betalanffy's "fan" of alternative futures.

Have you had other jobs? If so, were you able to work creatively while in these jobs?

I've served in eight previous positions in the Foreign Service, and in some of them it was indeed possible to work creatively. Prior to entering the Foreign Service, I worked as a graduate teaching assistant, editor, and freelance writer, not to mention my work as a musician, but I generally found that the more creative the position, the less it paid, or sometimes, the less steadily it paid. Perhaps the least-creative jobs were the least painful to me—working as a marketing analyst at the Fisher Nut Company in St. Paul was bland and uncreative, but I didn't mind it. Then again, I worked there for less than a year. I'd guess that eighteen months would be the maximum amount of time I could spend working in that sort of position. At least as a junior officer in the diplomatic corps, I was able to rotate from one job to another fairly quickly— visas, baby registration, passports, immigration visas.

What major changes/transitions have you experienced in your working life?

There's an old saying at the State Department: Every three moves is the equivalent of one house fire. This is true both literally and metaphorically.

What caused these transitions?

The simple answer is stress. I seem to be able to deal with the stress of travel and dealing with other cultures quite well. My former wife could not.

When you made changes in your working life, was there anyone whom you relied on for support and advice? If so, what did they do which was most helpful for you at these times?

My brother and my best friend from high school. They kept up a long conversation with me, lasting many months, so that I eventually realized once more that there is still intelligent life on Planet Earth.

How are you able to integrate relationships—as a parent, as a partner, as someone's child—into your working life?

So far, I haven't really been very successful at it.

CREATIVE ACCOMPLISHMENTS

What do you consider to be your most creative achievement?

My work on the development of U.S. policy toward Nigeria. This required all my resources—and I'm not sure it's been enough. My writing and music certainly were not as important.

In what area of your life are you most able to be creative?

Under less-stressful circumstances than the last year in Nigeria, I have managed to be most creative in my nondiplomatic writing, some of which is musical. There hasn't really been any time for anything like a creative outlet here because of the press of work.

What do you consider to be your creative attributes?

One of the main sources of my creativity is wordplay. This doesn't just include punning, but formulating parodies, dreaming of farces, and the like. In Nigeria, there is plenty of incentive to view the world as a tragic slapstick comedy anyway.

Another source of my creative impulse comes from my enjoyment of juxtaposition. A few years ago, I read a study of the Beatles called *Revolution in the Head*—written by Ian MacDonald; London: 1994, Fourth Estate, Ltd.; there's been a North American edition, but I don't know who published it back home—which discussed at some length the efforts of John Lennon and Paul McCartney to draw inspiration from the random joining of ideas or events. I was never really aware until I read this book that "random" art was a minor movement in the art world of the sixties. Did I absorb that interest in juxtaposition from growing up in that period? Probably. MacDonald's introductory essay struck me as a brilliant cultural history of the sixties; the bulk of the book is a close reading of the Beatles' recordings.

One of my creative weaknesses is clearly in coming up with the punch line to jokes. I can do the setting, create a lot of physical and verbal comedy, but I find it very hard to write jokes as such.

How would your close associates describe your creative attributes?

There's quite a range of response to somebody like me. For instance, my immediate supervisor, the deputy chief of mission, recently told me she admires me for my ability to look forward constantly, and my avoidance of getting stuck about thinking in terms of the past—in this case, a reference to the era of Nigeria's late dictator, General Sani Abacha. Others tend to think of me as a very witty person. Unfortunately, in the realm of music, my creativity has caused me some grief: I'm particularly good at improvisation, which is what jazz is all about, but not necessarily what rock is all about; I have had my share of arguments with lead-guitar players in particular who wanted everything to sound exactly—and I mean *exactly*—as it did on a recording we were covering.

What influences guide or constrain your creativity; for example, overall life purpose, career goal, financial burdens?

The short answer to this is that I made so much money in the music business that I had to take the Foreign Service test. The longer answer is that I sought out a career that required me to use my brain, that provided for intellectual growth, and that promised some sort of pension at a fairly early age—in the U.S. Foreign Service, you can retire with twenty years' service at age fifty. This quickly ruled out the military, although I considered it. Reading George Kennan's *Memoirs* as an undergraduate made me realize that I could contribute to our society through government service, and I did. People only a few years older than me were inspired to undertake government service by President Kennedy's inaugural address; although I remember watching it on TV at U.E.S., I guess I was a little too young to have been inspired by Kennedy's speech. What I didn't reckon with was the burden that such a career places on one's family.

The workload in the Foreign Service is such that you don't have the spare time you might have in a less-taxing job; especially in difficult places like Lagos or Washington—one's own capital is always the most demanding place in anybody's diplomatic corps—you have to use what spare time you have to recuperate and get ready to fight another day.

GENERAL QUESTIONS ON CREATIVITY

If you could provide educators advice for nurturing creativity in children, what would you share with them?

Highly creative children can be very disruptive; I know I was. But that's usually a child's response to boredom. In the "Sesame Street" era, attention spans are shorter than they were in the "Captain Kangaroo" era, making the potential for disruptive behavior even greater than before. Instilling in children a sense that learning is an adventure may help to overcome their impetus toward boredom. I think that's an approach that can apply to both boys and girls, though it was obviously more appealing to boys in my generation.

My own past has been remarkably channeled by my own desire to have a swashbuckling good time. An attitude no doubt exacerbated by reading Edgar Rice Burroughs in the mid-1960s; Michael Dirda recently wrote in 1999 in the *Washington Post* that he felt few kids can read Burroughs any more—true, as far as I can tell from my family members. The sciences drew me in when I was in my pre-teens, as I've mentioned above, because they represented adventure. Foreign affairs effected an analogous lure on me in the late teens.

If you could provide parents advice for nurturing creativity in children, what would you share with them?

I'm not well qualified to answer this one, considering that I have no children and have experienced a divorce. But I'm a very family-oriented person, and I spend a lot of time with my young relatives, and on the basis of that experience, I can say that they find the adventure of our times very appealing too.

If you could provide guidance to mentors working with highly creative youngsters, what would you share with them?

I think people need mentors, because they need a point of view from somebody other than their parents about themselves and what they're doing. Consequently, it's important for a mentor not to get into a position in which he or she is competing with the mentored person's family—easy to do if that person's family situation is significantly less than ideal.

If you could design a time capsule that represented you as a creative person, what would you include in this capsule? Say five to ten items?

The capsule would contain copies of my published works—so far that's two novels, a *Festschrift* translated from the German, and several handfuls of uncollected essays and short stories—some unpublished recordings, and a couple of films I made in college and graduate school. I'm told videotapes of the films still exist, but I don't have any in my possession.

What are your creative goals, aspirations, and dreams for the future? Please describe.

I've always wanted to work in the film industry—yes, another of my many career dreams—as both an actor and screenwriter. If I'm not promoted and the State Department doesn't offer me anything good after my next assignment, I will retire and try to get into the screen-writing Master of Fine Arts program at the University of Southern California as a means to this end. Of course, I'd still like to make ambassador, but that's not likely in the time limit of twenty years I set for myself, which ends in 2001. Along the way, I'd like to have a family again. Yes, I'm an ambitious person; maybe these goals are only slightly less than impossible to achieve.

Jim concluded the interview with the following comment:

Many of my closest friends refer to me as a many-layered person. I'm not sure that this exercise has explained that aspect of my psyche very well, but I think this structure plays an important role in my creativity. I'm aware that my associative mental processes "rub against" one another, producing the sense I have of new ideas bubbling up inside me. I feel that it's not my varied interests and talents that give the impression that I'm made up of many layers, but rather that my personality is somehow like a set of concentric spheres, and that people can see me moving from one part to another. In graduate school, I remember having a conversation about brain structure with a fellow student in the midst of which I made some sort of humorous aside. He replied that I must have no division between my right- and left-hand brain to make such a remark. It's more than twenty years ago, and I confess I can't remember what wisecrack I actually came up with. But I do remember thinking that the guy just didn't talk to many people with a sense of humor. Which is a long way of saying that I really do believe that creativity has some roots in a person's ability to break through one's own internal psychological barriers, and that it may well have a physical aspect that some people can sense going on inside them.

SUMMARY

The case study of Jim Young illustrates that his high creative potential as measured by the *Torrance Tests of Creative Thinking* in elementary school predicted later creative achievement as an adult. In addition, the significant factors of access to mentors, high focus, and persistence; using the skills of interdependence; and the freedom to play his own game continue to support Jim in his creative achievements.

Jim Young is one of the most creative of the group studied in Torrance's longitudinal study. He, by his own admission, is "frighteningly well rounded," and his elementary-school teachers thought that he was "too creative." He has interest and expertise in the fields of art, music, science, and social planning. His "radical right brain" has been put to good use in his current work as a diplomat and social planner in the U.S. Foreign Service. He still has ambitious goals to get back into the performing arts upon his retirement (2001) from his current work, and still expects to find time to "smell the roses." Mentors have played an important role in Jim's career. He cites eight or nine key individuals for whom he has deep respect and genuine affection. Among those mentors are elementary-school teachers; a university professor; some musician friends; and a couple of colleagues in the Foreign Service. Dr. Torrance was mentioned not as a mentor but as an individual who was clearly responsible for creating an outlet for his creativity when Jim was a student at University Elementary School.

During his elementary-school years, Jim had a few teachers who understood and cultivated his creative impulses. They encouraged his "off-beat" behavior. He still is in touch with his fourth-grade teacher. He has persevered despite the struggles he encountered as a young person (as a "holy terror" of a kid). His father passed away early in his life and he and his mother were deeply in debt. His music and art interests kept his dream alive and he had a clear future-career image: that of a writer and adventurer, which came to pass.

Jim has learned the skills of interdependence and has been recognized in his current job for his leadership to put a team together and keep them motivated. Finally, although he is not completely "free to play his own game" or "sing in his own key," he is now in a position to get the U.S. Government to listen to him, particularly on issues like the development of a facilitative approach to bringing communities, government, and the private sector together in the troubled Niger River Delta in Africa. In short, he has succeeded once —when it comes to Nigeria's troubled oil country—in getting others to play his game.

Jim's persona and career to date represents a "beyonder":

- a love and enjoyment of one's work
- persistence
- a purpose in life
- a diversity of experience
- high energy level
- sense of mission
- openness to change.

Indeed, a multitalented adventure seeker!

NOTES

1. Personal communication from Rod Myers to Garnet Millar, November 29, 1999, in possession of the author.

2. Personal communication from Wayne Kirk to Garnet Millar, December 2, 1999, in possession of the author.

3. Personal communication from Jim Young to Garnet Millar, December 22, 1999, in possession of the author.

4. Personal communication of Jim Young with Dr. E. Paul Torrance, May 17, 1998.

REFERENCES

Myers, R. E. (1980, October). "Creativity Revisited" (unpublished paper). Salem: Oregon Department of Education.

Young, J. M. (1979). *The Face of the Deep.* New York: Pocket Books.

Young, J. M. (1980). "How Bright the Vision: Social and Educational Structures in Modern Utopian Literature" (dissertation), University of Minnesota.

part three

THEMES FROM THE CASE STUDIES

Eighteen individuals from the original sample were selected for in-depth study (ten of these are included in part II). The majority of the interviews were conducted in Minneapolis, while a few individuals were interviewed over the telephone or, in one case, by mail. Part three summarizes all 18 interviews and discusses implications for the development of creativity in the home, school, and community. Five broad themes related to creativity are discussed for the case studies: early influences on creativity; career paths and transitions; creative accomplishments; response to the "Manifesto for Children" (Torrance, Henderson, & Presbury, 1983); and reflections on creativity by the individuals selected for case study.

The original sample of students (N=391) was composed of normal children, although the majority came from homes that were extremely supportive of schooling and education in general. The majority of the case studies (N=18), drawn from the original sample, were advantaged in that their parents had been well educated and had professional careers. The individuals in the case-study group carried on the tradition of post-secondary preparation and generally assumed professional careers. Certainly the level of intelligence was higher for the case studies than might be expected. The results and conclusions should be interpreted in the context of the individuals selected for case study.

twenty

EARLY INFLUENCES ON CREATIVITY

This chapter deals with the awareness of the individuals about their creativity and how it showed itself at an early age. Questions related to how schooling influenced their creative ability and what events may have impacted their chosen field of work are explored. In addition, the case studies are described through the "eyes" of their peers, and lessons learned about their creativity at this age are discussed.

One-half of the case studies recognized their creativity either before entering school, or during the elementary-school years (grades 3 through 6). Over one-third of the case studies were unaware of their creativity as children. One mentioned that in high school, he was able to "fix things" (mechanical and electrical) easily.

For those who recognized their creativity at an early age, involvement in some aspect of the "fine arts" was mentioned as a manifestation of creativity. They participated in drawing, sculpting, play-acting, music, dancing, and singing. Jim had a powerful singing voice, while Laurie wrote poetry and made journal entries "at the lake." Others stated that parents provided freedom at home to express themselves through music or creative dance. The University of Minnesota Elementary School was called "a creative place"—a school ahead of its time that rewarded students for creative behavior. Still others indicated that the creativity tests conducted at the schools provided awareness of creativity. Leadership qualities were recognized early in Cathy. She and the other girls were creative in getting her elected as class president. There were more boys than girls in her class. So they realized that they would have to influence two boys to win the election for class president. They bribed two boys with five cents to swing the vote. The girls won! Interestingly, Ted was in his forties before he realized that he was creative and "saw" things differently.

All case studies indicated that schooling overwhelmingly had a positive influence on their creative ability. Enthusiastic teachers who were creatively motivated and took the time to understand their students well were high on the list. These teachers used creative art and open-ended projects with their students. The teachers used a flexible curriculum allowing the students freedom; they graphed maps, designed automobiles, and made oral and visual presentations. Many students were able to read, unimpeded, great literary works, such as Robert Louis Stevenson. Creativity was not only encouraged, but also recognized at school by awards. The interaction with other bright and creative students in the two Minnesota schools also sparked the creative behavior of the students. After all, the majority of the students were from professional homes where the parents cared a great deal about the schooling and education of their children. A few students stated that living abroad in countries such as Denmark, Germany, and Austria with parents on sabbatical leaves provided enriching international experiences. Jim mentioned that a period of forced sickness while in elementary school created a great dependence upon his imagination. He later blazed through school far ahead of his peers and has become one of the most productive, creative students of the group studied.

The individuals in the case studies reported about people and activities in the school, home, and community that enabled their creativity to develop and excited their imaginations. At school, they remembered meaningful, cooperative projects on topics such as the United Nations, tasting foreign foods, writing imaginative stories, and various art projects. Several remember teachers who were inspiring, loved their work, and "mandated" that their students use creativity to think and learn. David K. vividly remembers his fourth-grade teacher, Rod Myers, challenging him by whispering in his ear, "Don't lose your creativity!" He never did and continues to be an extremely creative professional and human being. Students were encouraged to read widely (science fiction, relativity theory) and to study languages (Chinese, German). A couple of students remembered the positive reactions of research associates from the Bureau of Child Study at the University of Minnesota Elementary School in their responses to activities in the creativity tests.

The home provided activities and opportunities that also enabled creativity to develop. Musically involved parents instilled the desire in their children to learn and excel. Wendy H.'s father was a pianist and her mother was a singer, so she became an actress. Two boys, Ted and Jim K., were allowed by their parents to work on college-level algebra while in grade 5. Jim's father was a professor of mathematics and he would gladly "mark" their papers. Ted became a successful CEO of a company selling medical products, while Jim became a computer expert with Texas Instruments. The home also provided lots of books because the parents read widely. Some of the students in the case studies were not allowed to watch much television but were encouraged rather to use their minds in unstructured activities of their choosing.

The community also provided different opportunities and venues for creativity to develop. These included an encouraging church minister, touring museums in foreign countries, dancing for self-expression, and attending concerts and symphonies.

A number of activities and events were reported by the case studies at school and at home that impacted them in their choice of subsequent career or chosen field of work. However, the *home* had the greatest impact or influence on their eventual occupations. This is an interesting finding. However, it should not surprise anyone. Parents really *do* orchestrate their children's education. Schooling is only one component of a child's educational experience. Parents have much more influence than they seem to realize. The home has a great influence on the eventual careers their children choose.

While the schools attended by the case studies had an impact on them regarding their future vocation, it was not as influential as home-related factors. Both University Elementary School and Sidney J. Pratt School developed strong skills in the students and nurtured their strengths and passions, which led to positive self-esteem and self-confidence. In addition, the excellent elementary teachers displayed sensitivity to the learning needs of students by providing a flexible curriculum and catering to the individuality of students. In fact, one teacher is *still* considered to be a mentor to three students and communicates regularly with them—after 40 years!

The home influenced the case studies in many different ways. The value of books in the home influenced two students who became librarians. Parents who display a commitment and love for their work can affect their children's vocational choice. Kevin witnessed his father's love of his work—medicine. He eventually became a neurologist and pioneer-researcher in chemotherapy. In another case, Cathy's mother had an abiding interest in politics and law. Cathy eventually became a lawyer. Jim Y. had supportive parents who permitted him to pursue an interest in ancient civilizations and world crises (Vietnam War and Watergate); eventually he chose a career in the Foreign Service. Wendy W. was influenced by a neighbor's interest in photography. It became a life-long hobby for her. Ann's foreign travel with her parents as a young person enabled her to develop an interest in archaeology; she now "digs into" the human psyche as a psychologist. Alex, now a medical researcher, was encouraged by his parents to be observant and to read widely. Sarah was influenced by her parents' friends, beatniks who were nontraditional; it made her eager to try new things. Eventually, she became a fiber-optics specialist in the telecommunications field, considered to be a nontraditional job for women. Neil had an uncle who collected insects, which sparked an interest in science and learning; thereafter he became interested in neuropsychology. Just having parents who consistently demonstrate support by encouraging in children to "strive for the best" and making children's careers "first and foremost" has made the difference for Cathy. Finally, David K. feels a tremendous debt to his father, who invested huge amounts of time and interest in him; David is today a successful actor and teacher of theater arts.

The qualities most cited of teachers, parents, and others who had a strong influence on the case studies were individuals who demonstrated and lived the following characteristics:

- total commitment to their work (intellectual passion)
- positive role models
- somewhat nonconformist in word and action
- energetic
- implemented fair behavior restrictions
- valued creative action
- thoughtful/gentle/patient/calm.

ımber of opposing or antithetical characteristics were reportıe case studies to describe how others would have described uring the early period of their lives. Shy, introverted, and <id" topped the list. Others were described as friendly, like-

able, generous, and being a "good kid." Many were described academically as "top of the class," smart, and a good student. Still others were considered to be leaders, got along well with others, and were adventurous and fun to be around. Some were described as being dominating in personality, and others as followers and "geeks." These traits show a divergence in characteristics; some are the opposite of others. Recent research by Csikszentmihalyi (1996) reveals that creative individuals often present antithetical traits. He cites ten pairs of traits as follows:

1. Great deal of physical energy but are often quiet and at rest.
2. Smart (wisdom) yet also naive (childishness) at the same time. General intelligence is high among people who make creative contributions. He states that naiveté is the most important attribute of the genius.
3. Creative people are often playful (irresponsible/kicking things around/carefree) and disciplined (responsible/doggedness/perseverance).
4. They are imaginative (fantasy) and yet have a rooted sense of reality.
5. They tend to be extroverted (intense social interaction) and introverted (inner-directed reflection).
6. They can be remarkably humble (modest/self-critical) and proud (ambitious/accomplish a great deal) at the same time.
7. They may exhibit a tendency toward "psychological androgyny." A creative person may show an ability to be at the same time aggressive and nurturant, sensitive and rigid, dominant and submissive, regardless of gender.
8. Creative people are both traditional (conservative) and rebellious (iconoclastic/take risks/break with the safety of tradition).
9. They can be passionate (attachment) about work, yet they can be extremely objective (detachment) about it.
10. Finally, a creative person's openness and sensitivity can often expose them to suffering and pain, and yet also to a great deal of enjoyment.

The case studies displayed many of these antithetical traits of personality.

Finally, the most important lessons learned during the elementary-school years by the individuals in the case studies regarding their creativity were that:

- experience with many activities and topics is important
- creativity is fun
- all abilities and learning styles need creative outlets.

Another lesson cited was that creativity is your greatest strength. One person stated that creativity saved her from the effects of sexual abuse. She was able to use her creativity to gain the approval of others and escape the depression caused by sexual abuse. Another individual in the case studies stated that creativity helped him develop his imagination while sickness had curtailed his school attendance and athleticism. Finally, one boy realized the power of creativity when a teacher whispered a dictum into his ear in grade 4: "Don't lose your creativity!" It had a profound effect on his life as an actor and teacher.

GENERAL FINDINGS: EARLY INFLUENCES ON CREATIVITY

1. Half of the individuals in the case studies recognized their creativity either before entering school or during the elementary-school years.

2. Creativity manifested itself at an early age as involvement in the "fine arts," activities provided by parents, and schools that were staffed by teachers with a creative motivation.

3. Schools staffed by teachers who are creatively motivated and committed to teaching creatively can positively affect students. These teachers got to know their students well and offered a flexible curriculum with many options for students.

4. The home has the greatest impact or influence on a child's eventual career or occupation.

5. The most effective teachers were those who displayed a sensitivity to the learning needs of students by providing a flexible curriculum.

6. Those individuals (teachers, parents, others) who exerted a strong influence on students displayed a number of characteristics:

- commitment to their work
- positive role model
- energetic
- somewhat nonconformist
- value creative actions
- thoughtful/gentle/patient/calm.

7. A number of opposing or antithetical traits were used to describe the most creative students such as shy, introverted, and "quiet kid" to friendly, generous, and "good kid." This corroborates the findings of Csikszentmihalyi (1996).

8. Individuals in the case studies reported that the most important lessons they learned about their creativity as a young person were that experience with many activities and topics is important; all abilities and learning styles need outlets; creativity is fun; and finally, that creativity is your greatest strength in coping with the struggles of life as a young person.

twenty-one

CAREER PATHS AND TRANSITIONS

This chapter explores the types of jobs held by the case studies and how they deal with changes or transitions in their working life. In addition, trends are noted with respect to whom they relied on for advice and how they integrate relationships into their working life.

As illustrated in table 21.1, the case studies represent a variety of occupational choices, even though they came from similar school environments. The homes of the case studies represented different emphases, values, and expectations, and provided many different experiences. Is it a fair question to ask: What influences a child more, school or home environment? Certainly it must be the total education experience that shapes a child, including his genetic make-up.

In reporting how the individuals use creativity in their occupations and work, they essentially defined creativity, according to Torrance (1962), as the "production of something new or unusual as a result of the process of sensing difficulties, problems, gaps in information, missing elements; making guesses and formulating hypotheses about these deficiencies; testing these guesses and possibly revising and retesting them; and finally, communicating the results."

These key concepts of creativity are embedded in the following uses of creativity by the case studies:

TABLE 21.1

Specific Occupations* of the Case Studies (*N*=18)

Females		Males	
Caroline Dunn	public-service assistant, county library system	Alex Adams	medical researcher
		David Herr	lawyer
Wendy Henry	actress/singer/writer[L]	David Kwiat	actor/professor of theater arts
Cathy Gorlin	lawyer		
Sarah Kelley	fiber-optics telecommunications specialist[R]	Kevin Lillehei	neurosurgeon/professor of medicine
Sharon Kennedy	print buyer (social-styles instruments)	Frederick Puzak	construction/architect, self-employed
Laurie Larson	librarian	Neil Raab	neurodiagnostician[U]
Ann Lumry	psychologist in private practice	Fritz Reeker	lawyer
Joanne Mishek	elementary-school teacher[L]	Ted Schwarzrock	CEO/medical equipment[R]
		Jim Young	Foreign Service officer
Wendy Warfield	certified professional accountant		

*As of October 2000.
[L]On leave; [R]Retired; [U]Unemployed.

- *sensing difficulties, problems, gaps in information, missing elements*

  Several of the case studies indicated that they use their creativity to troubleshoot problems by gathering information and using the process of creative problem-solving. Kevin and David H. indicated that they identify problems to attack in medical studies and legal cases, respectively. Jim Y. uses creative problem-solving to develop a range of options for writing U.S. policy for Nigeria. Both Ann and Joanne used this aspect of creativity in planning and designing a community garden and playground. Fred uses his creativity all the time in designing and remodeling buildings and existing structures. Kevin also is applying this phase of creativity in his research to harness the immune system to eradicate malignant brain tumors.

- *making guesses or formulating hypotheses about these deficiencies*

  Some individuals use intuition a great deal in their work in order to generate hypotheses about problems. Ann, for example, relies on her intuition to come up with hypotheses when working with couples in therapy in order to build connections between people. Ted is using his creative skills, now, to help himself adjust to retirement: he is formulating hypotheses about how to spend his retirement (or refirement) years.

- *testing these guesses and possibly revising and retesting them*

David K. clearly says that staying open is his key in working with drama students. A readiness to explore and be available is important in his work as an actor and professor of theater arts. Neil, a neuropsychologist, is one who examines the true meaning of concepts. He, like his father, breaks down the meaning of concepts such as agnosia or anorexia nervosa to examine its true or multiple meanings.

- *and finally, communicating the results*

Several of the individuals in the case studies use creativity in teaching (elementary school and acting), writing articles, newspaper reporting, and photography to communicate ideas to others. Wendy W. developed a procedural checklist to be used as a "tool" by colleagues in an accounting firm.

The individuals apply their creativity as a process differently, but it approximates the definition as developed by Dr. Torrance nearly 40 years ago.

The individuals selected for the case studies have had a range of other jobs that required varying levels of creativity. For example, Ted was a student in medical school. His mother and father told him repeatedly that he wanted to be a doctor . . . and he believed them. He used his creativity to challenge the medical program and how the doctors delivered it. Sarah was a student in a Master of Fine Arts program. Although she didn't use her degree in her work as a fiber-optics splicer, she used it to design and build her home in Deep Haven, Minnesota. Ann was a clinical psychologist in a hospital setting for eight years. The job required a good deal of creativity because people presented a variety of "diagnostic puzzles" to her. She nearly burned out by overwork. Fritz was a tennis professional for a short time. He applied his creativity to this job in several ways: used patterns to analyze opponents in order to detect flaws; understood the geometry of the flight of the ball; and knew his own weaknesses. David H. worked as a waiter in a restaurant for a time. It taught him multitasking and how to do things well, but not to expect perfection. He applies these skills today to his law practice. Now he can juggle the various roles he plays in his work, can prioritize, and is always home in time for dinner. These examples demonstrate that creativity can be learned and applied in various types of settings.

A variety of reasons were given for major changes in the case studies' work lives. Some felt that the salary system was unethical and inconsistent for the commitment that was required. Two females indicated that they were married young (at age 21) and were not prepared for the responsibility of parenting children. Jim Y. was in the Foreign Service, and his constant moving from one country to another in assuming assignments caused marital difficulties. Ted's rebellious attitude was problematic at medical school as he "took on" authority, to his detriment. Both Fritz and Kevin realized that they were becoming workaholics and wanted to spend more time with their wives and families. Sarah experienced some gender discrimination because men preferred male supervisors, even though she was accepted by them— eventually. Ann struggled to make the transition from working in a hospital to working in the private sector as a psychologist. She was influenced by a strong female role model, and a course on "Women in Leadership" helped to provide her with the support and courage to change.

A number of reasons was given for the job changes. However, the influence and support from mentors and friends was the most dominant. Finding a better balance between work and home life, as well as the potential for more income, were also cited. The individuals in the case studies reported that they relied on best friends, teachers, parents, and spouses for advice when making career changes. Those who were particularly helpful provided encouragement and affirmation, advice, help in locating work, and just being themselves as models of integrity.

All individuals expressed a concern for maintaining a balance between work and home life. The majority continue to struggle with this challenge. Half of the case studies indicated that they were unsuccessful or had great difficulty balancing their work and personal life. Their passion for work "tips" the delicate work–home balance, often affecting marriage. Several have decided that family comes first. Fritz and David H. have committed time to spend with a disabled wife and a son with special needs. Still others have designed work schedules that allow for integration of roles. Ann, for example, can arrange her appointments with clients around her family schedule. If she wants to watch her daughter, Emilie, play soccer on Monday evening, she will not schedule clients at that time.

To maintain a healthy balance between work and home life, several strategies were proposed. Cathy learned from a colleague to say *"no"* to requests that will not make a real difference to her law practice. Fritz designs opportunities to meet and spend time with friends—for example, on the golf course. Ann's husband is extremely supportive of her work and does a great deal of housework and parenting. Wendy H. views her dependency on friends as a gift: it has given rise to many meaningful friendships. David H. has learned to prioritize his work and not to be a perfectionist.

The individuals in the case studies represent various careers and transition issues that are inevitable. The case studies reflect the important career messages for today and tomorrow; namely, that change is constant; follow your heart; be an ally/find an ally; focus on the journey; and keep on learning.

GENERAL FINDINGS: CAREER PATHS AND TRANSITIONS

1. The total education experience (school and home), including genetic endowment, shapes a child and ultimately determines what he or she will do.

2. The individuals in the case studies represent a variety of occupations, most of them professional in nature.

3. Creativity is applied by the case studies in their work in essentially four areas:

    - sensing difficulties, problems, gaps in information, missing elements
    - making guesses and formulating hypotheses about these deficiencies
    - testing these guesses and possibly revising and retesting them
    - and finally, communicating the results.

4. Creativity can be applied and learned from all types of roles and work settings.

5. Transitions from roles and jobs occur for many reasons, but basically they involve one's perception of balance between work and personal/family life.

6. During times of transition, the case studies turned to best friends, teachers, parents, and spouses for encouragement, support, and advice.

7. The work–personal-life balance represents a major challenge to the case studies.

8. Strategies to maintain this healthy balance include the following:
   - say *"no"* to requests that don't matter to you
   - design opportunities to meet and spend time with those who matter to you
   - enlist the support of your significant other
   - do your best and forget about being perfect.

9. Remember the key career messages for today and tomorrow:
   - change is constant
   - follow your heart
   - be an ally, find an ally
   - focus on the journey, not the destination
   - keep on learning (Millar 2000).

twenty-two

CREATIVE ACCOMPLISHMENTS

This chapter deals with the trends that resulted from a summary of the creative accomplishments of the 18 case studies. They were asked to describe their creative achievements and attributes; how they apply their creativity to their life; and what influences guide and constrain their creativity.

The individuals in the case studies indicated their most creative achievements in a number of personal and professional areas. The personal area was *most* frequently mentioned. Several stated that raising children was their most creative achievement. Others said that living with themselves creatively was itself a creative achievement. Wendy H. said clearly that she was her own most creative achievement. These achievements varied from one person to another: Fred's adventure trip to Southeast Asia in 1975; Joanne's involvement in a community project to help children of poverty; and Ted's breaking the cycle of physical abuse. As far as professional or public achievements are concerned, high on the list was writing books, articles, national newsletters, and monographs in various fields of specialization. For example, Jim Y. identified the U.S. policy he developed for Nigeria. Fritz has dealt successfully with 3,600 legal cases; Ted has established successful medical-equipment businesses; Ann's daily work as a counseling psychologist in private practice requires a lot of hard work, creativity, and humbleness; and David K. has been a successful actor. The struggle to maintain one's creativity and pass it on to children and loved ones was dominant in the responses.

Interestingly, both male lawyers in the case studies thought that creativity would not be useful to them in their work. David H. said: "Creativity in law would be a way to describe someone's desperation on the other side—they're resorting to creativity." He went on to say that "creativity is not valued by lawyers." They perceive that creative arguments are invalid. Their work is dictated by rules and facts. Facts provide answers. Other lawyers have failed to see that creativity is a process that they could use to generate possibilities and approximate the truth. Despite their concerns about using creativity in their work, both male lawyers in the study understand the importance of it as a process to generate possibilities.

Individuals felt most creative in raising a family and in positive personal relationships. They used the skills of listening, being perceptive, and solving issues and problems. Involvement in hobbies and in their careers were other areas of life in which individuals felt most able to be creative. Hobbies included the following: gardening, biking, quilting, photography, guitar, stained glass, cooking, and raising dogs. Careers in which individuals felt most success included: law, architecture, medicine, and acting. Writing poetry, science fiction, and music were other frequent responses as areas of life in which the case studies felt most creative.

Generally, two self-reported creative attributes stood out in the case studies: "making things happen"—getting people connected (a doer/finisher and empowering others); and "seeing solutions that others don't"—problem-solving. Ted is a good example of these attributes. He was extremely successful in establishing and maintaining a business selling medical equipment. He had a strong network with doctors because of his experience in the medical field and his ability to engage people. Also, he knew that a successful business venture involves people with different points of view. Several case studies reported intuition (getting to the essence quickly) and good communication and listening skills as creative attributes. For example, Ann uses visual aids as communication devices to help couples express ideas and feelings in counseling. Kevin, the neurologist, stated that his creative attributes were a willingness to question or challenge existing dogma and to be "unafraid of the untried." Actor David K. stated that his creative attributes are an "expressive face" and a "heightened level of energy."

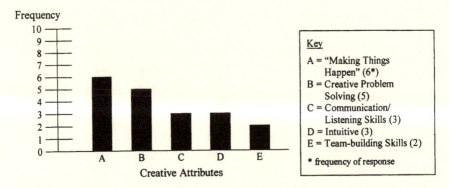

FIGURE 22.1 Creative attributes as perceived by self.

The creative attributes of the case studies are described by close associates in similar but somewhat different ways. The major creative attribute perceived by close associates is an expertise in human relations and outstanding people skills. Wendy H. and Ted would be excellent examples of individuals who have developed an extraordinary ability to relate to others and design a strong human network. Other perceived creative attributes are: the ability to ask good questions;

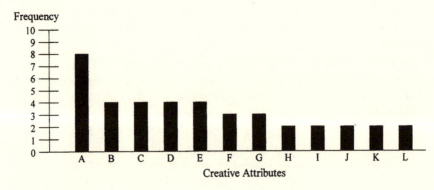

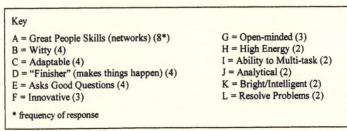

FIGURE 22.2 Creative attributes as perceived by close associates.

being a doer and finisher; the ability to solve problems; being adventurous; being open-minded (forward thinking); and being innovative. Figures 22.1 and 22.2 display the creative attributes of the case studies as perceived by themselves and by close associates.

The common creative attributes reported by the case studies themselves and by close associates deal with excellent people skills, the ability to solve problems creatively, and "making things happen" (follow through).

Individuals reported more influences that constrained their creativity than guided it. Generally, lack of time to accomplish all they wanted and being criticized by others and not measuring up to standards were deemed to be serious constraints. On the positive side, individuals felt that they needed a purpose or reason to create, as well as encouragement from friends to guide their creative development. Maintaining creativity is a struggle for them while being confronted by so many constraints. These influences that guide and constrain the creativity of the individuals in the case studies are reported, by frequency, in table 22.1.

TABLE 22.1

Influences that Guide and Constrain Creativity

Guide Creativity	*Constrain Creativity*
• reason to create/make a contribution to society ($f=8$)	• lack of time ($f=9$)
• encouragement of friends/mentors/parents ($f=3$)	• rules constrain creativity/judgment of others—not meeting standards ($f=7$)
• reading books, articles, etc., in various fields ($f=2$)	• feeling fatigued/emotionally demanding ($f=5$)
• need good "dose" of respect/confidence	• efforts to "balance" work with other areas of life/interests ($f=2$)
• attracted to an area that provided a good/early pension	• financial pressures (high lending rates) ($f=2$)
• use of "brain"	• caretaking role of family ($f=2$)
• opportunity to display integrity	• routine of work/always struggling
• opportunity to apply personal goals	• physical abuse ("goofy childhood") affected relationships/produced rebellious attitude
• opportunity to use education	• need to have others ask for your help
	• financial necessity (must work to maintain lifestyle)
	• fear of being limited
	• early marriage took away individuality
	• weather (gloominess in Minnesota!)
	• lack of information in field
	• political factors

Note: f = frequency of response.

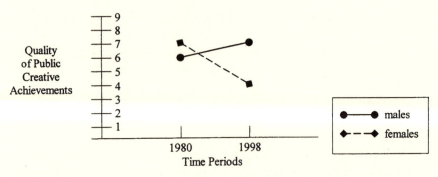

FIGURE 22.3 Interaction between males and females on quality of public creative achievements over follow-up time periods.

Studies (Kogan, 1974; Maccoby & Jacklin, 1974) have shown no evidence of the superiority of one sex over the other in terms of creative potential. However, the case studies demonstrate (see figure 22.3) that creative achievements of the females diminished over time. This is not the case for the males in the case-study group. It may be that our society does not support or encourage females to become or stay as productive as it does for males. Ann is an example of an individual who was very productive as a graduate student at the University of Minnesota and was publishing academic articles. She later decided that her husband and child deserved more of her time and chose a job as a psychologist in private practice that was not as demanding as far as academic publications were concerned. Kevin, on the other hand, became highly productive as a medical doctor and researcher in the area of cancer treatment. His wife supported his productivity, his family expected it, and the medical-research community valued it. I believe that society, generally, still favors males over females in relation to public creative achievements throughout their careers. Young people need to deal with the varying expectations of their parents and teachers. The finding that males are more productive than females in terms of public creative achievement may be attributed, at least in part, to the differing expectations of parents, teachers, and significant others in society. It may be that higher expectations are held for males than females, and this becomes a struggle for people to deal with.

GENERAL FINDINGS: CREATIVE ACCOMPLISHMENTS

1. Creative achievements occur more in personal areas than in professional and public areas.

2. Creative personal achievements included raising children, and living with themselves creatively.

3. Creative professional or public achievements centered on writing for publication (books, articles, newsletters, and monographs).

4. Individuals felt most creative in the following areas: raising children; in positive personal relationships; hobbies; and careers.

5. Two creative attributes were self-reported: "making things happen" and "seeing solutions to problems that others don't."

6. Close associates perceive the creative attributes of the case studies in seven main ways: having outstanding people skills; ability to ask good questions; being doers and finishers; being good problem-solvers; being adventurous, open-minded, and innovative.

7. More influences that constrain creativity than guide it were reported.

8. Major influences that *constrain* creativity are: lack of time; rules and standards; emotional fatigue; efforts to "balance" life; financial pressures; and caretaking role of family.

9. Major influences that *guide* creativity are: need for a purpose and reason to create; encouragement of friends and mentors; and reading in various fields.

10. Males appear to maintain and increase their public creative achievements as their careers progress. Conversely, females diminish in their public creative achievements over the course of their careers.

twenty-three

"MANIFESTO FOR CHILDREN"

Paul Torrance has said for years now that longitudinal studies are conducted not only to determine the predictive quality of a test but also to identify other influences that may affect the behavior being studied over time. Indeed his battery of tests, the *Torrance Tests of Creative Thinking*, administered to elementary-school children during the 1958–1965 period predicted their creative achievement as adults in 1998. However, he found at the 22-year follow-up in 1980 that there were other factors that supported and encouraged creative behavior in his subjects. These important factors are reported as creative principles in his "Manifesto for Children" (see Torrance, Henderson, & Presbury, 1983).

In 1998, 18 years after the first follow-up of the elementary-school children, the author and Paul Torrance wanted to determine if those principles or factors still persisted to influence the creativity of the case studies. Dr. Torrance will elaborate on the "Manifesto for Children" and the large sample in the longitudinal study in a book to accompany this one. A brief accounting of the case studies in relation to the factors contained in the manifesto is reported here.

Seventy-five percent of the individuals selected for case study indicated that they had *"fallen in love"* with their careers and/or hobbies.

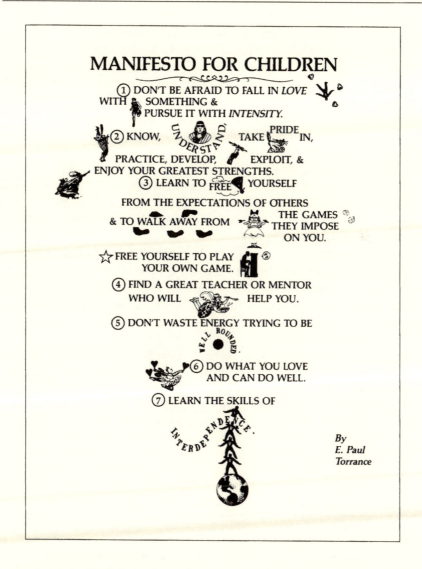

MANIFESTO FOR CHILDREN

① DON'T BE AFRAID TO FALL IN *LOVE*
WITH SOMETHING &
PURSUE IT WITH *INTENSITY.*

② KNOW, UNDERSTAND, TAKE PRIDE IN,
PRACTICE, DEVELOP, EXPLOIT, &
ENJOY YOUR GREATEST STRENGTHS.

③ LEARN TO FREE YOURSELF
FROM THE EXPECTATIONS OF OTHERS
& TO WALK AWAY FROM THE GAMES
THEY IMPOSE
ON YOU.

☆ FREE YOURSELF TO PLAY
YOUR OWN GAME.

④ FIND A GREAT TEACHER OR MENTOR
WHO WILL HELP YOU.

⑤ DON'T WASTE ENERGY TRYING TO BE
WELL ROUNDED.

⑥ DO WHAT YOU LOVE
AND CAN DO WELL.

⑦ LEARN THE SKILLS OF
INTERDEPENDENCE.

By
E. Paul
Torrance

Those responding positively used words or phrases such as: "un-equivocally in love"; "dedicated to work"; "constantly growing"; and "loves children." David H. stated that he has a "middle-aged" passion (more subdued!) toward his practice of law. Caroline expressed a passion about raising "kids in society." Wendy W. loves photography as a hobby that could easily become a job. Kevin described "a deep commitment to medicine." David K. found his "niche" (love of acting) early in life in the seventh-grade drama club. Others (25%) felt more negative toward work and wondered about other possible careers. Clearly, the majority had "fallen in love" with their work.

The two most dominant ways that the individuals in the case studies pursued their passion areas were by continuous study and networking with colleagues in their particular fields. Kevin, Alex, and Wendy W. are constantly reading, attending workshops/seminars, and writing in their respective fields of medicine, pulmonary care, and photography. David K.'s teaching of acting enables him to model his passion area and motivate others to pursue acting as an area of interest or profession.

Individuals reported a number of ways to *exploit* their *greatest strengths*. The most frequent was by using a creative approach to find and solve problems. Others mentioned that they dared to be different and were "carefully unconventional." Empathy, persistence, and motivation were other strengths.

The majority of individuals in the case studies felt that their creativity was affected by the *"expectations of others."* Some felt that they have learned the lesson, which is to please themselves, not others, but that it has been a struggle. The individual comments in table 23.1 are instructive and reflect how the case studies are affected by the expectations of others.

One individual was somewhat ambivalent and stated that he needed the approval of others; however, he was passionate about his area of expertise and pleased himself, not others. He felt that there needed to be ". . . an intertwining of expectations." He stated: "With all that's fragile that's wrapped up with being human and wanting

TABLE 23.1

Ways Creativity Is Affected by *"Expectations of Others"*

Not Affected (f=6)	Affected (f=9)
• ". . . used to be an issue—now freer"	• "society has certain expectations of women my age"—constrained by gender expectations (f=2)
• "learned lesson to please *self*, *not* others"	
• "I'm one of these solo thinkers and I'm not that impressionable"	• academic preparation affected by parental expectations
• "inner locus of control" (carrying on family attitude of self-direction)	• tries to meet expectations of others and conform to their expectations—"160 bosses [clients]"; "[she] does it their way"
	• ". . . not expected to lead"
	• ". . . not financially secure—need to attend to needs of children"
	• "aware of others' needs"

Note: f = frequency of response.

the approval of other people, and finding approval means so much in terms of our self-esteem. I would say that other people's expectations are inextricably intertwined in terms of trying to do the best you can."

The majority (77%) of individuals felt that they were "free to play their own game" or could "sing in their own key." Comments such as: "less driven and know self better"; "private practice allows me to be in charge"; "economic situation allows freedom"; and "within the limits of my responsibility as a medical doctor" support the majority and enable them to "play their own game" and "sing in their own key."

Clearly, the individuals in the case studies indicated that mentors and then their spouses were most helpful to them in achieving their potential. Mentors were ranked in order of importance as follows: parents, teachers, university advisors, professional colleagues, and grandparents. Spouses provided mentorship with help in self-acceptance, self-knowledge, and general support.

The individuals described their relationship with their mentors as displaying unconditional belief in potential; expressing ideas freely and without hurting feelings; and holding high expectations. Mentors possess a large number of qualities and skills. The individuals studied reported that their mentors enabled them to see the "large picture," communicate "big ideas," and were overtly accepting and open. Other qualities and skills mentioned are:

- great care/concern
- somewhat counterculture
- expended effort
- answered questions
- provided encouragement/understanding
- recognized "gifts"
- expressed opinions freely
- intuitive
- mature
- experienced/well traveled
- good listener
- realistic (keeps one "grounded")
- holds high expectations.

The majority of individuals in the case studies felt great admiration, genuine affection, and gratefulness toward their mentors. Fritz has had a mentor for 38 years, and the above sentiments describe his feelings toward his then-fourth-grade teacher and now mentor. Feeling a closeness towards the mentor is most important in the relationship.

The majority of the individuals in the case studies demonstrate the "skills of interdependence" and are involved professionally in furthering the careers of others by mentoring their own children and teaching to enhance the careers or personal lives of others. Professional interactions were reported with junior officers in the Foreign Service; young lawyers; college students; and colleagues. Children were mentored by parents "being available" and helping with school activities, such as reading the Great Books series with classes and supervising on field trips.

Collaboration (with peers, fellow doctors, lab partners, etc.) in a professional sense is the principal way that others interact with the individuals in the case studies to enhance their own careers.

The majority (89%) of the individuals in the case studies felt more able at *some* things than others. Only two individuals described themselves as "well rounded." One of these individuals is particularly multitalented—inordinately strong in a number of areas: history, physics, science, art, and music. The results reported in table 23.2 are dramatic in response to "being well rounded."

GENERAL FINDINGS: "MANIFESTO FOR CHILDREN"

1. The majority of the case studies had "fallen in love" with something (careers and/or hobbies) and were "pursuing it with intensity."
2. Continuous study and networking with colleagues were ways identified to "pursue your passion" areas.
3. "Exploiting your greatest strengths" was frequently accomplished by using a creative approach to problem-finding and -solving.
4. Creativity was affected by the "expectations of others."
5. Some individuals had learned to please themselves, not others. However, it had been a struggle.
6. The majority of individuals felt "free to play their own game" or that they could "sing in their own key."
7. Mentors were most helpful in achieving the creative potential and achievements of the case studies.

TABLE 23.2

Case Studies' Responses to "Being Well Rounded"

Well Rounded (f=2)	*More Able at Some Things than Others (f=16)*
• very well rounded ("frighteningly so!"). Practices weekly in various areas—writing, science, foreign language, music, art	• targets *only* a few interests (not good at mechanics) (*f=8*)
	• interest areas are neglected *now* due to demands of job (law and medicine) (passion areas take time) (*f=2*)
	• well rounded *with* notable exceptions
	• a specialist but tries to keep up with current events, etc.
	• better at management skills
	• fitting parts together
	• only well rounded in certain areas/talented academically and athletically
	• "right-brain dominated"
	• thought worthwhile life entailed keeping up with everything—*now* values "internal self"
	• needs to prioritize interests
	• relies on others for help
	• broad-based problem-solver
	• socially deficient/backward
	• enjoys abstraction but has difficulty communicating thoughts

Note: *f* = frequency of response.

8. Mentors are likely to be: parents, teachers, friends, faculty advisors, professional colleagues, spouses, and grandparents.

9. Mentors displayed unconditional belief in the mentee; express ideas freely; and uphold high expectations. In return, affection, admiration, and gratitude are felt toward the mentor.

10. The individuals in the case studies demonstrated the skills of *interdependence* by furthering the careers of others and mentoring their own children.

11. The majority of individuals felt more able at some things than others. They did not waste their time and energy to attempt to be well rounded.

twenty-four

REFLECTIONS ON CREATIVITY

The individuals selected for case studies were asked to comment on key areas of creativity that related to them and to provide advice for others. Their comments included: their creative goals/aspirations; advice to educators, parents, and mentors for nurturing creativity; and finally, what they would leave behind in a time capsule that would represent them as a creative person.

Regarding creative goals and aspirations for the future, the most creative individuals wished to pursue new areas and ambitious projects. One stated: "All my goals are slightly less than impossible to achieve." For example, Jim Y., who holds a doctoral degree and enough credits for two more undergraduate degrees, wishes to return to school to obtain a Master of Fine Arts degree so that he can pursue a career in the film industry as an actor and writer. He also stated that he would aspire to be an ambassador in the U.S. Foreign Service. David H. has the desire to "argue" in the U.S. Supreme Court and be a judge some day. Others wished to do something different, such as work at the Salvador Dali Museum in Florida or start up a medical company to develop an antibody to combat AIDS. Some of the case studies wished to continue to contribute in their respective fields of specialization, such as medicine, psychology, and law. Several wanted to spend more time traveling and to spend more time as a parent. Two individuals wished to start a family at the mid-point in their lives. Wendy H. has succeeded in this aspiration and has recently become the mother of twins. Other creative goals and aspirations can be categorized in the areas of work-related or personal development. These are reported in table 24.1. One individual who was unhappy in her work stated that she must "move on."

TABLE 24.1
Creative Goals and Aspirations for the Future

Work Related	Personal Development
• Make more money during the next ten years • Stay open and be receptive to possibilities and keep exploring • Get back into field (telecommunications) • Stay teaching • Continue to act	• Become more spiritual • Develop more relationships outside of work • Desires stability and comfort • Live in a more hospitable climate • Do a yearly self-assessment of aspirations • Display photographs in a formal showing/be a published photographer

Although the individuals in this 40-year predictive validity study were quite advantaged and had ample opportunities and freedom to develop their creative abilities, the results *do* indicate that creativity tests administered in the elementary-school years can predict real-life adult creative achievements. However, other factors have been identified that may be equally important to sustaining and supporting creative behavior in adulthood, such as having a mentor, having teachers who value creativity, and being in love with one's work.

The struggle to maintain one's creativity is fragile and can be "squashed" at any age or time. Perhaps what parents, teachers, and mentors can do is to recognize creativity in children, encourage it, and then "get out of their way!," setting them free to play their own game and be the very best that they can be. Several suggestions and ideas were advanced as advice to educators about nurturing creativity in children in the school environment. Much of the advice is interrelated, but will be treated separately in this discussion.

The most common piece of advice was for educators to value divergence (differentness) in students. It is important for teachers to recognize that students have different ways of learning and varying degrees of ability and interest. One individual stated that teachers need to be vigilant of the quiet student who possesses a great deal of potential. Teachers need to foster and encourage student strengths. Children seem to learn best through experiential activities. Finally, educators must understand the emotional and psychological needs of children and plan curricular activities accordingly. Often educators look for the learning problem in students and/or in their environment. The problem might be with the way or method the teacher is using with that particular student. In 1972, the term I used for this "academic illness" is *dysteachia* (Millar, 1972), where indeed the problem for some student learning lies within the teacher's inappropriate method(s) in presenting subject matter.

Several individuals mentioned the importance of instilling adventure and fun into learning to relieve boredom. Science and social studies were mentioned as two subject areas that could be exciting for both boys and girls at school. Jim Y., who provided this advice, was tremendously excited as an elementary student and was constantly asking questions about prehistoric life and was preoccupied with dinosaurs and drawing them.

Teachers need to allow for "creative space," but yet establish boundaries and structure in the classroom. One individual stated "that absolute freedom frightens." It is not enough to provide exercises in creativity to students, the teacher must be creatively motivated and committed to it. A good instrument to use in gauging a teacher's commitment to teaching creatively is the *Creative Motivation Scale* (Torrance, 1995).

Another way to nurture creativity is to allow students to ask good questions and to tolerate different answers. One individual in the case studies indicated that teachers must develop "a tolerance for more than one answer." In 1992, my colleague Ralph Himsl and I published an instrument to measure the quantity and quality of student questions (Himsl & Millar, 1992). In addition, I wrote a handbook for teachers (Millar, 1992) of strategies to use to encourage students to ask good questions. One of the individuals in the case studies stated that "I didn't learn to ask questions until I was in college—I was frightened to ask as a student." Encouraging a healthy skepticism is desirable behavior for students and should be welcomed by educators.

"Listen to students" was another suggestion made by several of the case studies. By knowing what their interests and values are, teachers will be better able to inform their instruction and design meaningful learning activities.

Teachers need to be clear about distinguishing between *excellence* and *perfection*. Students need to know that "it's okay to make mistakes" and "to be the best they can be." Advice was also given by the case studies that basically said that students need "to learn something, not everything." Most students and people, in fact, are not well rounded and cannot be expected to excel in all subject areas at school. A few individuals in the case studies believed that teachers should set higher expectations for students, especially those who demonstrate high potential.

Other comments made by the case studies for educators to consider are listed below.

- staff schools with high-quality teachers (enthusiastic, love for kids, intelligent)
- be open
- provide a *safe* climate for children to learn and create
- respect children as friends
- teachers need to be involved in writing the curriculum
- be friendly to students (need to have a chemistry with kids)
- use good classroom-management skills
- allow for success to happen
- connect students with mentors (others who have an interest in an area)
- seek and reward the unusual responses
- push students to work hard
- design learning plans for *all* students.

Many suggestions were put forward by the individuals in the case studies to help parents nurture creativity in their child(ren). Providing choices for children was the dominant theme. Children should be allowed to follow and pursue interests and to access a variety of experiences. As one individual put it: "So find it, nurture it, and don't suffocate it."

Several reported that parents need to provide the emotional support so that children can securely operate in their environments and be willing to try new things. Needless to say, parents need to provide their child(ren) with unconditional love, support, encouragement, and respect. *Cradles of Eminence* (Goertzel & Goertzel, 1962) is a provocative study of the childhood of over 400 famous twentieth-century men and women. Among the 400 were Albert Einstein, Eleanor Roosevelt, Winston Churchill, Marie Curie, Sigmund Freud, Robert Frost, Kahlil Gibran, Pope John XXIII, and Helen Keller. While 80 percent of the total group showed evidence of being unusually intelligent or exceptionally talented, *none* were given an opportunity to ask meaningful questions or pursue their interests and talents at school. In fact, 60 percent of the 400 *disliked* school. A number of reasons were given: a too-rigid curriculum; dull, irrational, and cruel teachers; and fellow students who bullied, ignored, or bored them. The book points out that the majority had parents who demonstrated a strong drive toward intellectual or creative achievement and a love of learning. This they communicated to their children.

Another piece of advice was to control and monitor the amount of television viewed by children. Some said: "Turn the TV off!" Much research shows that violence and sexuality are modeled by young people who watch too many undesirable and violent programs. In fact, there is a growing movement in the United States by the Parents' Television Council (February 29, 2000) to stop the killing, violence, promiscuous sex, and vulgarity on television that is "desensitizing an entire nation." Their mission is to bring back family-safe television programming.

A number of suggestions were given that dealt with parents' relationship with their child(ren). Talk *with* (not *to*) children about ideas. They need to hear what you think and share their views on world events, work-related issues, and sport and family activities. Provision of materials to make sample things or art projects would help children to "create" things. Even though it is important to involve children in clubs and music and sports lessons, try not to "over-program" their free time. Children *do* need time to be solitary, to read or just to think. Parents need to provide a structure and set limits for children so that they know what is expected of them and so that they can pursue their interests. To develop an open relationship with your child(ren), present everyday problems to everyone in the family, so that it may be solved cooperatively. Children will learn to solve problems creatively. A few individuals in the case studies felt that one parent should stay home with the children to facilitate their optimal growth and development. Other advice provided for parents included:

- enjoying the outdoors (interact with nature)
- providing a variety of books
- avoiding modeling "bad habits" (such as alcoholism)
- asking good questions.

Rod Myers's advice[1] to parents and teachers on how to encourage creativity in children, is to respect the children and value their ideas by showing by your *actions* that you do. Wayne Kirk, a sixth-grade teacher at University Elementary School (1959–1963) stated: "I've often reflected upon those students. Sometimes the best thing I did was encourage them and then get out of the way."[2]

Celebrating the individuality of creative youngsters and paying attention to their ideas and questions were reported as the most important considerations for mentors. Notice should be given to those who may be either disadvantaged and/or withdrawn *but* who have real potential. Torrance (1962) recognized early that sustained creative achievement was facilitated by having a mentor. The 1980 follow-up of the elementary-school students demonstrated that having a mentor facilitates creative achievement (Torrance, 1984). Torrance, Goff, and Satterfield (1998) demonstrated that mentoring can help disadvantaged students who live in poverty to qualify for gifted programs. Other advice provided for mentors was to make the relationship fun: provide a different, yet noncompetitive perspective from parents; focus on problem-solving and encourage questioning.

Generally, the individuals indicated that they would represent themselves as creative persons by placing six "objects" in time capsules that could be opened years later. The six deposits in the "creative time capsule" would be: published and unpublished works; representations of an embedded concept; photographs; samples of artwork; videotapes; and awards. Typically one would expect public achievements to represent the case studies' creative accomplishments. Table 24.2 displays these accomplishments.

The second highest category of items to be placed in the time capsules would be objects that represented an underlying or embedded

TABLE 24.2
Published and Unpublished Works in Time Capsules ($f=25$)

• books	• poems
• novels	• letters written to family
• essays/short stories	• cookbook
• scientific journal articles	• one-man play
• research reports (antibiotics/brain tumors)	• brief presented in court
• films	• yearbooks of medical students
• recordings	• stage manager's prompt book
• newspaper articles/reviews	• portfolio of course syllabus and student handouts

Note: f = frequency of response.

concept. For example, Laurie placed a red party dress, which represented the "fun" part of her. Ann placed an e-mail message from a
fellow therapist, which represented sharing ideas and the importance to her of continuous learning. Other representations are found
in table 24.3.

TABLE 24.3
"Objects" Representing an Embedded Concept
in Time Capsules (*f*=20)

- hologram of me ("Creative Person-at-Large") talking about how I feel about creativity, and how it saved me
- a seashell, representing the attraction of the ocean
- something that reflected lust for adventure and desire for knowledge outside of our society
- symbol to represent the end of physical abuse
- blank paper (in order to create *own* designs)
- flower (cultivating beauty/growth)
- some sunshine ("gone when opened"); "temporalness" of life relating to earthly life as opposed to heavenly
- system developed to do quick mathematical calculations
- drawing/painting/illustrating the complex role of women
- some items from my cabin at the lake, representing escape and serenity
- vial of water from the St. Croix River, representing escape from city life
- sample minutes from a meeting chaired, representing leadership role
- something depicting role model for students/inspirational father and good husband
- "Dixie Cup," which represented my naughtiness at school (prevented me from experiencing a visiting author in elementary school)
- copy of *curriculum vitae* signifying achievements/success in career
- poster—two people communicating heart-to-heart—essence of life
- photo of a river north of Lake Superior to illustrate connection with spirituality
- draft-board letter earning me the status of conscientious objector during Vietnam War

Note: *f* = frequency of response.

The photographs to be placed in the time capsules were mainly
those of loved ones, namely, children, spouse, parents, and brothers.
Others were of themselves in leisure pursuits: playing tennis, swim-
ming in the Caribbean, and adventure traveling. Samples of artwork
was another category of objects. Art pieces represented here were
sewing and knitting, fabric art, line drawings, and a son's drawing.
Videotapes represented another category. Two individuals would
represent themselves dancing with their partners. A videotape of a
one-man play would represent another creative accomplishment. A
digitized video of a construction site "walk through" would show

how the space was used creatively. The last category would be tangible awards (plaques) for community service and high ranking in competitions.

Upon analysis, the major themes depicted are: public and personal achievements and recognition, photos of loved ones and concepts such as the search for serenity, self-expression, lust for knowledge and/or adventure, creative expression, personal happiness, importance of humor and levity, leadership, philosophic stance on important issues, and the desire to be good spouses and parents. This time capsule concept illustrates that there is a relative balance between public creative achievements and personal creative endeavors. It shows that creativity can and should be applied to all that we do in our careers, and lives in general.

GENERAL FINDINGS: REFLECTIONS ON CREATIVITY

Goals and Aspirations

The creative goals and aspirations of the most creative individuals in the case studies were to pursue new areas and ambitious projects. One stated that "all my goals are slightly less than impossible to achieve." Interestingly, two individuals wished to start a family at the mid-point of their lives and succeeded in doing so!

Schooling

1. Educators can nurture creativity in students by valuing divergence ("differentness"):
   - know that students have different learning styles/interests/abilities
   - notice "quiet" students with high potential
   - incorporate "experiential learning"
   - understand the emotional and psychological needs of students.
2. Educators need to instill adventure and fun into learning.
3. Educators need to allow "creative space" for students, with reasonable boundaries and structure.
4. Educators need to be creatively motivated and committed to teaching creatively.

5. Educators need to encourage an attitude of "healthy skepticism" and curiosity in students by welcoming questions.
6. Educators need to help students strive for excellence, not perfection.
7. "Learn something, not everything."

Parenting

1. Parents can nurture creativity in their children by providing choices:
   - follow/pursue interests
   - involvement in a variety of experiences
   - "so find it, nurture it, and don't suffocate it."
2. Parents need to provide emotional support to their children.
3. Parents need to control and monitor the amount and kind of television viewed by their children.
4. Parents need to be aware of their relationship with children:
   - talk *with*, not *to*, children about ideas/concepts
   - provide materials so child can "create"
   - don't "over-program" their free time
   - provide a structure in the home and set limits
   - present problems that can be solved with the assistance of children
   - one parent should stay home, if possible
   - provide books and computer access
   - ask provocative questions and provide fewer answers.

Mentoring

1. Mentors need to celebrate the individuality of the child, especially the disadvantaged and/or withdrawn.
2. Mentors need to pay attention to the questions children ask.
3. Mentors should provide a different, yet noncompetitive perspective from parents.

Creative Representation

1. Creative persons represent their creative achievements in a balance between public and personal achievements.

2. Public creative achievements include published and unpublished works: books, articles, poems, films, short stories,
cookbooks, plays, and newspaper articles.

3. Personal creative achievements include a wide variety of
"objects": photographs, samples of art, videotapes, awards,
and other objects representing an embedded meaningful
concept (fun, loyalty, humor, integrity, etc.).

NOTES

1. Personal communication from Rod Myers to Garnet Millar, November 29, 1999, in possession of the author.

2. Personal communication from Wayne Kirk to Garnet Millar, December 2, 1999, in possession of the author.

twenty-five

KEY MESSAGES FOR CREATIVE LIVING

EARLY INFLUENCES ON CREATIVITY

1. Creativity is normally recognized by individuals before entering school or during the elementary-school years.

2. Creativity manifests itself at an early age as involvement in the "fine arts" in activities provided by parents; and in schools that are staffed by teachers with a creative motivation and commitment.

3. Schools staffed by teachers who are creatively motivated can positively affect the creative achievements of students.

4. The most effective teachers are those who display sensitivity to the learning needs of students by providing a flexible curriculum.

5. The home has the greatest impact or influence on a child's eventual career or occupation.

6. Individuals (teachers, parents, others) who exerted a strong influence on students display a number of characteristics:

- commitment to their work
- positive role model
- energetic
- somewhat nonconformist
- values creative actions
- thoughtful/gentle/patient/calm.

7. A number of opposing or antithetical traits are used to describe the most creative students. The traits range from shy, introverted, and quiet, to friendly, generous, and being a "good kid." This corroborates the findings of Csikszentmihalyi (1996).

8. The most important lessons that one can learn about creativity at an early age is that:
- all abilities and learning styles need outlets
- experience with many activities is important
- it's an individual's greatest strength
- it's fun!

CAREER PATHS AND TRANSITIONS

1. The total education experience (school and home), including genetic factors, shapes a child and ultimately determines what he or she will do.

2. Creativity as a process is applied by individuals to their work in four areas:
- sensing difficulties, problems, gaps in information, missing elements
- making guesses and formulating hypotheses about these deficiencies
- testing these guesses and possibly revising and retesting them
- and finally, communicating the results.

3. Creativity can be applied and learned from all types of roles and work settings.

4. Transitions from roles and jobs occur for many reasons, but basically they involve efforts to balance work and personal/family life.

5. During times of transition, individuals turn to best friends, teachers, parents, and spouses for encouragement, support, and advice.

6. The "work–personal-life balance" represents a major challenge to creative people.

7. Strategies in maintaining a healthy balance between work and home life include the following:
   - saying "no" to requests that don't matter to you
   - designing opportunities to meet and spend time with those who matter to you
   - enlisting the support of your significant other
   - doing your best and not being concerned about being perfect.

8. Recognize and remember the key career messages for today and tomorrow:
   - change is constant
   - follow your heart
   - be an ally/find an ally
   - focus on the journey, not the destination
   - keep on learning.

CREATIVE ACCOMPLISHMENTS

1. Generally, the creative promise of youth is reflected in creative performance in adulthood for both men and women.

2. Creative achievements generally occur more in personal areas than professional or public areas.

3. Creative personal achievements include raising children and living with oneself creatively.

4. Creative professional or public achievements center on written publications (books, articles, newsletters, and monographs).

5. Individuals feel most creative in the following areas: raising a family; involvement in positive relationships; hobbies; and careers.

6. Two creative attributes identified by creative people are: "making things happen" and "seeing solutions to problems that others don't."

7. Close associates perceive the creative attributes of colleagues in seven main ways: outstanding people skills; ability to ask good questions; a doer and finisher; good problem-solver; adventurous; open-minded; and innovative.

8. More influences constrain creativity than guide it. It is a struggle to maintain.

9. Major influences that *constrain* creativity are: lack of time; rules and standards; emotional fatigue; efforts to "balance" life; financial pressures; and caretaking role of family.

10. Major influences that *guide* creativity are: need for a purpose or reason to create; encouragement of friends and/or mentors; and reading in various fields.

11. Males increase their public creative achievements as their careers progress, while females' achievements diminish.

VALIDATING THE "MANIFESTO FOR CHILDREN"

1. Tests that purport to measure creativity, such as the *Torrance Tests of Creative Thinking* (*TTCT*), identify creative potential and predict creative achievement in adulthood. However, there are other factors that are necessary to support and facilitate the persistence of creative behavior over time. Torrance (1999) identified these factors in his *Manifesto for Children*.

2. The majority of creative people *fall in love* with something (careers or hobbies) and *pursue it with intensity*.

3. Continuous study and networking with colleagues are ways to *pursue your passion* areas.

4. *Exploiting your greatest strengths* is accomplished by using a creative approach to problem-finding and -solving.

5. Creativity is generally affected by the *expectations of others*. Some creative individuals learn to please themselves, not others. However, it is an ongoing struggle.

6. Creative persons feel *free to play their own game* and *sing in their own key*.

7. Mentors are most helpful in achieving the creative potential of creative persons.

8. Mentors are likely to be parents, teachers, friends, faculty advisors, professional colleagues, spouses, and grandparents.

9. Mentors display unconditional belief in the mentee; express ideas freely; and hold high expectations. In return, affection, admiration, and gratitude are expressed toward the mentor.

10. Creative persons often demonstrate the skills of *interdependence* by furthering the careers of others and mentoring their own children.

11. The vast majority of creative individuals feel more able at some things than others. They do not waste their time and energy trying to be *well rounded*.

REFLECTIONS ON CREATIVITY

1. The creative goals and aspirations of most creative individuals are to pursue new areas and ambitious projects. One individual from the case studies stated: "All my goals are slightly less than impossible to achieve." Interestingly, two individuals wished to start a family at the mid-point of their lives.

2. Educators can nurture creativity in students by valuing divergence ("differentness"):

- knowing that students have different learning styles/interests/abilities
- noticing "quiet" students with high potential
- incorporating "experiential learning" in and out of the classroom
- understanding the emotional and psychological needs of students.

3. Educators need to:
  - be creatively motivated and committed to teaching creatively
  - help students strive for excellence, not perfection
  - present a curriculum that allows students to "learn something, not everything"
  - allow "creative space" for students, with reasonable boundaries and structure
  - encourage in students an attitude of "healthy skepticism"
  - instill adventure and fun in learning.

4. Parents can nurture creativity in their children by providing choices to enable them to pursue interests.

5. Parents need to:
  - decide whether one parent should stay home
  - provide structure in the home and set limits
  - be aware of their relationship with children
  - provide children with emotional support
  - provide materials so child can "create"
  - talk *with*, not *to*, children about ideas/concepts
  - ask questions and provide fewer answers
  - provide books and computer access
  - present problems that can be solved with the assistance of children
  - not "over-program" their children's free time
  - control and monitor the amount and kind of television programming viewed by their children
  - "so find it, nurture it, and don't suffocate it."

6. Mentors need to:
  - celebrate the individuality of the child, especially the disadvantaged and/or withdrawn ones
  - pay attention to the questions children ask

- provide a different, yet noncompetitive perspective from parents.

7. Creative persons represent their creative achievements in a balance between public and personal achievements.

8. Public creative achievements include published and unpublished works: books, articles, poems, films, short stories, cookbooks, plays, and newspaper articles.

9. Personal creative achievements include a wide variety of "objects"—photographs, samples of art, videotapes, awards, and other objects representing an embedded meaningful concept such as loyalty, integrity, fun, and so on.

NOTE

These key messages for creative living have been derived from selected cases in the Torrance Longitudinal Study of Creative Behavior.

appendix a

DESCRIPTION OF CREATIVE FACTORS AND CREATIVE STRENGTHS

RATIONAL FACTORS

These factors have largely resulted from the work of J. P. Guilford and represent a rational view of the creative process. These factors include fluency, flexibility, originality, and elaboration.

Creative Factor A

Produce and consider many alternatives. (*Or:* Think of lots and different kinds of ideas.)

DESCRIPTION   This factor actually involves two creative elements: *fluency* and *flexibility*. Fluency is simply the production of a number of ideas. Flexibility has to do with an individual's ability to shift mental categories or to produce and consider ideas and alternatives that are categorically different from one another.

Creative Factor B

Be original. (*Or:* Be inventive!)

DESCRIPTION   *Originality* is the ability to produce ideas that are different and unique. It requires looking beyond the obvious and mundane to the novel and inventive. Rarity and unusualness of response characterize this factor.

Creative Factor C

Elaborate. (*Or:* Add some extras.)

DESCRIPTION   The addition of detail to an idea, plan, or drawing is *elaboration*. It involves the embellishment of whatever is being produced. It is the "flesh" that rounds out the "skeleton" of an idea.

SUPRARATIONAL FACTORS

Creative Strengths

Since 1979, Paul Torrance and his associates have developed a set of factors that fall outside the realm of pure reason. These factors move creativity toward the further reaches of creative potential and are termed "creative strengths." Torrance's tests utilize these factors in the scoring scheme.

Creative Strength 1

Highlight the essence. (*Or:* Get to the heart of the matter.)

DESCRIPTION   This ability requires a whole range of subskills, from simplication and clarification to condensation and summarization. It involves a process of distinguishing between relevant and irrelevant material. The ultimate goal of highlighting the essence is to identify the dominant problem or idea.

Creative Strength 2

Keep open. (*Or:* Don't take the easiest way out.)

DESCRIPTION   In order to prevent premature closure, an individual must resist the natural impulse to accept the first idea or solution that comes to mind. Deferment of judgment until a problem is fully understood and a number of solutions have been explored is crucial to avoiding premature closure.

Creative Strength 3

Be aware of emotions. (*Or:* Know and express your feelings.)

DESCRIPTION   *Feelings* affect thinking and creative production. Emotional commitment is required and emotional factors play a role in the achievement of a genuine breakthrough or "eureka!" Many ideas and solutions related to a problem originate in emotions. Although the most meaningful creative insight will arise in conjunction with knowledge and persistence, without the ability to tap the emotions, it may not occur at all.

Creative Strength 4

Put your ideas in context. (*Or:* Get the big picture.)

DESCRIPTION   Ideas do not function in isolation from other ideas. This creative strength is the ability to see the relationship between and recognize the large-scale implications of ideas and events.

Creative Strength 5

Combine and synthesize. (*Or:* Get it together.)

DESCRIPTION   This strength is an ability to bind an array of ideas and factors together to develop a new idea. The new idea is more than the sum of the parts that make it up. The parts may be very diverse, and the process of connecting and joining them in a novel and pleasing combination is the essence of this creative strength.

Creative Strength 6

Visualize it richly and colorfully. (*Or:* See things in all their splendor.)

DESCRIPTION   Creative production demands an ability to visualize concepts, ideas, processes, and plans. The visualizations need not be original, but are of necessity vivid, distinct, intense, and colorful. The image produced often appeals to and stimulates more than one of the sense modalities.

Creative Strength 7

Fantasize. (*Or:* Use your imagination.)

DESCRIPTION   *Fantasizing* is the ability to go beyond what is real into the realm of imagination. The ability to extend one's thoughts beyond concrete reality and, just for a while, to believe that the impossible is possible, which is the essence of fantasy. It is an ability that can wither quickly under the pressure to conform and face up to reality.

Creative Strength 8

Enrich imagery. (*Or:* Feel it, smell it, touch it, taste it, hear it.)

DESCRIPTION   *Imagery* is enriched when more than one sense modality is incorporated in the experience. Idea-flow appears to be increased when an individual is kinesthetically and auditorally active.

Creative Strength 9

Have an unusual visual perspective. (*Or:* See things from a different angle.)

DESCRIPTION   An *unusual visual perspective* is achieved when an individual perceives an object, person, or event in a different and new light. A creative individual may look at everyday objects and see something novel and exciting. This ability is one of the single most-effective predictors of adult creative achievement.

Creative Strength 10

Have an internal visual perspective. (*Or:* Don't judge a book by its cover!)

DESCRIPTION   An *internal visual perspective* is attained by examining inner elements of an object, problem, or idea. An interest in what makes a machine "tick," or determining the core components of an idea, is an internal visual perspective. This ability involves looking beyond exteriors to hidden possibilities.

Creative Strength 11

Breakthrough—extend the boundaries. (*Or:* Break habit-thinking.)

DESCRIPTION   Breaking away from an image or idea to go beyond its boundaries is what is meant by *breakthrough*. It requires looking past the problems or images themselves to the systems that they function in and around. It involves removing barriers imposed by habit and tradition and reformulating the problem or solution.

Creative Strength 12

Have a sense of humor. (*Or:* Laugh a little.)

DESCRIPTION *Humor* involves an ability to see incongruities, to combine ideas or images in an unusual way, or to surprise. The most important component of this strength is not necessarily the ability to produce humor, but to see and pick up on the humor in situations, events, and images. This ability to see humor, or to be humorous, requires a certain detachment that is similar to the critical perspective necessary to look at problems and situations in a creative way.

Creative Strength 13

Decentrism—glimpse infinity. (*Or:* Get out your crystal ball.)

DESCRIPTION *Decentrism* simply means a concern for things outside of the self. It involves a concern for the future and a willingness to adapt to changes that the future holds, and to be a part in shaping the future. An acceptance of the uncertainty of the future and remaining open to it is an important component of this creative strength.

TORRANCE LECTURE DELIVERED BY WENDY HENRY AT THE UNIVERSITY OF GEORGIA, OCTOBER 20, 2000

ONE CREATIVE VOICE

"Looking Back Through the One-Way Mirror–40 Years Later!"

First of all, I want to thank you so much for inviting me here. It isn't very often that you get to meet someone who has known you for 40 years!

I also want you to know how much it means to me to be here. When I got the call from the Torrance Center inviting me to speak, I was thrilled. I remember telling friends that if I had had a choice between being offered a lead role in a Hollywood movie, or this, I would have chosen this, because this gives me the chance to talk about the thing that is the most important to me in the world and to share myself.

I'm going to talk this afternoon about my experience in the longitudinal study, my life as a creative person and how it has manifested in my life, what the creative process feels like to me, the gifts and the struggles in being a creative person, and, based on my own experience, what I would tell teachers or others who work with creative kids of all ages. I'll also be tossing in some of my personal opinions—which I do all the time anyway!

But first, I'd like to sing a poem I wrote for Dr. Torrance. I call it a poem because the melody is always different when I sing it:

"Dr. T"

You've known me forty years
I don't know you at all

2·0·0·0
E. Paul Torrance
Lecture Series

Guest Speaker:
Wendy Feder Henry

October 20-21, 2000

Sponsored by:
The Torrance Center for Creative Studies
University of Georgia • Athens

Program cover

That's why I am so pleased
To be here with you this Fall.

You gave me lots of tests
Apparently I passed
Isn't it strange how forty years
Can travel by so fast?

I hear you have a file on me
Down in your house below
Maybe you can fill in some gaps
About me that I don't know

I see there is a crowd
That values what you've done
For a world without creativity
Is like earth without the sun

Now, what I have to share
Doesn't come from school or a book
I bring you forty-eight years of me
And the pathways that I took.

Thank you.

A STORY ABOUT A LITTLE GIRL AND A STUDY

Once upon a time, about 40 years ago, there was a little girl. She loved to draw and make things out of doodles and sing and dance in the fantasies of her own little head and she loved to imagine and dream all sorts of wonderful things.

Even before the little girl was born, her parents had her on a waiting list for a special nursery school way over in Minneapolis, on the other side of the great Mississippi River at a place called Pattee Hall at the University of Minnesota.

When she was two years old, in 1954, the little girl's parents drove her to the special nursery school in Minneapolis, way over on the other side of the great Mississippi River. She remembers being walked into a big brick building, down a long, wide hall to a room in the corner and being left there. She especially remembers the red and white striped pants she wore because those were her favorites.

Her memories of nursery school and elementary school are vague: she remembers naps on little mats in the early years and the crowded coatroom in the first grade. She remembers being in a classroom and seeing the 1961 *Mad Magazine* issue where the cover could be turned upside down and the year looked the same. She remembers liking her third grade teacher and getting glasses that year. She remembers Ronnie Falk, the first boy she ever loved. She remembers admiring Katie Thomes and wanting to be close to her and sleepovers at her house and chasing Rip Rapson around the schoolyard because she had a big crush on him and wanted to kiss him.

She remembers naps in kindergarten where her very large teacher would pull tables together and sleep on them.

She remembers wandering around Pattee Hall feeling lonely and being taken next door to the psychology building for different tests. She later thought that they were psychology graduate students.

She remembers inkblots and images, objects and pictures, clapping hands and being one of only a couple of Jewish kids in the class and covering her mouth whenever the names Jesus or Christ came up in Christmas carols when they were all singing. Which was a lot, especially around Christmas.

She remembers one-way mirrors and feeling like she was being watched all the time and feeling uncomfortable and not liking it very much. She remembers wondering who was on the other side.

But the tests were fun.

She liked looking at blobs of ink and pictures and seeing what they looked like. She always liked the attention of nice people who seemed so interested in her answers. She liked clapping her hands on TV in a demonstration group. She liked a lot of things. She just didn't like being watched.

She was surprised to learn, many years later, that there had only been two big questionnaires in the 40 years because it seemed to her that they were a part of her life always. On some level she always expected one and was never surprised when they came.

Even though she was well beyond childhood when they first began coming, they made her very anxious and overwhelmed her in a certain way. They were straightforward enough, but she had a hard time answering all of those specific questions on those straight little lines because it was always so important to her to be known truly as who she was—and how can you draw a picture of a person on a straight little line?

She never even managed to send in the final one—but demanded to meet the Canadian stranger when he was in town doing interviews, even though it wasn't the rules, not having finished the questionnaire, but after all—You've gotten to know me! I want to get to know you! she said. I want to know who was on the other side of those one-way mirrors!

And so she did, and the man she met from Canada was so kind and sweet and interested in all she had to say that she was forced to drop all of the bad pictures she ever had of who those people might have been, and she got the biggest chance in her whole life to express who she really was because this man—let's call him Garnet because he is such a gem—was so ready to listen and listen and listen and she came so ready to talk and talk and talk and she brought all sorts of things for him to see.

"Because don't you see" her little heart screamed out, "I don't fit on the lines of a questionnaire!" And guess what? That little girl who was now a 47-year-old woman never appreciated herself as much, or knew herself so much until she finally had the chance to say all that was in her heart about who she was and what mattered to her to someone who wanted to hear and was interested in all she had to say.

The moral of this story: Children of all ages need to be heard and validated by another to fully experience and appreciate who they are.

And there is another moral: If you ever have the opportunity to spend a couple of hours with Garnet Millar, grab it! Garnet has a special gift for appreciating people and he makes you feel it.

O.K. Now what's it like to *be* a creative person? Well, it's pretty hard to be objective since I've never been anyone else! What I can say, is that most of the things in my life that I've done have sort of happened to me. Things come up and I volunteer. Sort of like doodles as a kid.

When I was little, I had a favorite game. I used to say to my mother, "Mommy, make me a doodle!" She would do a scribble on a piece of paper and give it to me, and I would make something out of it . . . I've been given things and then I've made things out of them. In a sense, I feel as if I've volunteered for my life. Here is a piece I've written about that called:

I'LL DO IT

I can't say that I've ever planned to do things much.

Most of the time things would just come up. I'd volunteer and my life would take a new path.

When Mr. So-and-So appeared before my fifth grade class and said, "We need someone to play cello in the orchestra," my hand shot up—"I'll do it! I'll do it!!!—I said out loud or in my thoughts.

I just said, "Yes."

I said "yes" before I knew I would play cello for many years. I said, "Yes" before I ever knew I would take lessons from a cellist in the Minnesota Orchestra who wouldn't figure out for a while that I never practiced, I just got better from lesson to lesson.

I said, "I'll do it" before I ever knew that my essays to get into college would be about the cello, and before I knew I would eventually stop playing because of a dream I had one night—while I was still in college.

I said, "I'll do it" before it even registered what a cello was.

I said, "I'll do it" when a director friend said he needed a portrait painted for the play he was doing. I had never painted a portrait before, but I knew I could.

I said, "I'll do it" when a local artist told me I could get some interesting effects if I mixed watercolors and salt, and I ended up with a series of 50.

I said, "I'll do it" when a friend of mine vacated her position as a reporter on the *Navajo Times* newspaper and I became a journalist.

I said, "I'll do it" when two friends asked me to sing at their weddings.

I said, "I'll do it" when a woman I knew while taking some "grad-student-at-large" classes at an Arizona University asked me if I was an actress, and if I wasn't I should be, and told me to audition for a play she was directing. I remember feeling strange when I overheard that a professor was talking about me to his large freshman acting class, calling me the next Vivien Vance. I said, "I'll do it" to a number of other directors who offered me roles that year.

I said, "I'll do it" when a community theatre on the Navajo Indian Reservation said they needed a president and "I'll do it" when I was told that some of the best acting schools in the country were auditioning in San Francisco.

I said, "I'll do it" when, as an artist-in-residence after earning my MFA, the Head Acting Coach said he needed someone to help him teach his undergraduate acting class, and "I'll do it" when a director from the school asked me to play a leading role in the first show of the New England Repertory theatre.

I said, "I'll do it" to moving to New York City because fellow actors said that was the place to go and they were going, and "I'll do it" when I met a woman who was an art therapist at a nursing home in Brooklyn and I thought, "I could do that." And I did.

I said I'll do it when, living in Greenwich Village, a woman I met said, "Uta Hagen's studio is only a few blocks from you—you should audition, and I became a master class student of hers . . . and then, "I'll do it, too" to an actor friend leaving New York City to move to Minneapolis bringing me back home.

I said, "I'll do it" to a Minneapolis director looking for actors for a two person collaborative touring show about shame and recovery, and "I'll do it" to a man I knew who said, when I was flying out to Montana for a wedding, "They're auditioning for an ABC miniseries here when you'll be here—you should bring your resume." I said, "I'll do it" when they cast me as Custer's sister, Maggie Calhoun, and asked me to come back to Montana for filming.

On the first day of filming, I saw that Rosanna Arquette was going to be riding sidesaddle and Maggie Calhoun was supposed to ride with her. Nobody was paying much attention to me, so I snuck over to where the horses were and asked someone to teach me. When our scene came up and they asked me if I could ride, I said, "I'll do it."

When a woman I knew from a class told me she thought I would be a great keynote speaker and gave my name to her paraprofessional group, I said, "I'll do it."

When a woman I knew said she was forming a swing dance demonstration group, I said, "I'll do it."

When, after dating for three months, that beautiful blonde man you see in the audience said we should get married and have a baby, I said, "I'll do it." I must have said, "I'll do it" twice because we now have twins.

Wendy and Stuart with twins Jake and David

I really don't know what specifically my future will hold beyond continuing to grow as a person, a mother, a partner and a friend. I suppose it will depend on the questions asked.

The moral of *this* story: You don't always have to know where you're going to get to some pretty interesting places.

Now I'd like to say a little bit about what the creative process feels like to me.

As most of you know, I'm pretty busy these days with my 9-month-old twin boys, Jake and David. An actor/director friend of mine recently asked me if I was missing being on the stage and thinking about acting again. I told him that I was missing doing *something* creative, but I didn't know specifically what I was wanting to do next.

The reason being that no matter what particular thing I'm doing—whether it's acting, singing, song writing, painting, dancing, or whatever—the experience I have on the inside is pretty much the same.

Let's say I'm about to do a painting. I'll choose this because it's easy to visualize. I'm sitting at my dining room table with a big, empty white piece of paper in front of me, a bunch of watercolors, some salt, and whatever else happens to be there . . .

At first I feel some resistance. The paper is blank. I have to start. I do something—a crayon mark. Or a color. It's a little slow at first and my concentration is still a little scattered. I continue until, all of a sudden, I'm swept away, caught in the colors, my hands reaching for paint or salt or crayon, the colors mixing and moving and the sheet of paper is evolving and I am lost, captured, moving, filled.

It's sort of like walking to the riverbank and looking at the water. Will it be cold? I resist. Soon I put my toe in, and then my foot. Do you know those little whirlpools, those eddies near the riverbank? For a while I fall into one, swirling around in a circle, going nowhere, and then suddenly I shoot out into the main current, carried away, pulled downstream with a force that takes me. There is no longer any effort, just movement. I am relaxed, peaceful, full, lost in time, happy. There is no effort. I feel a sense of connectedness, unity, esteem. There is no sense of time.

That's what the creative process feels like to me—no matter what particular creative thing I'm doing.

So, when it comes to the gifts of creativity in my life—obviously, the great pleasure and freedom I get from the process is a big one.

Then there is the sense of esteem, which comes during the process—a feeling of power and solidity as part of a larger flow. And then the esteem that comes afterward when, lo and behold, something outside of you that is beautiful has been created.

There is the ability to get things out of you—to express things. It's sort of like—do you know the feeling you get when you are trying to remember or find the perfect word to express something? It's so close and you just can't grasp it? Creativity offers endless languages from which to choose. If you can't find the words, perhaps what you need to say can be danced, or painted or sung or written.

For me, my creativity has been a great source of healing. Like many others, my childhood home life wasn't very happy. I suffered some abuse, and had little recognition or support for who I was. So I was hurt, cut off, and lonely, with no one who would or could really listen.

My creativity gave me a means to express myself. Through drawing or singing or dancing, I had a way out. In a sense, I had a way to express myself to myself. I truly believe that this enabled me to come out of my history and still develop into a full and healthy human being with meaningful relationships.

I consciously began to pursue my recovery when I moved back to Minnesota in 1988. I was in a great deal of pain at the time. One day I brought my guitar to my friend Violet and sang for her. Violet looked at me and said, "Wendy, when you sing, there is no pain in your voice." It was true. No matter what was happening in my life then or now, no matter how painful, the creative part of me was never touched. It was always a place for me to go that was safe, pure, fulfilling, beautiful and good.

I've also had struggles as a creative person. I've felt lonely and estranged at times, feeling different or not understood—expressing things that make perfect sense to me and having people look at me like I'm speaking a language from another planet. At those times I've wondered about myself, thinking that perhaps something was wrong with me.

Again, my friend Violet helped me. I consider her to be one of my first real mentors, someone who was enough like me to understand where I was and the path I was on, and from her own experience, helped me to feel less alone and more courageous in my journey.

She was the first person to recognize who I was in a certain way, and helped me to see it too. I remember the day she took a piece of paper and drew three lines on it, one above the other. The top line was short, the middle line was long, and the bottom line was short.

She pointed to the short line on the bottom and said to me, "Wendy, this line represents all of the people in the world who, for some reason or another, can't function completely—those who are disabled in some way."

She pointed to the long middle line and said, "Now this line represents most of the world. These are the people you see walking around Lake Harriet, having barbecues and doing all of the normal things. This line represents most of the people."

Then she pointed to the short line on the top. "Now these," she said, "are the artists. This is where you are. And your problem is," she said, making an arrow pointing from the short top line to the long middle line," is that you keep wanting to fit yourself in down here. You belong up here. It's lonelier, because there aren't so many of you."

This was the first time I had ever been truly "seen" in a certain way. I was told something about who I was and was reassured that it was not only, not crazy, but it was good.

Now I'd like to share some of my "creations" and how they have served me in my life. First, an example of "I'll do it" in my life.

Almost immediately after I started playing the guitar, which I taught myself as a freshman in college, I began to write songs. I would sit in the stairwell of my freshman dorm, play the few chords I knew—which are the primary chords I still play now after 30 years!—and start singing my thoughts. Songs began to come out.

The summer after my freshman year, a friend of mine asked me if I'd write him a song. I said, "About what?" He said, "About my back."

I thought it was sort of an odd request, but I'd like to sing you what I wrote:

"Your Back Is Delicious"

Your back is delicious, your spine is divine
You're lucky your rib's in a cage
And each vertebrae alerts me to say
I wish all of your pieces were mine

Your knees really please me, your arm has got charm
I've grown very close to your feet
Your shin is a winner, your ears are so dear
Your smile really makes my heart beat

So, if you should fall for me, be prepared for what I'll do
You mean so much to me that I'll go to pieces for you

And when we've grown older, our hair's turning gray
The years have really taken their toll
Your skin may be wrinkled, your eyes a bit dim
But I'll still love the parts of your whole

If you should fall for me, be prepared for what I'll do
You mean so much to me that I'll go to pieces for you

Your back is delicious, your spine is divine
You're lucky your rib's in a cage
And each vertebrae alerts me to say
I wish all of your pieces were mine

Now, here is an example of a song I wrote, when I couldn't find words to express myself.

I was in graduate school for my acting training, and I developed a huge crush on this fellow who was in my class. Obviously, I couldn't tell him—the crush was way too big and I felt way too vulnerable, so I wrote this song. I like it because it also describes a little bit how I hid behind my creativity, before I did a lot of my healing.

SONG

Would you like to do a scene with me?
A love scene would do me just fine.
I could pretend to pretend, to feel what I feel
And no one has to know that it's real.

Romeo and Juliet, Stanley and Stel
Antony and Cleopatra are few
Of the lovers you see that feel the same as me
When I walk into class and see you

So would you like to do a scene with me?
A love scene would do me just fine
I could pretend to pretend to feel what I feel
And no one has to know that it's real

Oh God, you're coming toward me
What am I going to do?
What? What's this I hear?
You say you'd like to do a love scene—or two
Oh God, it's going to be a great year!
So would you like to do a scene with me?
A love scene would do me just fine
I could pretend to pretend to feel what I feel
And no one has to know that it's real

Finally—is it O.K. if I sing one more? O.K. This was a song, simply expressing my joy one day.

I was living in New York City, and I had just dropped off a good friend on his way to the airport after a great visit. I was on the subway, and feeling wonderful, and I had absolutely no money in my pocket, only five subway tokens. So I came out of the subway singing this:

Five tokens in my pocket, Manhattan
I've got you in the palm of my hand
Just dress me up in heels and red satin
No thank you, I've got more than I can stand
Don't worry if you're down to a dollar
Cus' money can't afford everything
As long as you can get into a shower
You know that you can always sing!

Finally, I'm sure all of you read in the program bio about me that I like to "channel" my favorite grandmother. I had a very special grandma, a little old Jewish lady from the "old country" who was well under five feet tall and continued to get shorter until she died in her nineties about 13 years ago. I was very close to her and was with her when she died. I think I dealt with my grief by, very simply, keeping her with me. I "do" Grandma Clara. I get to say all of the things that she said, and that she might have said, and not only does that keep her alive for me, it allows me to say all sorts of things I never could say as myself!

A few moments from *GRANDMA CLARA AD LIB*—(not exact, but the general gist!)

*Hello dahlings, how are you? You came to see my granddaughter Vendy. She's
so vonderful, she's so good, I tink it's so vonderful dat you invited her here. She
desoives it, my Vendy.*

*Dat goil is so creative, she can do anyting. Ask her to do someting for you,
she'll do it. . . . She draws, she paints, she sings, she vrites, anyting you ask,
she can do. Except find her keys. DAT GOIL COULDN'T FIND HER KEYS
OUT OF A PAPER BAG!!!*

*Did you meet her beautiful husband? Her Stu? Vat a dahling. He's so
beautiful, he's so good he's so blonde! He's so good to my Vendy. And their two
babies. Do you know them? Jake and David. Ach. Such dahlings. I can't tell
you. WHAT ARE YOU ALL DOING HERE? YOU SHOULD BE OVER
AT THE HOLIDAY INN VISITING THOSE BABIES!!!*

*And Dr. Torrance. Hello Dahling. I hear you just had a boitday. Happy
Boitday, Honey. You know, from where I sit, you're a very young man. Anyvay,
Vendy has told me so much about you! Especially these past couple years. She
tells me she met people who love you so much!*

*You know, dahling, I think ve're a lot alike you and I. Everybody loved me.
Venever somebody said to me, "Clara, you're so vonderful, everybody loves
you," I vould just say, "You know, honey, I'm lucky dat vay."*

*Dat's how you and I are alike, Dr. Torrance. People love us so ve're the
riches ones in the vorid. You and I, dahling. Ve're lucky dat vey.*

Happy boitday, honey. Let me kiss you.

Now I'd like to talk a little about what I would say to teachers or
those who work with creative kids of all ages, based on my own experience.

I had two great acting teachers when I was living in New York
City.

These two teachers were Uta Hagen and Michael Shurtleff. Uta
Hagen is a Broadway actress and probably the most famous acting
teacher in the United States. Michael Shurtleff was a leading casting
director on Broadway for many years. They had many things in common as teachers.

First, there was an underlying sense of respect in their classes. The
respect that was asked for was reasonable and uncomplicated. Miss
Hagen expected us to be on time and to be prepared. If we were late,
we did not get to do our scenes, even if we had hauled our entire
apartments to class to create a set.

By the same token, the sort of respect we got, was a solid sense
that if put into words would go something like this: "You should
know, just by the fact that I've invited you into this class, that you are
very special and extremely talented. I expect a lot from you, and I am
eager to see what will come."

It wasn't pressure or demand, really, more a sense that there was the *assumption* of valuable things to happen.

That assumption felt good. It made me eager to show what I had, excited to bring things forth knowing that there was a wanting, interested, invested audience/teacher/guide.

There were no tricks, no traps, no hidden agendas. The basic beliefs, the thoughts and judgements about us, spoken or unspoken were good, and we could feel it. The relationship between teacher and student was, very simply, respectful.

I felt "known" by each teacher and was treated personally regardless of the number of students in each class. Rather than give a single exercise for the entire class, or leave it up to us to choose, we were each assigned specific scenes that seemed designed to challenge us or draw something out of us, to make us grow in some way. We were treated as unique individuals with unique differences, and it felt good.

They were both unabashedly generous with praise when it was deserved.

I remember when Michael Shurtleff gave a scene from *Rosencrantz and Guildenstern Are Dead* to another woman and me. The scene was written for two men.

We came up with a very physical, very playful, very childlike scene. When we were finished performing it for the class, Michael looked at us, with such respect, almost awe, then turned to the whole class and said simply, "That was brilliant."

Nothing else. No criticism (which both teachers give honestly and freely), no holding back. And no competitiveness. Just appreciation and a sense of gladness in being able to give such honor.

Sometimes I think teachers think, mistakenly, that even if something is wonderful, if they hold back just a little a student will respond by giving even more. I don't believe that is true. In my experience stinginess, competitiveness, and withholding have caused me to feel hopeless and to shut down. Praise!! Recognition for something wonderful has made me want to give more.

Now if a scene was not good. Neither teacher would shame us. They both seemed to take some responsibility our development. Miss Hagen would think for a minute, then assign some acting exercise. Mr. Shurtleff would make comments, then either give some suggestions or assign another scene. Both acted like it was their job to find the right key to unlock you (as long as, of course, the basic respect was there and you were doing your work).

So both teachers were respectful, personal, generous with praise, eager for and interested in seeing their students succeed, and both expected much in a way that made us feel honored and important. Both were firm in their boundaries and only told the truth. We were neither shamed nor coddled. Being treated like a capable and gifted artist made me want to live up to those expectations.

Now, I want to share my completely personal opinion about why all of this matters, and my hopes for all of you who may be spending your life invested in researching creativity.

My hope is that you won't forget what's important. The products of creativity may be beautiful, but if you think that's where the real value is, I think you're missing the point.

I think that what really matters is what happens inside us when we are creating something. Something inside awakens, comes alive, struggles, giggles, groans, moves, hopes, blooms, wanting expression in the world. Out of that process comes, let's say, a painting like the *Mona Lisa*. Then millions of people walk by, and in looking at that painting, something lights up and happens inside of them.

That, I believe, is where the true value in all of this work lies. Creativity offers a world of fuller, brighter—in the light sense, and more alive people. People who, like our friend Bee Bleedorn, have an inner pilot light that just keeps growing. I believe our creativity makes us richer, more joyful, more alive and more human.

I want to leave you with something I wrote in the middle of the night a couple of months ago while preparing for this lecture:

"Just Say Yes to Me"

Just say yes to me
Don't ask me why I do what I do
Just tell me you want more
Just tell me you wish you could do what I do
Just tell me there's a place on your refrigerator that needs me to fill it
Just say yes when I ask you to look at what I've done.
Just say yes when I say can I show you something
Just say yes when I ask you if you like it
Just say yes when I look into your eyes and say "really?"
Just say yes when I ask you if you need more
Just say yes when I ask if you'd like to see something
Just say yes when I ask if you have a minute
Just say yes when I ask if you'd like one
Just say yes when I ask if I can come back
Just say yes

*I never really knew exactly what I wanted to be. I could never choose. And I
thought there was something wrong with me*

Just tell me I don't have to choose

*I was always taught that you had to decide to be one thing and pursue it. I never
knew you could be many*

Just tell me I can be everything that I am

I always thought that things that came easily couldn't be very important.

Encourage me to enjoy what I am able to do.

I was always told that I was talented, but not that talented.

Tell me I have it in me to do anything.

Tell me I'm special

Tell me you love what I'm able to do.

*Tell me you wish you could do what I can do, but since you can't you are so glad
you know me so I can help you try.*

Tell me you don't understand exactly, but you think it's wonderful.

Just appreciate me

Tell me I don't have to have a reason, it's wonderful just to do it.

Tell me you love me

Tell me you admire me

Tell me it doesn't matter if I can't find my keys, not everyone can draw

Tell me you'd like to hear me sing something

*Tell me you'd like to close your eyes and imagine you are somewhere and could I
create the place for you?*

Ask me to use my imagination

Ask me if I could show you how

Tell me you'd like to hear about it.

---

*Performances, speeches, art shows . . . they're all well and good . . . but it's the every-
day expressions . . . the joy in the doing of it. The beautifully wrapped packages and
the fruit plate with the fresh flowers on it. The table set with atmosphere, the meals
made without recipes, the one-liners, the birthday cards that are made, not bought.*

You know art can heal anything, don't you?

It lives in a place inside of you that no abuse can touch

Not sexual abuse, not criticism, not judgments, not crushing competition

Even if it gets stuck and sits there for years, you can't kill it.

*You can ruin the joy, but it can't be destroyed. It's always just waiting there to
be freed.*

Thank you so much. I'm proud to be a "Torrance kid."

Wendy Henry and Garnet Millar receive Torrance Awards from Dr. Torrance

PRATT AND UNIVERSITY ELEMENTARY SCHOOLS 1980 FOLLOW-UP QUESTIONNAIRE AND SUPPLEMENTARY INFORMATION

PRATT AND UNIVERSITY ELEMENTARY SCHOOLS
FOLLOW-UP QUESTIONNAIRE

DIRECTIONS: Please answer the following questions. Skip those which do not seem applicable to you or which you prefer not to answer. Any information you provide will be of use to the study, so please return the questionnaire regardless of the number of questions you choose to answer. Feel free to add information on the back of pages or on extra pages. Thank you for your cooperation.

> E. Paul Torrance, Professor
> Department of Educational Psychology
> Aderhold Hall
> University of Georgia
> Athens, Georgia 30602

I. General Information

1. Name: _____
   First   Middle/Maiden   Last

2. Current address: _____
   _____
   _____

3. Current phone number: _____

4. Name and address of person who will always know how to contact you:

_____

_____

_____

5. Sex: Male _____ Female _____

6. Your age: _____

7. Are you: 1) single _____ 2) married _____ 3) widowed _____

   4) divorced _____ 5) remarried _____

8. Your age at marriage(s) _____

9. Number of children: _____

10. Do you expect to have more, or any, children? Yes _____ No _____

11. Do you consider yourself politically: 1) conservative _____

   2) liberal _____ 3) radical _____ 4) other (please specify) _____

   Your political affiliation: _____

II. Educational Information

12. Are you currently a student? Yes _____ No _____

   If yes, are you enrolled: Full time _____ Part time _____

   Anticipated date of graduation (if you are in a degree program):

   _____

   Degree you will receive and major field: _____

   _____

13. If you have never attended college, please state your reasons for not doing

   so: _____

   _____

   _____

   _____

   _____

14. If you did not attend college, what did you do first after high school?

_____

_____

_____

_____

15. Undergraduate school(s) attended:

institution	dates of attendance	major field(s)	degree earned

16. Graduate school(s) attended:

institution	dates of attendance	major field(s)	degree earned

17. If you attended college or graduate school but never finished, please state the reason for your decision to leave: _____

_____

_____

18. Have you completed any training programs in skills that were not primarily academic (such as an apprenticeship, or crafts, technical, drama, musical, etc., training)? Please describe the nature of the program(s) and its value to you:

_____

_____

_____

_____

19. Do you have further formal educational plans? Yes _____ No _____

    If yes, please describe: _____

    _____

20. Please list any scholarships, honors, awards, assistantships, or notable achievements of your undergraduate years: _____

    _____

    _____

    _____

21. Please list any scholarships, honors, awards, assistantships, or notable achievements of your graduate years: _____

    _____

    _____

    _____

III. Career Development

22. List the full time positions you have held since graduating from high school. Check those relevant to your current position:

position	employer	dates

23. List significant part time, summer and volunteer positions you have held since graduating from high school. Check those that are relevant to your current position:

position	employer	dates

24. Please list any career related honors, awards or special recognition you have received:

_____

_____

_____

25. Briefly describe the duties you perform in your present position:

_____

_____

_____

26. What are your career ambitions; for example, what position, responsibility or rewards do you wish to attain? What do you hope to accomplish?

_____

_____

_____

_____

27. Are you considering a major career change at this time?

Yes _____ No _____. If yes, what change do you plan to make?

_____

_____

_____

28. Have you ever had a "time out" (a period of six months or more) during which you interrupted your education or career to pursue something entirely unrelated?

Yes _____ No _____.

If yes, how long did you stay "out"? _____

_____

What were your reasons for taking this break and what did you do with the time?

_____

_____

_____

_____

29. What are your current interests and hobbies, unrelated to your career?

_____

_____

_____

30. Indicate whether you achieved any of the following <u>in high school</u> by underlining the appropriate words. On the line before any item you have underlined, indicate the number of times you have achieved it.

_____ a patentable device

_____ scientific paper published in a scientific journal

_____ original paper at a scientific meeting sponsored by a professional society

_____ prize or award for scientific work or study

_____ participation in a National Science Foundation summer program for high school students

_____ first, second, third place in a state, regional, national science contest

_____ poems, stories, essays, or articles published in public newspaper or magazine, state or national high school anthology

_____ literary award or prize for creative writing

_____ editing of school paper or literary magazine

_____ writing of an original play which was given a public performance

_____ lead in high school or church-sponsored play

_____ minor roles in plays, not school or church-sponsored

_____ first, second, third place in a state, regional, national speech or debate contest

_____ composition of music which has been given at least one public performance

_____ performance with a professional orchestra

_____ organization of dance or jazz band

_____ rating of Good or Excellent in state or national music contest

_____ exhibition in a state-wide, regional, or national show of a work of art (painting, sculpture, photography, etc.)

_____ cartoons, photographs, drawings published in public newspaper or magazine

_____ appointment, nomination, or election to student office

_____ organization of school political group or campaign to change institutional rules, procedures, or policies

_____ organization of own business or service

_____ Junior Achievement award

_____ award or special recognition for leadership of any kind

List below any high school creative achievements that are not covered by the above list:

_____

_____

_____

31. Indicate whether you have achieved any of the following by underlining the appropriate words. On the line before any item you underline, indicate the number of times you have achieved it since graduating from high school:

_____ invented a patentable device

_____ published an article in a scientific or professional journal

_____ presented an original paper to a scientific or professional society

_____ received a prize or award for scientific or professional paper or project

_____ received a research grant for scientific, literary, education, art, or other project

_____ published a poem, short story, feature story, or book

_____ received a literary award or prize for creative writing or other journalism

_____ edited a professional or literary paper or magazine

_____ wrote or directed a play or choreographed a dance that was given at least one public performance

_____ performed the lead role in a play or dance

_____ received an award or prize for original work in drama or dance

_____ received an award or prize for performance in drama or dance

_____ composed music which was given at least one public performance

_____ published original musical composition

_____ performed with or organized a professional musical group

_____ received an award or prize for musical composition

_____ received an award or prize for musical performance

_____ held an exhibition of paintings, sculpture, photographs, etc.

_____ published art work (cartoon, photograph, illustrations) in a newspaper, magazine, or book

_____ received prize or award for work in art

_____ created advertising ideas that were implemented

_____ created original educational materials that were used by a wide audience

_____ won election to public office

_____ organized a political campaign

_____ organized own business, service, or professional organization

_____ received an award or special recognition for leadership of any kind

_____ conducted in-service education or training for co-workers

_____ suggested modifications of existing practices or policies that were adopted by superiors or co-workers

List below any creative achievements that are not covered by the above list:

_____

_____

_____

_____

32. Describe below what you consider your three most creative achievements since high school graduation. These may be in any area of life:

_____

_____

_____

_____

33. What do you consider your greatest spur for continued achievement?

_____

_____

_____

_____

_____

34. What do you find the greatest obstacle(s) to continued achievement?

_____

_____

_____

35. Have you ever had a mentor—an older person in your occupational field or educational experience who "took you under his/her wing?"

Yes _____ No _____ (If no, please skip to question 36.)

If you have had more than one mentor, please select the one that influenced you most:

Was this person: Male _____ Female _____

What was this person's official position? _____

_____

_____

How long was this person your mentor? _____

Approximately how much older than you was this person? _____

What did this person do that influenced you the most? _____

_____

_____

_____

If you no longer consider this person your mentor, what were the circumstances of the termination of the mentorship?

_____

_____

_____

_____

How do you feel about this person now? Why do you feel this way?

_____

_____

_____

_____

_____

_____

Have you adopted any of the qualities of this person as your own?

Yes _____ No _____.

If yes, please specify. If no, please discuss why you chose not to adopt any of his/her qualities:

_____

_____

_____

_____

36. How would you describe your current ambition for:

	Not Very Important		Somewhat Important		Very Important
a. excellence in work	1	2	3	4	5
b. recognition for achievements	1	2	3	4	5
c. career success	1	2	3	4	5
d. financial success	1	2	3	4	5
e. success in family life	1	2	3	4	5
f. success in friendships	1	2	3	4	5
g. useful service to others	1	2	3	4	5
h. joy in living	1	2	3	4	5

37. How would you rate your satisfaction with your current attainment in:

	Not Very Important		Somewhat Important		Very Important
a. work	1	2	3	4	5
b. recognition	1	2	3	4	5
c. challenge	1	2	3	4	5
d. income	1	2	3	4	5
e. marital status	1	2	3	4	5
f. children	1	2	3	4	5
g. leisure activities	1	2	3	4	5
h. friendships	1	2	3	4	5
i. community involvement	1	2	3	4	5
j. opportunity for independent action	1	2	3	4	5
k. creative output	1	2	3	4	5
l. joy in living	1	2	3	4	5

38. In general, would you describe your current lifestyle as:

Not Very Important		*Somewhat Important*		*Very Important*
1	2	3	4	5

39. What do you see as the primary frustrations (if any) in your life?

_____

_____

_____

_____

_____

_____

40. If you could do or be whatever you choose in the next ten years, what would it be?

_____

_____

_____

_____

_____

_____

41. Please add any information about your current lifestyle or concerns that you feel are important to you, but that this questionnaire has not tapped:

_____

_____

_____

_____

_____

_____

_____

_____

_____

_____

SUPPLEMENTARY INFORMATION
UNIVERSITY ELEMENTARY/PRATT ELEMENTARY CREATIVITY STUDY

DIRECTIONS: Please complete this form as completely as you can. However, skip those questions which do not seem applicable to you or which you prefer not to answer. Any information that you supply will be useful, so please return the questionnaire even though you do not care to respond to all items. Feel free to add information on the back of the questionnaire or on extra sheets.

1. Name: _____

2. Current address: _____

_____

3. Many participants in the study have expressed an interest in obtaining the address of their former classmates and elementary teachers. We are willing to prepare and distribute such a list, if enough participants are willing for their addresses to be included and would be interested in having this information.

Would you be willing for your name and address to appear on such a listing?

Yes _____ No _____ (check one)

Would you like to receive such a listing? Yes _____ No _____.

4. Can you recall an incident in elementary school when a teacher encouraged you to use your creative abilities and this made a real difference in your later career? If so, please describe the incident and tell what influence it had on you. If you need more space, please use the back of this page.

_____

_____

_____

_____

_____

_____

_____

_____

_____

_____

_____

5. Please give the name of the teacher: _____

6. Please describe an incident which occurred during the past month and which you think illustrates best the creativity that you display in your day to day life. It may be something that happened in your professional life, in your home, in your community—or anywhere:

_____

_____

_____

_____

_____

_____

_____

_____

_____

_____

7. To whom would you be most likely to turn for assistance and encouragement on a difficult project, time of crisis, or for general "morale building" and psychological support?

_____

_____

_____

8. How does your life today compare with your expectations of the future when you were graduated from high school?

_____

_____

_____

_____

_____

_____

_____

9. To what do you attribute any differences between dream and present reality?

_____

_____

_____

_____

_____

_____

_____

_____

_____

_____

_____

10. Within the past five years, have you?:

_____ organized an action-oriented group (e.g., an environmental pressure group, community service group, food cooperative, etc.)

_____ designed and taught a new course

_____ designed a house

_____ designed a garden

_____ been instrumental in starting a new educational venture (e.g., a preschool, special tutoring program, free school, program for the elderly, etc.)

_____ participated in a group experience designed to foster personal change (e.g., encounter group, T-group, consciousness-raising group, Outward Bound, etc.)

_____ planned and led such a group

_____ joined a new religion

_____ had a striking religious experience

_____ taken up meditation

_____ completed a poem, story, novel, or article that was not published

_____ completed a musical composition that was not performed

_____ choreographed a dance that was not performed

_____ completed a painting or other artwork that was not publicly exhibited

_____ made original designs for clothing

_____ planned and carried out an unorthodox journey (e.g., bicycling through the Gobi Desert, transcontinental camel ride, rowing to Alaska, etc.)

_____ been instrumental in bringing about a significant change in rules or operating procedures in an organization

_____ worked out a new way of doing an everyday task (e.g., housework, getting to work, routine office matters, etc.)

_____ learned a new skill

_____ became seriously involved in a new sport

_____ became seriously involved in a new hobby

Note below any creative activities that are not covered in the above list:

_____

_____

_____

_____

11. How would you assess the current division of housekeeping duties in your home?

| task | *Approximate percentage of responsibility assumed by:* | | | |
	self	*spouse*	*other(s)**	*paid outside help*
cooking	_____	_____	_____	_____
food shopping	_____	_____	_____	_____
housecleaning	_____	_____	_____	_____
child care (preschool)	_____	_____	_____	_____
child care (school age)	_____	_____	_____	_____
child care in emergencies or illness	_____	_____	_____	_____
transportation of children to school and activities	_____	_____	_____	_____
accommodating social activities of children	_____	_____	_____	_____
laundry	_____	_____	_____	_____
entertaining	_____	_____	_____	_____

gardening and lawn care   _____   _____   _____   _____

car maintenance and repair   _____   _____   _____   _____

household maintenance
(repair and remodeling)   _____   _____   _____   _____

household decorating
(selecting furnishings,
arranging rooms, etc.)   _____   _____   _____   _____

financial decision-making   _____   _____   _____   _____

bill-paying   _____   _____   _____   _____

*Please describe briefly the nature of the "other(s)" (for example, roommate, partner, child, etc.), if that category is used:

_____

_____

_____

12. How much creativity or ingenuity do you think you bring to such house hold tasks? Give one example.

_____

_____

_____

13. What is your father's highest educational degree?

_____

14. What is your mother's highest educational degree?

_____

15. What is the occupation your father spent most of his adult life performing?

_____

16. What is the occupation your mother spent most of her adult life performing?

_____

17. Did your mother work outside the home while you were a:

	full time	part time	not at all
preschooler	_____	_____	_____
elementary-school student	_____	_____	_____
high school student	_____	_____	_____
adult	_____	_____	_____

If you are an only child, skip to question 21.

18. How many brothers and sisters (living and deceased) do you have who are older than you:

    Sisters _____ Brothers _____ .

19. How many brothers and sisters (living and deceased) do you have who are younger than you:

    Sisters _____ Brothers _____ .

20. Do you feel that your siblings were supportive and encouraging of your work, dreams, and ambitions while you were:

	Yes	No
a child?	_____	_____
a teenager?	_____	_____
a young adult?	_____	_____
currently?	_____	_____

21. Do you maintain close ties with any of your high school friends?

    Yes _____ No _____ .

    If yes, please describe briefly the nature (i.e., infrequent meetings, frequent contact & similar lifestyle, etc.) and the value of the friendship(s) to your present life.

    _____

    _____

    _____

    _____

    _____

    _____

22. Do you maintain close ties with any of your college friends?

Yes _____ No _____.

If so, please describe briefly the nature and the value of the friendship(s) to your present life.

_____

_____

_____

_____

_____

_____

23. Do you live:

_____ alone

_____ with relatives (if so, please indicate relationship _____

_____)

_____ with a group of nonrelatives (commune, group of agemates, etc.)

_____ with husband

_____ with husband and children

_____ with children

_____ with opposite-sex partner

_____ with same-sex partner

_____ with an opposite-sex roommate

_____ with a same-sex roommate

_____ other (please describe _____)

24. In what ways does the person(s) you live with support and encourage your professional and/or personal activities and interests?

_____

_____

_____

_____

_____

_____

If you have never married, skip to question 29.

25. Did you change your surname when you married?

    Yes _____ No _____.

    Please discuss briefly the reasons for your decision:

    _____

    _____

    _____

26. Do you use any combination of your maiden name and your husband's name, such as:

    _____ maiden name as middle name

    _____ hyphenated, maiden-husband or husband-maiden

    _____ other (please specify _____)

    _____ no combination

27. Do you vary the name you use in different situations (i.e., your own name at work, your own name on published or exhibited work, your husband's name socially, etc.)?

    Yes _____ No _____.

    If yes, please describe:

    _____

    _____

    _____

28. What is your husband's occupation? _____

    _____

If you do not have children, skip to question 31.

29. To what extent does someone else participate in the care of your children?

Never		Sometimes		Very Frequently
1	2	3	4	5

30. Is this assistance provided by:

_____ husband?

_____ living companion?

_____ hired help?

_____ day-care facilities?

_____ relatives?

_____ other? (please specify _____)

Do you feel satisfied with this assistance? Yes _____ No _____.

31. How many voluntary services do you work with (school, church, social agencies or other service-oriented organizations for which you do not receive money for what you do)?

_____

_____

_____

On the average, how many hours per week do you spend in voluntary service? _____

32. How any social and civic organizations do you belong to (groups such as AAUW, garden clubs, women's clubs, political-activist groups, which are not organized primarily to provide voluntary services)?

_____

_____

_____

On the average, how many hours per week do you spend in such activities? _____

33. How many professional organizations do you participate in (groups such as teachers' organizations or bar associations, which are primarily related to professional or career interests)?

_____

_____

_____

On the average, how many hours per week do you spend in such activities? _____

34. Please name the organizations in which you invest the major portion of your time and energy. Circle those which you feel offer you significant support in return. (Support may be defined as feelings of worth or self-confidence, opportunities to develop leadership skills, or, more tangibly, financial, career or crisis assistance, etc.)

_____

_____

_____

35. Have you been involved in any formal women's groups (such as NOW, a professional caucus, etc.) that are a source of particular support to you?

Yes _____ No _____.

Have you been involved in any informal women's groups (such as consciousness raising or close friendship/support, etc.) that are a source of particular support to you?

Yes _____ No _____.

If you answered YES to either question, please describe briefly:

_____

_____

_____

_____

_____

_____

36. Please add any comments about your current lifestyle or concerns, or this questionnaire, that you feel would be of use to this study:

_____

_____

_____

_____

_____

_____

_____

_____

FORTY-YEAR FOLLOW-UP QUESTION-NAIRE FOR UNIVERSITY ELEMENTARY AND PRATT SCHOOL PARTICIPANTS, 1998

FORTY-YEAR FOLLOW-UP STUDY QUESTIONNAIRE FOR UNIVERSITY ELEMENTARY AND PRATT SCHOOLS STUDY PARTICIPANTS

Please answer the questions in this questionnaire to the best of your ability. Please keep in mind that your responses will be treated in strict confidence.

When you have completed this questionnaire, no matter how many or how few of the questions you have answered, put it in the self-addressed and stamped envelope, along with your book selection.

Your cooperation is deeply appreciated!

E. Paul Torrance
Georgia Studies of Creative Behavior
183 Cherokee Avenue
Athens, Georgia 30606-4305
Tel: (706) 543-9674

PART I: DEMOGRAPHIC DATA

This part of the survey will provide general biographical data for the study.

A. Personal Information

1. Name: _____

             Last (maiden)   First   Middle   Married Name

2. Current address: _____

_____

_____

3. Current phone number: _____ work or _____ home (_____)_____

4. Name and address of person who will always know how to contact you:

_____

_____

_____

5. (Please circle the appropriate answer.) Are you?

(a) single   (b) married   (c) widowed   (d) divorced   (e) remarried

6. Number of children: _____

7. Birth date: _____

8. Your present occupation: _____

9. Your spouse's occupation: _____

B. Educational Information

1. Highest level of education attained: _____

2. Highest degree attained, if any: _____

Where attained? _____

3. Undergraduate college(s) or other post–high school(s) attended:

_____

_____

_____

4. Graduate and/or professional school(s) attended:

_____

_____

_____

5. List any fellowships, scholarships, assistantships, grants or prizes that you have been awarded in conjunction with your professional education:

_____

_____

_____

C. Career Information

List any jobs that you have held for at least twelve months during the period 1980–1997:

_____	19 ___ – 19 ___
_____	19 ___ – 19 ___
_____	19 ___ – 19 ___
_____	19 ___ – 19 ___
_____	19 ___ – 19 ___

PART II: CREATIVE ACHIEVEMENTS

A. Public Achievements

In this section, try to answer all questions in terms of the period 1980–1997. Listed below are a variety of activities and achievements. On the right-hand side is a column headed "Number of Times." Under this column indicate the number of times each of the items on the left applies to you. If you discover that the achievement listed is done with regularity as part of your professional or avocational life, you may wish to indicate so with an "R" instead of a numeral. Please feel free to add comments if you wish.

achievements and activities	*number of times*
1. Published poem	_____
Published song	_____
Published short story	_____
Published feature story	_____
Published play	_____
2. Published book	_____

3. Published article in scientific or professional journal _____

4. Wrote unpublished scientific or professional paper _____

5. Directed or produced a play, choreographed play, etc. _____

6. Created an original dance, choreography, etc. _____

7. Received research grant for scientific, literary or art project _____

8. Conducted in-service education or training for co-workers _____

9. Suggested modifications of existing practices or policies which were adopted by superiors and/or co-workers _____

10. Received prize or award for scientific paper or project _____

11. Presented an original paper at a professional meeting _____

12. Invented a patentable device _____

13. Designed and constructed an original piece of scientific apparatus _____

14. Founded a business or other professional organization _____

15. Received award or special recognition for leadership _____

16. Received literary award or prize for creative writing _____

17. Received award or prize for work in art _____

18. Received award or prize for musical composition _____

19. Received award or prize for musical performance _____

20. Received award or prize for creative work in drama _____

21. Received award or prize for creative work in dance _____

22. Received award for performance in drama _____

23. Received award for performance in dance _____

24. Held exhibition of paintings, sculpture, photography, etc. _____

25. Composed music which was given at least one public performance _____

26. Had a musical composition published _____

27. Had a cartoon published in a newspaper, magazine, book, etc. _____

28. Illustrated a book, magazine, advertising, etc. _____

29. Created advertising ideas that were executed _____

30. Created and/or produced a radio and/or television program _____

31. Created original educational materials _____

32. Elected to public office _____

List below creative achievements in business, politics, science, medicine, the arts or any other field not covered by, or that don't seem to "fit," the above list:

_____

_____

_____

_____

_____

B. Personal Creative Achievements

Between 1980 and 1997 have you (please check *yes* or *no*):

1. Organized an action-oriented group (e.g., an environmental pressure group, community service group, food cooperative, etc.)   yes _____ no _____

2. Designed and taught a new course   yes _____ no _____

3. Designed a house   yes _____ no _____

4. Designed a garden   yes _____ no _____

5. Been instrumental in starting a new educational venture (e.g., a preschool, special tutoring program, free school, program for the elderly, etc.)   yes _____ no _____

6. Participated in a group experience designed to foster personal change (e.g., encounter group, consciousness-raising group, Outward Bound, etc.)   yes _____ no _____

7. Planned and led such a group as described in question no. 6   yes _____ no _____

8. Joined a new religion   yes _____ no _____

9. Had a striking religious experience   yes _____ no _____

10. Taken up meditation   yes _____ no _____

11. Completed a poem, story, novel, or article that was not published   yes _____ no _____

12. Completed a musical composition that was not performed   yes _____ no _____

13. Choreographed a dance that was not performed   yes _____ no _____

14. Completed a painting or other artwork that was not publicly exhibited   yes _____ no _____

15. Made original designs for clothing   yes _____ no _____

16. Planned and carried out an unorthodox journey (e.g., bicycling through the Gobi Desert, climbing the Canadian Rockies, transcontinental camel ride, rowing to Alaska, etc.)   yes _____ no _____

17. Been instrumental in bringing about a significant change in the rules or operating procedures in an organization   yes _____ no _____

18. Worked out a new way of doing an everyday task (e.g., housework, getting to work, routine office matters, etc.)   yes _____ no _____

19. Learned a new skill   yes _____ no _____

20. Become seriously involved in a new sport   yes _____ no _____

21. Become seriously involved a new hobby   yes _____ no _____

22. Written an unpublished book   yes _____ no _____

23. Written an unpublished monograph   yes _____ no _____

24. Written an unpublished lengthy report   yes _____ no _____

25. Written an unpublished poem   yes _____ no _____

26. Written an unpublished song   yes _____ no _____

27. Written an unpublished short story   yes _____ no _____

28. Written an unpublished play   yes _____ no _____

Please note below any personal creative activities that were not covered in the above list:

_____

_____

_____

_____

_____

PART III: STRENGTHS AND WEAKNESSES

1. (a) What kind of work do you do? _____

_____

_____

(b) Would you say that you are in love with your work?

_____

_____

(c) At what point of your career did you fall in love with your work?

_____

_____

(d) Do you have any hobbies that you love? _____

What are they? _____

_____

_____

(e) What do you consider the most creative thing or things that you have done in your hobby or hobbies?

_____

_____

_____

(f) On the average, how much time do you spend on your hobbies in a week?

_____

2. (a) What do you consider your greatest strength(s)?

_____

_____

(b) How did you become aware of these strengths?

_____

_____

(c) What have you done to practice, enjoy, and explore your strengths?

_____

_____

3. (a) Have you been able to free yourself of the expectations of others and "play your own game"?

_____

_____

(b) What kind of conflicts did you encounter in doing this?

_____

_____

_____

_____

(c) What were the expectations that others (parents, teachers, spouse, employers) had of you?

_____

_____

_____

_____

4. (a) Did you have one or more great mentors who helped you achieve success?

_____

(b) What was the occupation or role of the person who helped you most?

_____

(c) At what period of your life did this relationship occur?

_____

_____

(d) How did this occur? _____

_____

(e) How did this person help you? _____

_____

(f) How long did this relationship last? _____

_____

5. (a) Do you consider yourself "well rounded"? _____

_____

(b) Describe some of the pressures you experienced, if any:

_____

_____

_____

_____

_____

(c) In what ways, if any, did you give in to these pressures?

_____

_____

_____

_____

(d) In what ways, if any, did you resist these pressures?

_____

_____

_____

_____

_____

6. (a) Have you done what you love and can do well?

_____

(b) When you were young, did you have opportunities to do the things that you loved and could do well? _____
In elementary school? _____ In high school? _____ In college or other post–high school education? _____

(c) During what period in your life did you have the best opportunities to do what you loved and could do well?

_____

_____

(d) What forces have you had to cope with in doing what you loved and could do well?

_____

_____

7. (a) Describe some of the experiences you have had in using skills of interdependence: _____

_____

_____

_____

_____

(b) Were you encouraged to develop skills of interdependence? In elementary school? _____ In high school? _____ In college or other post–high school situations? _____

(c) What are some of the skills that you depend upon others for?

_____

_____

_____

_____

(d) What are some of the skills that other people depend upon you for?

_____

_____

_____

_____

Would you be available for a personal interview?_____

Comments: _____

_____

_____

_____

_____

_____

_____

_____

_____

INTERVIEW FORM, 1998

CREATIVE LIVES IN PROGRESS . . .

SELECTED CASE STUDIES FROM THE FORTY YEAR FOLLOW-UP TO
THE TORRANCE LONGITUDINAL STUDY ON CREATIVITY (1958–1998)
ELEMENTARY GROUP (MINNEAPOLIS-ST. PAUL AND AREA)

GARNET MILLAR

Name: _____

Date: _____ Time: _____

Potential Interview Questions

1. *Early Influences on Creativity*

   a) At what age were you first aware of your creativity?

   b) How did this show itself?

   c) At elementary age [if appropriate to first answer] what influence did your schooling have on your creativity ability?

   d) What specific incidents can you remember in your childhood which enabled your creativity to develop?

   e) Was there any influence at elementary age which you now recognize as having had an impact on your subsequent career or chosen field of work?

f) What were the qualities/skills/behaviors of [whoever is identified at this age]?

g) What would you say was the most important lesson you learned with regard to your creativity at this age?

h) How would your peers have described you at that time?

2. *Career Paths and Transitions*

a) What is your present job?

b) How do you apply creativity to this work?

c) Have you had other jobs? If so, were you able to work creatively while in these jobs?

d) What major changes/transitions have you experienced in your working life?

e) What caused these transitions?

f) When you made changes in your working life, was there anyone whom you relied on for support and advice? [If so] What did they do which was most helpful for you at these times?

g) How are you able to integrate relationships [as a parent, as a partner, as someone's child] into your working life?

3. *Creative Accomplishments*

a) What do you consider to be your most creative achievement?

b) In what area of your life are you most able to be creative?

c) What do you consider to be your creative attributes?

d) How would your close associates describe your creative attributes?

e) What influences guide or constrain your creativity [overall life purpose, career goal, financial burdens]?

4. *Questions Related to the "Manifesto for Children"*

a) When did you fall in love with . . . ? Describe this for me, please.

b) In what ways do you pursue . . . ? Describe this for me, please.

c) What are your greatest strengths? Describe this for me, please.

d) In what ways is your creativity affected by the expectations of others?

e) Are you "free to play your own game" or "sing in your own key?"

f) What relationship has been most instrumental in helping you to achieve your potential?

g) Describe your relationship with this individual/mentor?

h) What qualities/skills does your mentor have?

i) What do you feel for your mentor?

j) How important is this to the quality of the relationship?

k) In what ways do you interact with others to enhance their career/ personal lives?

l) In what ways do you allow others to interact to enhance your life?

m) Would you describe yourself more as well rounded, or more able at some things than others? In what ways?

5. *General Questions on Creativity*

a) What are your creative goals and aspirations for the future? Please describe.

b) If you could provide educators advice for nurturing creativity in children, what would you share with them?

c) If you could provide parents advice for nurturing creativity in children, what would you share with them?

d) If you could provide guidance to mentors working with highly creative youngsters, what would you share with them?

e) If you could design a time capsule that represented you as a creative person, what would you include in this capsule? (5–10 items?)

f) If Dr. Torrance were with you at this moment, what question would you ask him regarding his work in the field of creativity?

Comments:

references

Alumni News. (1961). "A program of dedication to the science of children." Minneapolis: University of Minnesota 63(5): 12–19.

Black, A. (1985). *Mind design*. Athens, GA: Crea8ing Places Press.

Cohen, G. D. (2000). "C = me^2: The creativity equation that could change your life." *Modern Maturity 43R*(2): 30–35.

Cox, C. (1926). *The early mental traits of three hundred geniuses*, vol. II in the *Genetic Studies of Genius Series*, ed. L. M. Terman. Stanford, CA: Stanford University Press.

Csikszentmihalyi, M. (1996). *Creativity: Flow and the psychology of discovery and invention*. New York: HarperCollins.

Goertzel, V., & M. Goertzel. (1962). *Cradles of eminence*. Boston: Little, Brown.

Himsl, R., & G. W. Millar. (1992). *Measure of questioning skills*. Bensenville, IL: Scholastic Testing Service.

Hoffer, E. (1973). *Reflections on the human condition*. New York: Harper & Row.

Kirton, M. J. (1987). *Kirton adaption-innovation inventory*, 2nd ed. Herts, AL: Occupational Research Center.

Kogan, N. (1974). "Creativity and sex differences." *Journal of Creative Behavior 8*: 1–14.

Maccoby, E. E., & C. N. Jacklin. (1974). *The psychology of sex differences*. Stanford, CA: Stanford University Press.

Millar, G. W. (1972). "Dysteachia: New academic illness isolated." *News*. Ontario Public School Men Teachers Federation, Toronto.

———. (1992). *Developing student questioning skills: A handbook of tips and strategies for teachers*. Bensenville, IL: Scholastic Testing Service.

———. (1995a). *E. Paul Torrance: "The creativity man."* Norwood, NJ: Ablex.

———. (1995b). "Toast to the 'creativity man.'" Unpublished speech delivered at the Hargrett Library, University of Georgia.

———. (2000). "Key career messages for youth." Research paper completed for the Student Commission, Toronto, ON.

Parents' Television Council. (2000, February 29). "TV is leading children down a moral sewer" (advertisement). *Athens* [Georgia] *Daily News Banner-Herald*, 5A.

Renzulli, J. S. (1977). *The Enrichment triad model: A guide for developing defensible programs for the gifted and talented*. Wethersfield, CT: Creative Learning Press.

Rubin, H. J., & I. S. Rubin. (1995). *Qualitative interviewing: The art of hearing data*. Thousand Oaks, CA: Sage Publications.

Sheehy, N., A. J. Chapman, & W. Conroy. (1997). *Biographical dictionary of psychology*. New York: Routledge.

Sinetar, M. (1998). *The mentor's spirit: Life lessons on leadership and the art of encouragement*. New York: St. Martin's Press.

Stratton, P., & N. Hayes. (1993). *A students' dictionary of psychology*. New York: Routledge, Chapman and Hall.

Strauss, A., & J. Corbin. (1990). *Basics of qualitative research: Grounded theory, procedures, and techniques*. Newbury Park, CA: Sage Publications.

Terman, L. M., ed. (1925–1959). *Genetic studies of genius series*. Stanford, CA: Stanford University Press.

Terman, L. M., & M. H. Oden. (1947). *The gifted child grows up: Twenty-five years' follow-up of a superior group*, vol. IV of the *Genetic Studies of Genius Series*, ed. L. M. Terman. Stanford, CA: Stanford University Press.

———. (1959). *The gifted group at mid-life: Thirty-five years' follow-up of the superior child*, vol. V of the *Genetic Studies of Genius Series*, ed. L. M. Terman. Stanford, CA: Stanford University Press.

Torrance, E. P. (1954a). "The development of a preliminary Life Experience Inventory for the study of fighter inceptor pilot combat effectiveness." *Research Bulletin* (AFPTRC-TR-54-89). San Antonio, TX: Lackland Air Force Base.

———. (1954b). "The making of jet aces." Paper presented at the Western Psychological Association, Long Beach, CA (in Torrance Archives, Hargrett Library, University of Georgia).

———. (1954c). "Portrait of an ace." *Time Magazine 38*.

———, ed. (1960). *Talent and education*. Minneapolis: University of Minnesota Press.

———, ed. (1961). *New educational ideas: Proceedings of the third Minnesota conference on gifted children*. Minneapolis: University of Minnesota, Center for Continuing Study, General Extension Division.

———. (1962). *Guiding creative talent*. Englewood Cliffs, NJ: Prentice-Hall.

———. (1966). *Torrance tests of creative thinking: Norms-technical manual* (research edition). Princeton, NJ: Personnel Press (published in 6 languages).

———. (1971). "The courage to be creative." *Retail Credit Company Inspection News* 56(4): 8–11.

———. (1974; 1993). *Torrance tests of creative thinking*. Bensenville, IL: Scholastic Testing Service (published in 35 languages).

———. (1981). "Predicting the creativity of elementary school children (1958–80)—and the teacher who 'made a difference.'" *Gifted Child Quarterly* 25(2): 55–62.

———. (1984). *Mentor relationships: How they aid creative achievement, endure, change and die*. Buffalo, NY: Bearly Limited.

———. (1995). *Creative motivation scale*. Athens: Georgia Studies of Creative Behavior.

———. (1999). *Manifesto for children*. Designed by G. M. Mendoza for the Torrance Center for Creative Studies, Athens, GA.

———. (2000). *Research review of the* Torrance Tests of Creative Thinking—*figural and verbal forms A and B*. Bensenville, IL: Scholastic Testing Service.

———. (2001). *The Manifesto: A guide to developing a creative career*. Westport, CT: Ablex Publishing.

Torrance, E. P., K. Goff, & N. Satterfield. (1998). *Multicultural mentoring of the gifted and talented*. Waco, TX: Prufrock Press.

Torrance, E. P., M. Henderson, & J. Presbury. (1983). *Manifesto for children*. Athens: Georgia Studies of Creative Behavior.

Torrance, E. P., R. E. Wilk, & J. Harmon, eds. (1960). *Studies in Minnesota education*. Minnesota Society for the Study of Education, Eta Chapter of Phi Delta Kappa and Epsilon Center of Pi Lambda Theta.

index

About the Author

GARNET W. MILLAR lives in Edmonton, Alberta, Canada. He is an education consultant in private practice and former provincial coordinator for guidance and counseling with the Alberta government. Specific jobs in his career include teacher, counselor, school psychologist, assistant superintendent of schools, and visiting scholar/professor. He is currently an adjunct professor in the educational psychology department at the University of Alberta and holds a research fellowship at the University of Georgia.

For the past 16 years, Dr. Millar has been affiliated with the Torrance Center for Creative Studies at the University of Georgia. He presented the annual Torrance Lecture in 1990 and wrote the biography of Dr. Torrance, *E. Paul Torrance: "The Creativity Man"* (Ablex Publishing, 1995). He has written several articles and books related to creativity.